P9-DIB-931

WITHDRAWN

Prospects for Privatization

Prospects for Privatization

LIBRARY
BRYAN COLLEGE
DAYTON, TN 37321

Proceedings of
The Academy of
Political Science

Volume 36
Number 3

ISSN 0065–0684

Edited by Steve H. Hanke

New York, 1987

100473

Prospects for Privatization marks the final volume of the *Proceedings of the Academy of Political Science* to be produced under the direction of Professor C. Lowell Harriss as executive director of the Academy.

Lowell's contributions to Columbia University and to the Academy have been outstanding. Not only has his work been marked by high quality and scholarship; for those of us who have known him and worked with him, it has also been marked by a wonderful spirit of collegiality. As Lowell assumes new responsibilities with the Academy as senior adviser, we wish him the very best for long and continued success.

FRANK J. MACCHIAROLA
President and Executive Director

Copyright © 1987 by The Academy of Political Science

All rights reserved

Library of Congress Catalog-Card Number 87-70470

Cover design by Cynthia Brady

Printed by Capital City Press, Montpelier, Vermont

Contents

Preface

For many years and in various ways, governments have undertaken an increasing range of activities that were by no means inherently governmental. The results were not uniformly satisfactory. Performance quality was often unacceptable and costs were excessive. Assertions that the private sector could do better stimulated discussion of the desirability of government provision. Many services were transferred to the private sector under the rubric "privatization."

The Academy of Political Science undertook to sponsor a project on privatization. Professor Steve H. Hanke of the Johns Hopkins University agreed to plan the volume. He was able to draw upon his extensive knowledge of the subject and to obtain essays from a group of distinguished scholars. The resulting volume covers a wide range of issues. One outstanding feature is the emphasis on results, on experience gained under varying circumstances. Some of the papers were presented at a public conference at Columbia University on 20 November 1986.

The Academy extends its thanks for financial support to the Glenmede Trust Company, the Robert Schalkenbach Foundation, the John M. Olin Foundation, the Earhart Foundation, and the Signal Companies, Inc.

The Academy also thanks William Farr, Eric C. Banks, Brian Keizer, and Ingrid Sterner for skillfully editing the manuscripts and overseeing the production of the volume.

The views expressed are those of the authors and not necessarily those of any of the organizations with which they are associated. The Academy of Political Science serves as a forum for the development and dissemination of opinion on public-policy questions, but it does not make recommendations on political and social issues.

C. LOWELL HARRISS
Senior Adviser

Contributors

WALTER F. BABER is director of the MPA program, University of Nevada, Reno. He is the author of *Organizing the Future: Matrix Models for the Post-Industrial Polity*.

ROBERT W. BAILEY is assistant professor of political science, Columbia University. He has served on the staffs of the Emergency Financial Control Board for New York City, the New York City chancellor of schools, and the city's commissioner of consumer affairs. He is the author of *The Crisis Regime: The MAC, the EFCB and the Political Impact of the New York City Financial Crisis*.

JAMES T. BENNETT, Eminent Scholar and William P. Snavely Professor of Political Economy & Public Policy, George Mason University, is the author of *The Political Economy of Federal Government Growth* and the coauthor, with Thomas J. DiLorenzo, of *Destroying Democracy: How Government Funds Partisan Politics*.

STUART M. BUTLER is director, Domestic Policy Studies, the Heritage Foundation. He is the author of *Privatizing Federal Spending* and *Enterprise Zones*.

LOUIS DE ALESSI is professor of economics, University of Miami, Coral Gables, Florida.

THOMAS J. DILORENZO is the John M. Olin Visiting Professor, Center for the Study of American Business, Washington University at St. Louis. He is the coauthor, with James T. Bennett, of *Destroying Democracy: How Government Funds Partisan Politics*.

BARNEY DOWDLE is professor of forestry and adjunct professor of economics, University of Washington.

PETER J. FERRARA, an attorney with the firm of Shaw, Pittman, Potts and Trowbridge, has served as senior staff member, White House Office of Policy Development. He is the author of *Social Security: Averting the Crisis*.

PHILIP E. FIXLER, JR., director, Local Government Center, Reason Foundation, has served as legislative assistant, City of Los Angeles. He edits *Fiscal Watchdog*, a monthly newsletter on privatization.

JOHN C. GOODMAN, president, National Center for Policy Analysis, is the author of *Privatization* and *Economics of Public Policy*.

STEVE H. HANKE, formerly senior economist, President's Council of Economic Advisers, is professor of applied economics, the Johns Hopkins University. He is the author of *Studies in Water and Wastewater Economics.*

C. LOWELL HARRISS is professor emeritus of economics, Columbia University; senior adviser, the Academy of Political Science; and associate, Lincoln Institute on Land Policy.

STEPHEN MOORE is policy analyst, Heritage Foundation. He is the author of *Slashing the Deficit: A $122 Billion Savings Strategy to Avoid the Gramm-Rudman Ax.*

ROBERT W. POOLE, JR., president, Reason Foundation, has served as chairman, Local Government Center. He is the author of *Cutting Back City Hall* and the editor of *Unnatural Monopolies.*

JAMES B. RAMSEY is professor and chair, Department of Economics, New York University. His most recent book is *The Economics of Exploration for Energy Resources.*

GABRIEL ROTH is president, the Services Group. He is the author of a forthcoming book titled *Private Provision of Public Services in Developing Countries.*

FRED L. SMITH, JR., is president, Competitive Enterprise Institute.

PAUL STARR is professor of sociology, Princeton University. He is the author of *The Social Transformation of American Medicine,* winner of the 1984 Pulitzer Prize for Nonfiction and the Bancroft Prize in American History.

A. A. WALTERS is economic adviser to the vice president, Operations Policy, World Bank. He has served as personal economic adviser to Prime Minister Margaret Thatcher. He is the author of *Britain's Economic Renaissance: Margaret Thatcher's Reforms, 1979–1984.*

STEPHEN J. K. WALTERS is associate professor of economics, Loyola College in Maryland.

PETER YOUNG is executive director, Adam Smith Institute (USA). He was formerly head of research, Adam Smith Institute in London, which specializes in privatization policy.

Privatization versus Nationalization

STEVE H. HANKE

It is perhaps difficult to realize today how limited the functions of government were through most of American history. Until World War I, the Federal government exercised only a narrow range of functions and imposed essentially no taxes other than the tariff. Most states assumed only a few responsibilities. Local governments had a wider range of activities, but not many by present standards.

Gradually, government participation in economic and business activities increased. Franchises granted exclusive privileges to a few businesses, notably public utilities. Regulation of some private operations increased. For various reasons, municipal-reform movements developed in some cities in the late nineteenth century and after. In some cases these movements led to "municipalization" of functions that had been performed privately. By 1930 municipalities were performing many functions that were by no means inherently governmental, yet the number of municipal- and state-performed business activities was only a small percentage of the total economy. The Federal government ran the post office but provided few other services except national defense.

Over the past fifty years, however, governments have assumed a greater role in the economic affairs of most countries. There has been more emphasis on macroeconomic planning and management. In addition, public-sector budgets have grown in absolute terms and also in relation to the size of private-sector activity. This growth has been the result of rapid increases in welfare programs, military expenditures, and a vast increase in the range and scale of so-called public infrastructure and services. Many countries have also increased the scope of government by embracing the concept of an entrepreneurial state—one that is allegedly the engine of growth and development as well as one that attempts to achieve growth by either operating nationalized industries or intervening heavily in the operation of private firms (state capitalism). Of course, some countries have adopted or—more often—had socialist and communist economic systems imposed on them.

This trend toward more government involvement in economic affairs has been accompanied by a literature dominated by arguments that, in one way or another, attempt to rationalize public-sector activity. This imbalance has been reflected in popular dictionaries and specialized reference works. For example, before 1983, Webster's New Collegiate Dictionary contained an entry for nationalization but not for privatization. The Encyclopedia of the Social Sciences also omits privatization and includes an entry for nationalization.

Since about 1980, the trend toward more government spending, ownership, and intervention has been seriously questioned. This has sparked new debate about the merits of private versus public ownership. Privatization, which is the transfer of assets or service functions from public to private ownership or control, has emerged as the focal point of the debate. Consequently, the word privatize has been recognized, and the imbalance between nationalization and privatization has begun to be redressed. For example, privatize appeared in Webster's Ninth New Collegiate Dictionary in 1983, and the word will also be in The New Palgrave—a four-volume economics dictionary to be published by London's Macmillan Press Ltd. in 1987. The purpose of Prospects for Privatization is further to redress the imbalance in the literature between nationalization and privatization.

Although the objectives of privatization vary, the most frequently cited include: (1) the improvement of the economic performance of the assets or service functions concerned; (2) the depoliticization of economic decisions; (3) the generation of public-budget revenues through sale receipts; (4) the reduction in public outlays, taxes, and borrowing requirements; (5) the reduction in the power of public-sector unions; and (6) the promotion of popular capitalism through the wider ownership of assets. The first section of this volume, "Privatization as a Means to Control the Growth in Government," focuses on the second, third, fourth, and fifth objectives cited above. The second section, "The Economics of Privatization," addresses the first objective. "A Status Report on Privatization," the volume's final section, covers all six objectives in the context of ongoing privatization programs at local, state, and Federal levels of government in the United States and also internationally.

With the exception of the third section, "The Case against Privatization," the authors in this volume strongly support privatization. In doing so, they break new ground. The ground that they break, however, was originally tilled rather carefully by the father of modern economics, Adam Smith. In the Wealth of Nations, Smith concluded that "no two characters seem more inconsistent than those of trader and sovereign."[1] Adam Smith argued that this was the case because people are more prodigal with the wealth of others than with their own. He thought public administration was negligent and wasteful because public employees do not have a direct interest in the commercial outcome of their actions.

Despite allegations by critics of privatization, the authors are in good company. It is also important to debunk another allegation made by critics who assert that government must supply various goods and services because the poor cannot afford the prices that private suppliers would have to charge to recover costs. This assertion is incorrect. Whether the poor can or cannot afford privately supplied goods and services should not bear on the choice between private and public supply.

The decision about the appropriate means of supply should be based on which *supply* alternative, private or public, can produce a given quantity and quality of goods and services at the lowest cost.

If private enterprise can *supply* a given quantity and quality of goods and services by utilizing fewer resources than public enterprise, then private enterprise should be employed. If the broad polity deems that private *finance* — which operates through consumer sovereignty and private charity — does not allow the poor to purchase adequate quantities and qualities of goods and services from a cost-effective private enterprise, then the polity must choose the method and level of public finance to be used to assist the poor. This choice between private and public finance is separable from the choice between private and public supply. The separability of *supply* and *finance* allows the authors properly to concentrate the issues surrounding the choice between private and public supply, without considering the method to be used to finance the desired supply.

The authors demonstrate that, in order to improve the manner in which goods and services are *supplied*, the first step should be to privatize public enterprises. Then — to the extent that the polity desires to alter the level or mix of goods and services produced by private enterprises entities — the merits of modifying the manner in which goods and services are *financed* should be considered.

NOTE

1. Adam Smith, *Wealth of Nations*, Modern Library (New York: Random House, 1937 [1776]), 771.

Changing The Political Dynamics of Government

STUART M. BUTLER

When most scholars and public officials consider privatization, they tend to think of it strictly as a method of cutting the *cost* of government. Hence the discussion usually revolves around the relative efficiency of private versus public provision of goods and services in a society. While this is an important dimension of the debate, it conceals a deeper feature of privatization that is of far greater importance: by changing the pattern of demand for services, privatization may prove to be a potent *political* strategy to reverse the momentum toward ever-larger government in the United States.

Trying to bring some semblance of sanity to the scope and size of government in the United States has long been a source of frustration to politicians and voters in general and to conservatives in particular. Administration after administration has come to power pledged to cut the size of government by ending wasteful and irrelevant programs yet left office with government even larger and with few programs eliminated. The Reagan administration has been more successful than most; but even David Stockman, as director of the Office of Management and Budget, achieved little more than a slowdown in the rate of growth of Federal spending. To judge from the media coverage, one might conclude that the budget cuts were Draconian. On the contrary, all that Stockman managed to do was to slow down the remorseless growth of government programs, not reverse it. The share of output going to the government has continued to increase. Indeed, during the first Reagan term the proportion of the country's gross national product (GNP) spent by the government reached a post–World War II peak and has remained consistently above the proportion of the "big spender" Carter years.

The expansion of government cannot be explained by the defense buildup; the share of GNP devoted to defense spending is still well below that of the Kennedy administration. Despite David Stockman's successes in achieving cuts in several areas of domestic spending, the proportion of GNP devoted to nondefense spending still exceeds that of previous administrations. In particular, means-tested welfare spending has continued to rise. And more important, the entitlement programs benefiting middle-class Americans, such as Social Security, Medicare, and Federal retirement benefits, expanded by more than 17 percent in constant dollars during Reagan's first term. By the end of that term, David Stockman had come to discount as "dreamers" all who believed that a significant reduction could be made in entitlement programs. In a 1984 *Fortune* article, he maintained that "the minimum size of government achievable appears to be 22 percent to 23 percent of GNP."[1] This failure transformed Stockman into a cynic and an advocate of tax increases as the only way to halt the spiraling deficit.

The reason for this inability to control the growth of government has nothing to do with a lack of determination — who could be more resolute or persuasive than Reagan? The lost Battle of the Budget has little to do with a lack of will but much to do with obsolete political weaponry. The key fact is that little has been done to change the underlying political dynamics that favor increased Federal spending. The critical mistake has been to adopt the traditional conservative strategy of trying to contain spending by seeking legislation to slow down the flow of money leaving Washington. This "supply-side" view of the budget has led the Reagan administration to try to thwart the goals of powerful constituencies intent on securing benefits from government by pressuring or inducing lawmakers to vote for spending programs. The rising tide of government spending is a clear indication that the strategy has not worked.

Only through the alteration of those dynamics can government activity become more rational, and hence more efficient. As long as constituencies see it in their interest to demand government spending, and as long as politicians risk electoral damage when they vote against those demands, it is going to be very difficult to restrain spending. Thus a strategy to control the size of government needs a powerful "demand-side" element if it is to be successful. Conditions must be created in which the demand for government spending is diverted into the private sector. This is the beauty of privatization. Instead of having to say "no" to constituencies, politicians can adopt a more palatable approach to cutting spending. They can reduce outlays by fostering private alternatives that are more attractive to voters, thereby reducing the clamor for government spending. Changing the political dynamics of government spending in this way is the secret of privatization.

The Public Spending Ratchet

To appreciate how privatization can change the politics of spending, it is first necessary to review why government programs are so resistant to cutbacks. A government program generally begins in one of two ways. The more noticeable case is a response to a perceived crisis or threat to society. The Federal space program, for instance, was a direct response to the challenge posed by the Soviet Union's launching of *Sputnik* in 1957. Similarly, pressure for the massive extension of the Federal role implicit in the New Deal grew out of the calamity of the Great Depression. But a less spectacular, though more common, case is a program that develops as an offshoot of an existing government activity—usually a traditional all-American pork-barrel project to help some politically sensitive constituency or region. There is often no grand debate on these issues, and the general public may not even be aware of the program. Yet in both instances the result is the same: a coalition is created around the program that seeks to expand it and defend it from political assault. Normally, such a coalition consists of four distinct groups.

1. *Beneficiaries and near-beneficiaries.* Beneficiaries of spending programs have every reason to press for more spending and to oppose any future attempt to cut outlays. They have every incentive to form associations to protect their interests by lobbying for more spending. In addition, those who do not quite meet the eligibility criteria of the program think they are just as worthy as those who do. They may have a few too many employees to qualify for small-business assistance, or have a bit too much cash income to be eligible for welfare. Yet they strongly believe that they meet the intent of the law. These "near-beneficiaries," like those actually eligible for the program, have every reason to campaign for more generous eligibility criteria. Since the political cost of accommodating these constituents is usually much less than the cost of resisting their demands, officials and politicians tend to absorb them into the program. But once such a group of near-beneficiaries joins the program, another aggrieved group, claiming "unfair" treatment, quickly appears.

2. *Administrators.* The officials who administer a program are also a key element of the coalition determined to preserve and expand it. They may be motivated for various reasons. Some, of course, see the program as the key to their own livelihood and support it out of self-interest. But it is also common for both career and political officials to come to the conclusion that their agency and its programs are critical to the solution of the country's problems. Brookings Institution scholar Martha Derthick, for instance, noted in her analysis of the growth of the Social Security Administration (SSA) that Robert Myers, chief actuary at the SSA for many years, was shocked by the "religious zeal" of many of the staff. Derthick found that the overarching philosophy was that the answer to many of the country's most difficult social problems lay in the hands of the SSA. She noted: "The prevailing technique of policy analysis [within SSA] was to identify a social problem, such as lack of health care, and to develop the arguments and methods for dealing with it through social insurance."[2]

3. *Service providers.* The private sector itself can become a powerful advocate for government spending. A new Federal highway project means money and jobs for Americans engaged in construction work. Increased welfare spending means more money for nonprofit groups and professional service providers who care for the poor. A defense buildup means more jobs for defense contractors. A new program quickly attracts a host of such private-sector interests: corporations and individuals who may be strong critics of excessive government spending while believing, of course, that their own work is essential to the national interest.

4. *Political activists.* In addition to those with a proprietary interest in a government program, there are those who join public-spending coalitions for strictly

philosophical or political reasons. Many of the more ideologically motivated liberal politicians, for instance, see an expanding public sector as synonymous with the public interest itself. And outside the legislative process a host of organizations engages directly in the public-policy debate. These organizations span the political spectrum, but the liberal groups tend to be extremely effective in defending programs under attack.

The elements of these coalitions work together to advance the programs they support. Civil servants keep in close touch with the beneficiaries of a program and tend to represent their interests within an administration. Similarly, the political activists in and out of Congress cooperate with other elements of the coalition to create favorable political conditions for the program. Of course, those wishing to reduce or terminate a program also seek to establish political conditions that are conducive to their goals. Yet there are reasons why the political balance tilts heavily in favor of those who wish to preserve programs.

First, as scholars of the "Public Choice" school of economics point out, a narrow coalition benefiting from a program tends to have more political influence than the far greater number of taxpayers who are paying for those benefits. The relatively small number of people who receive most of those benefits have a strong incentive to spend part of them lobbying hard for the program. It is rational for them to spend time and money trying to influence lawmakers. On the other hand, the costs of programs are spread so widely and thinly that an individual taxpayer has little incentive to devote much effort to attacking the program. A $100 million highway project, for instance, means enormous benefits for a few construction firms and a few thousand motorists. They can be expected to fight hard for the program that awards such contracts. But the average Federal taxpayer will contribute about $1 to that project—hardly enough to encourage him to campaign against it. Whenever the programs dispensing such concentrated benefits are attacked, of course, the coalition has a strong incentive to lobby vigorously. If the program is terminated, while the average taxpayer can expect little change in his life, no rebate would be sent to him, nor would he likely notice any reduction in his tax bill.

Second, the Federal system makes these spending dynamics even more intense at the national level. The beneficiaries of a program are likely to have the edge over the taxpayers who finance the program at any level of government, but the further up the Federal system the program is found, the greater is that edge. The supporters of the program receive the same benefits, whether the check comes from the Federal Treasury or from local coffers. But the higher up the Federal system the program is financed, the more widely and thinly the tax costs are distributed—and the more diluted is the potential opposition. Thus it is no surprise that those who support a particular government-spending program rarely miss an opportunity to advocate that it be transferred to a higher level of government—simply to increase the likelihood that it will be preserved and expanded.

The political dynamics, in other words, favor increases in government spending but act strongly against any attempt to reduce outlays. Like a ratchet, the dynamics tend to operate in one direction only—toward growth. The opponents of ever-larger Federal spending tend to face this public-spending ratchet with a mixture of frustration and despair. Some, like David Stockman, have exhausted themselves with steadily less effective efforts to rally public support against the public-spending coalitions, only to conclude that the battle is hopeless. Others believe that only changes in the Constitution, such as a balanced-budget and spending-limitation amendment, can possibly alter the underlying pressure to spend.

Creating a Private-Sector Ratchet

Trying to overcome these spending dynamics by constitutional innovations or through a legislative war of attrition, however, is like engaging in political Sumo wrestling, in which each superheavyweight wrestler uses bulk and muscle to force his opponent out of the circle. The problem is that the would-be budget-cutters are perpetually at a weight disadvantage. The inherent imbalance in favor of the public-spending coalitions inevitably make it extremely difficult for the budget-cutter to achieve and sustain reductions in program outlays. Over the long run, those who wish to expand spending programs invariably win the wrestling match.

The privatization strategy, on the other hand, is more like a political form of judo, in which the opponent's own muscle and weight is used against him. Stated simply, privatization does not require the political strategist to wrestle out of the ring all those who demand services from the government but to create the conditions whereby the momentum of these demands is deflected into the private sector. Privatization does this by reversing the public-choice dynamics that currently favor beneficiaries over taxpayers. By establishing incentives and changing regulations, privatization involves the concentration of benefits on those who freely choose a private method of service delivery over the public provision of the same service. In this way, those who opt for a private method to satisfy their demands are heavily rewarded, while the "cost" of such incentives (to the extent that a tax break or regulatory relief on one person could be construed as a burden on everyone else) is spread widely and thinly.

This approach of offering an attractive "price" to those who choose to consume private services as an alternative to government services addresses the budget problem in a very different manner from the traditional approach of the budget-cutter. Instead of trying to contain spending by holding back the *supply* of dollars, privatization uses incentives to influence the *demand* for dollars. And instead of influencing spending decisions at the national macrolevel, it draws from microeconomic pricing policies to influence individual microdecisions. This strategy of influencing individual demand decisions is the key to privatization. It has been dubbed "micropolitics" by one of the leading privatization theorists, Madsen Pirie of Britain's Adam Smith Institute:

> Micropolitics is the art of generating circumstances in which individuals will be motivated to prefer and embrace the alternative of private supply, and in which people will make individual and voluntary decisions whose cumulative effect will be to bring about

the desired state of affairs. The process of transfer from [the] public to [the] private economy is most securely achieved when its progress is evolutionary, arising from free decisions.[3]

In its most refined form, the strategy leads to the creation of private-sector coalitions that are mirror images of the coalitions currently pressing for public-sector spending. By concentrating rewards on distinct groups of beneficiaries, near-beneficiaries, and private service providers, a lobby is created both to oppose the coalition demanding public provision and to press for an expanded private role. These privatization coalitions can be used to create a "privatization ratchet" to counter the public-spending ratchet. Members of the coalitions can be expected to lobby for deeper incentives for private choices and to fight hard against any attempt to eliminate the privatization option. Similarly, near-beneficiaries — those not quite eligible for the privatization incentive — will demand to be included, adding to the political momentum.

The privatization strategy is thus a reversal in the traditional public-choice dynamics of government spending. Political momentum is directed toward lower taxation (if the reward for private choice is a tax break) and for private rather than public programs. Moreover, each legislative or administrative victory won by the coalition will serve to strengthen it, just as each addition to a spending program increases the size and power of a public-spending coalition, thereby enhancing its ability to win more concessions. And if skillfully designed, the privatization incentives can be made attractive to members of existing public-sector coalitions, encouraging them to "jump ship" in favor of privatization. In this way the growth of a countervailing privatization movement can be at the *expense* of a coalition dedicated to larger government.

Three examples, drawn from the United States and Europe, illustrate the political potency of privatization dynamics.

Public housing constitutes approximately one-third of all the housing in Britain. By the 1960s it was clear that it had become a classic case of an irreversible government program supported by an irresistible political coalition. Substantially below-market rents made the housing very attractive to tenants but a constant drain on taxpayers who either owned their homes or rented in the private market. The construction industry had few complaints about a program that financed a constant demand for new units. Socialist politicians were eager to encourage an ever-larger public housing sector by maintaining rents even below maintenance costs, knowing that the implicit tax cost was spread widely throughout the country. And not surprisingly, near-beneficiaries clamored to have access to the sizable benefits. The result of these pressures was that the public sector expanded, and the quality — and expense — of public housing rose markedly to accommodate the demands of an increasingly blue-collar and middle-class tenant population.

Conventional strategies to reverse the tide proved totally ineffective, because they sought to deny benefits to the powerful constituency that benefited from the program. The threat of higher rents or the eviction of more affluent tenants guaranteed a flood of votes against any candidate who took such a stand.

Since Margaret Thatcher came to power in 1979, however, there has been a remarkable turnaround in the politics of public housing in Britain. More than 1 million public-housing units and their tenants have been transferred to the private sector and are thus no longer a drain on the taxpayer. And the Labour party has formally agreed to continue the privatization policy if it wins power in the next election.

The key to this abrupt and dramatic change was the deliberate, conscious creation of a coalition to reverse the policy by awarding a benefit to tenants who chose a private option — previous, unsuccessful strategies had centered on taking away existing benefits from the tenants. In this case, the benefit for those choosing privatization was an asset transfer. Any tenant agreeing to buy his or her unit may do so at up to a 70 percent discount from the market valuation. From the government's point of view, the privatization program makes good economic sense. The privatization of public housing allows the British Treasury to recoup at least part of the value of a housing asset that otherwise could never be realized and that currently involves an operating loss. The asset-transfer strategy also has had strong political and social implications. The immediate benefit of home ownership at a discount is far more popular among public-housing residents than the prospect of a future stream of benefits in the form of below-market rents. So there has been a strong demand for more sales — and the politicians resisting that have incurred the wrath of the near-beneficiary tenants who wish to join the program.

A similar coalition to privatize public housing is emerging in the United States. Some years ago various housing authorities began to experiment in dilapidated or troubled projects with the idea of resident management, in which the tenants themselves were given the responsibility for collecting rent and managing the property. In several cases these experiments have proved to be highly successful. But increasingly, effective tenant managers have come to the conclusion that their efforts are yielding savings to taxpayers and housing authorities but not to themselves. Consequently, momentum is growing for a British-style home-ownership program, so that the residents will gain directly, in appreciated property value and reduced housing costs, from their cost-cutting efforts.

The British have also been very successful at building coalitions around another form of asset transfer, stock offerings of previously nationalized companies. During Margaret Thatcher's tenure, these sales have amounted to almost $20 billion worth of commercial assets, including Jaguar Motors, British Telecom (the country's entire telephone system), and, among the most recent sales, British Gas. Each of the latter two offerings shattered the previous world record for a stock sale.

As in the case of public-housing sales, the privatization of these companies was enormously popular because sizable benefits were concentrated on those who chose to take part in the sale. In the case of British Telecom, for instance, the government broke down the coalition normally supporting public ownership and turned it instead into an enthusiastic proprivatization lobby. This was accomplished by offering key constituents free or discounted stock, together with below-market pricing of the issue, so that the stockholders could be sure of an immediate benefit through an appreciation of their holdings.

The employees of the nationalized company, who normally would have been expected to resist any attempt to take them out of the protective cocoon of public ownership, defied union instructions to boycott the sale and accepted a package of free and discounted stock. Indeed, no fewer than 96 percent of the staff bought into privatization in this way. Telephone customers agreeing to purchase stock were also provided with special stock options and vouchers to offset future telephone bills, in order to diffuse potential concern about the pricing policies of a private company. And to ensure a solid base of political support for retaining the company in the private sector, preference in the offering was given to small investors. Underpricing ensured an overdemand and a price rise immediately after the offering was floated on the stock market. The result was that the sale created 2 million stockholders, each of whom enjoyed a significant appreciation on the initial investment. Moreover, the success of the British Telecom sale generated enormous interest in future sales, thereby building momentum for more privatization.

The third example involves the use of tax benefits as the focus for a privatization coalition. It is also a case of possible privatization in the making, not privatization already achieved.

Social Security in the United States is a perfect example of the Federal ratchet in operation. Created in 1935 to supplement the retirement savings of working Americans, the system has mushroomed into a program that accounts for about one-fourth of all Federal outlays. Over the years, political pressure has caused the program to take on more and more functions, from disability payments to medical coverage, and with each expansion a new group of beneficiaries and service providers has been incorporated into the Social Security coalition. As politician after politician has discovered, it is extremely unwise to challenge that lobby. Talk of limiting Social Security may win a trickle of votes from young workers who begrudge the high payroll taxes they are forced to pay for benefits that many are skeptical of ever receiving, but it invariably leads to a torrent of lost votes from retirees and those nearing retirement, who have a great deal to lose from any cutback in the system.

In 1981, however, tax legislation made it possible for a powerful coalition for a private alternative to Social Security to emerge. A provision was included in the Economic Recovery Tax Act of 1981 to allow all working Americans to open tax-deductible Individual Retirement Accounts (IRAs). The $2,000 annual deduction became a significant, immediate benefit concentrated only upon those choosing to open such a private pension account, while the cost of the deduction (in the sense that a deduction to one taxpayer is seen as a comparative burden to all other taxpayers) was spread widely and thinly across all taxpayers.

As soon as this deduction was established, banks, stockbrokers, and other financial institutions saw it in their interest to join the coalition. They advertised heavily, persuading far more Americans to open IRAs than the Treasury had expected and thereby strengthening the lobby for this private version of Social Security. Near-beneficiaries also entered the picture. Nonworking spouses, who were allowed only a $250 IRA deduction under the 1981 law, claimed that there was discrimination against homemakers and demanded equal treatment. And perhaps most significant of all, the medical industry and certain policy institutes proposed that a medical IRA be established to enable working Americans to save or purchase insurance to cover retirement medical costs—a form of private Medicare.

The expansion of the IRA alternative was halted by the Tax Reform Act of 1986, which put new limits on IRAs. Yet the debate over that legislation demonstrated the power of the coalition. Few tax breaks were as vigorously defended as the IRA and none led to more constituent mail. Instead of ending the deduction, as many strong proponents of tax simplification intended, they had to settle for a limitation. And just as failing to eliminate a spending program leaves its coalition intact, the IRA coalition continues, ready to renew its campaign whenever conditions permit.

Privatization strategists think that if the campaign is eventually successful in creating a private retirement saving system, operating parallel to Social Security and incorporating health care, disability, and other features, the chances of controlling the growth of Social Security will improve immeasurably. An IRA-based "private Social Security system" would make it easier to persuade workers to press for the right to opt out of Social Security.

These examples indicate how decisively a privatization initiative can change the political climate for a reduction in the activities of government. Since World War II, Britain has seemed completely unable to break out of the straitjacket of nationalization. Occasionally a Conservative government managed to make some progress, but the coalitions supporting public ownership seemed secure. Yet privatization has shattered their tight grip. By creating and entrenching privatization coalitions, the size of the public sector in Britain is declining and seems destined to remain smaller even if a Labour government is returned to power, simply because the constituency benefiting from private ownership of public housing and nationalized firms is so strong.

This general strategy of changing the demand for public-sector goods by altering the incentive structure and thus creating self-interest coalitions has many variations. The examples cited involve the most obvious and widely used techniques—transferring an asset and providing a tax incentive. But there are other methods that the strategist can use. Simply deregulating an activity, for instance, allows private firms to enter a market that had been monopolized by the public sector, thereby encouraging private-sector providers to bid for the consumer's attention. The partial deregulation of bus transportation in both Britain and the United States, for instance, has been used as an instrument to stimulate privatization.

In addition, various forms of incomplete privatization can be achieved when complete privatization is neither desirable nor politically possible. Vouchers, for example, do involve government funding of a service; by giving those funds directly to the beneficiary, however, a wedge may be driven between that beneficiary and other members of the public-spending coalition, reducing the pressure for government control. In the case of education, for instance, the voucher has helped to isolate the teacher unions that many believe operate the public school system in their own interests.

The techniques available to the advocate of privatization are extensive and sophisticated. But if the strategy is to be successful, it must be carefully designed and executed. In Britain the coordination of the privatization strategy has been at the cabinet level, and a single office within the Treasury has acted as the tactical "command center." This has enabled the Thatcher government to minimize mistakes and to lay careful groundwork before a privatization initiative is launched. In this way the Thatcherites have been able to move swiftly and decisively to build up the necessary coalitions for privatization and to concentrate on the weak points of the potential opponents.

The record in the United States has been less successful, mainly because these important lessons have been ignored so far. Rather than centralizing its privatization strategy, the Reagan administration has allowed each department to operate almost independently. That has led to repeated political mistakes and confusion in the minds of the public. For instance, the attempted sale of a tiny portion of the 750 million acres of land owned by the Federal government quickly became a dispute over environmental considerations and states' rights. Little or no attempt was made to target benefits to environmentalists or ranchers, who felt threatened by the proposal, and so a wall of opposition doomed the idea. A similar inability to learn from experience led the U.S. Department of Transportation into serious opposition when it sought to sell Conrail, the federally owned freight railroad. Preferring to sell the railroad to a single buyer instead of considering a British-style public offering, the Reagan administration managed to unite almost every interest group against the sale. Unless the management of the strategy is improved, there will be little progress and many more missed opportunities.

Although it is important to design privatization initiatives carefully, if the political dynamics are to be altered decisively, privatization—unlike conventional budget-cutting approaches—does not require constant leadership from the top to be successful over the long run. Federal programs grow because the coalitions supporting them are always pushing at the margin, constantly urging small new additions; those wishing to restrain spending have the nearly impossible task of guarding all political fronts. Privatization operates in a similar manner. Once a privatization coalition begins to form, it is constantly looking for new opportunities to shift related functions to the private sector, and then it is the defenders of the public sector who must be ever-vigilant. That is why privatization is such an insidious, and effective, tool to control the size of the public sector.

NOTES

1. P. W. Bernstein, "David Stockman: No More Big Budget Cuts," *Fortune*, 6 Feb. 1984, 54.

2. Martha Derthick, *Policymaking for Social Security* (Washington, D.C.: Brookings Institution, 1979), 25.

3. Madsen Pirie, *Dismantling The State* (Dallas: National Center for Policy Analysis, 1985), 29.

The Role of Tax-Funded Politics

JAMES T. BENNETT
THOMAS J. DILORENZO

Extensive research on privatization has revealed that private firms are almost always far more efficient than government enterprises in providing a wide array of services, from airport administration to zoo maintenance. Quality is also generally superior when services are produced by private businesses rather than by public employees. The evidence is so consistent and compelling that there is currently a worldwide movement away from state production and control of resources and toward privatization. But despite some successful privatization efforts at the state and local levels of government in the United States, there has been little movement in that direction at the Federal level, because of the intense political opposition of those who benefit most from public provision. The principal beneficiaries are members of Congress, who value their claim to the service benefits; bureaucrats who administer the programs; and political pressure groups that promote government programs ranging from consumer-protection regulation to environmental protection to welfare. Thus, despite clear evidence that the public would gain from privatization, such policies have been effectively forestalled by powerful special interests.

That well-organized special interests often dominate the relatively unorganized taxpayers in politics is nothing new. This essay discusses an important aspect of the political process that, until recently, has received little attention: tax-funded politics, the use of tax revenues to finance special-interest politics. Government at all levels provides hundreds of millions of tax dollars each year in grants and contracts to political pressure groups, ostensibly for admirable purposes, such as protecting consumers and the environment and helping the unemployed, the elderly, and minorities; but some of the funds are partly diverted for advocating increases in the size and scope of government in various ways, including opposition to privatization. Thus, a major (if not *the*) reason that privatization initiatives have not been successful at the Federal level is that the special interests that oppose it are well financed by taxpayers.

The ABCs of Tax-Funded Politics

Government provides hundreds of millions of tax dollars each year to a wide variety of political pressure groups. Examples include over $100 million annually during the 1970s and early 1980s to food-stamp advocates; more than $154 million to the National Council of Senior Citizens, the largest senior-citizen lobbying group, from 1978 to 1981 (this group is administered by union executives who compose eleven of the thirteen members of its board of directors); over $100 million annually to the National Urban League and its affiliates; more than $5 million to Jesse Jackson's Operation PUSH from 1978 to 1981; at least $300 million annually to the Legal Services Corporation, which has used the funds for such purposes as suing state governments to pay for sex-change operations, to preventing statewide literacy tests as a prerequisite for graduation from high school, and paying professional lobbyists to oppose a tax-reduction referendum in California; in excess of $167 million to labor unions from 1977 to 1982; and millions more to such political organizations as Ralph Nader's Public Interest Research Groups, environmentalist pressure groups (e.g., the Sierra Club, Wilderness Society, Friends of the Earth, Environmental Action, National Wildlife Federation, Natural Resources Defense Council, Environmental Defense Fund); and even various conservative groups have received support from the taxpayer. Tax-funded politics pervades the governmental process, and although the amounts involved are "only" in the range of hundreds of millions of dollars annually, these sums are highly leveraged. If the $375 million expended by all candidates (incumbents and challengers) in the 1984 congressional elections is important to the political process, then the even larger sums spent on tax-funded politics must also be.

A major difference between campaign expenditures and tax-funded politics is that the former is legal, whereas the latter is not. Congress has repeatedly prohibited the use of Federal funds for political activities and has made it a criminal offense for Federal officials to spend appropriated funds to encourage political advocacy: "No part of the money appropriated by any enactment of Congress shall, in the absence of express authorization by Congress, be used directly or indirectly to pay for any personal service, advertisement, telegram, telephone, letter, printed or written matter, or other device, intended or designed to influence in any manner a member of Congress, to favor or oppose, by vote or otherwise, any legislation or appropriation by Congress, whether before or after the introduction of any bill or resolution proposing such legislation or appropriation."[1] In addition, many appropriation bills contain specific riders that also ban the use of tax dollars for political purposes. Even the Supreme Court has ruled that a person cannot be required (through taxation) "to contribute to the support of an ideological cause he may oppose."[2] These restraints, however, have had no perceptible effect on the widespread misuses of taxpayer dollars for political purposes.

The notion that neither members of Congress nor public employees are aware of these abuses can be dismissed out of hand. Hundreds of millions of dollars are routinely given to organizations that lobby, make campaign contributions, and engage in grass-roots organizing and lobbying. For those who deal frequently with political pressure groups, it is nonsense to suggest that they do not know how the funds awarded through grants and contracts are used. Nor is the issue of tax-funded politics a new one; the U. S. General Accounting Office reported violations forty years ago. Moreover, by repeatedly legislating against the use of tax funds for political purposes, Congress has shown that it is fully cognizant of the scope and magnitude of these abuses. Congress, however, has not rigidly enforced those legislative restrictions; otherwise, the imposition of repeated prohibitions for over a decade would not have been necessary.

Members of Congress must benefit from passing legislation banning certain activities, for it allows them to assure their constituents that they are unalterably opposed to these practices without having to enforce the law. As the record shows, Congress has been adept at ignoring its own laws. For example, even though two laws have been passed requiring a balanced Federal budget, deficit spending continues at unprecedented rates. Congress has also frequently exempted itself from laws that apply to the private sector: its members can legally discriminate in hiring and promotion, are exempt from affirmative action and equal employment opportunity laws, can pay their staffs less than the minimum wage, and can legally ignore health and safety regulations. Evidently, Congress is frequently more concerned about appearances than substance and considers itself above the law.

If it appears that a large and powerful constituency supports a special cause, politicians respond to its demands by passing laws and regulations or appropriating funds for its programs. The most important measures of the size and power of an interest group are the resources that the group can bring to bear on the political process, such as campaign contributions, votes, lobbyists, and media attention.

Funds are required for advocacy groups to make campaign contributions, hire lobbyists, produce studies that support particular policy initiatives, maintain offices, develop news releases, hold press conferences, and publish newsletters, brochures, and pamphlets. The greater its resources, the more effective an advocacy group should be. The resources available for a particular cause are a good measure of the intensity of feeling on the issue if support for the group advocating the issue comes solely from voluntary contributions. A large number of people with strong views can express their preferences by contributing to a group that promotes that issue. Tax-funded politics, however, allows a small group of people with access to the public purse to obtain resources from government to advance its views even though few may share the group's philosophy. Whenever government aids any political advocacy group, it effectively penalizes the groups that advocate opposing public policies and provides a distinct advantage to the group or groups that it favors.

The role of public employees in the public-policy process is frequently misunderstood. It is widely assumed that bureaucrats are passive agents, that is, they merely administer and carry out the programs that Congress designs and funds. The term *civil servant* suggests that bureaucrats only execute the orders of the elected members of Congress or, ultimately, the taxpayers. This characterization, however, ignores the entrepreneurial role played by public employees. Civil servants, like everyone else, are primarily concerned with their own self-interests: salary, perquisites, rank, prestige, and opportunities for promotion. Because career prospects for bureaucrats are improved when their agency's activities and budget are expanding, they have strong incentives to promote and stimulate a perceived need for their own programs. The bureaucracy, therefore, lobbies vigorously.

There are many examples of bureaucratic lobbying expenditures. In fiscal year 1984, the Department of Agriculture with a budget of $6.5 million officially employed 144 full-time public-affairs persons. The department, including subagencies, employed 704 people to work in public affairs. The Department of Education had a full-time public affairs staff of 46 persons and a budget of $2.4 million; the Department of Transportation had 21 public-affairs professionals and a $1.5 million budget. The Pentagon listed 1,066 full-time public-relations employees. Similar programs undoubtedly exist in other agencies.

Even though large sums of tax revenues are formally appropriated to promote the activities of the Federal bureaucracy, these sums are apparently inadequate to ensure the expansion of agency budgets to the extent desired by bureaucrats and politicians. Tax-funded politics is a way of diverting even more tax revenue for the purpose of self-promotion by the support of various special-interest groups that are formally outside government. The grants and contracts may ostensibly be given to "aid the poor," "protect the consumer," and so forth, but a portion of the money is intended for political advocacy in behalf of the government agency that awarded the funds and the agency's patrons in Congress. By channeling tax dollars in this way, the bureaucracy rewards its friends and provides support for those who reciprocate by lobbying and campaigning for increased program expenditures.

Like bureaucrats, politicians pursue their self-interests by increasing their income, prestige, and perquisites of office. Political advocacy funded by the taxpayers plays an important role in this process. Many students of public policy view members of Congress, state legislators, and elected local officials as passively responding to the will of the people; but this view ignores the entrepreneurial role that politicians play in diverting tax dollars to advocacy groups as a means of obtaining resources to win reelection campaigns.

A politician's income, power, prestige, and perquisites depend on winning reelection; money and other resources (such as telephone banks and campaign volunteers) are the lifeblood of electoral politics. Advocacy groups that receive tax dollars repay their political debt by promoting the political careers of incumbents who support them. The groups often make campaign contributions, provide campaign workers and volunteers, and register and organize low-income people, who normally do not participate actively in politics. Once reelected, the politician has strong incentives to reward these advocacy groups with tax dollars that are used to keep the incumbent in power. Grass-roots organizing is a labor-intensive and costly activity, but when the taxpayers bear the cost the incumbent has an important edge over challengers.

Even if not facing serious opposition to reelection, the incumbent has an incentive to spend time and energy seeking campaign contributions from every possible source, including advocacy groups that receive taxpayers' funds. The incentive is simple: members of the U.S. House of Representatives can divert leftover campaign funds to their personal use. Under a law passed on 8 January 1980, all members of Congress at the time of enactment could legally use excess campaign funds for personal expenses (other members do the same, even though it is illegal).

Campaigning can be very profitable under such a law. Consider the case of Rep. Joseph G. Minish (D-N.J.), who had $326,568 in his campaign account when, three weeks before the election, he managed to raise an additional $85,919, apparently to wage a major effort to retain his seat for a twelfth term. According to the Federal Election Commission (FEC), however, Minish was able to spend only $142,958, and $269,529 remained when he was defeated. Minish's report to the FEC indicated that more than $13,000 was received "on four days—Nov. 9, 15, 19, and 21—after the election."[3] Minish refused to comment on the planned use of the funds, but he dismissed the possibility of returning it to contributors, because it would have been difficult to decide how much to give each donor. Other defeated or retiring members of Congress have also retained substantial sums; for example, Geraldine Ferraro, the vice-presidential nominee of the Democratic party in 1984, left Congress with more than $105,000 in her congressional campaign account.

The rule with regard to campaign contributions in the Senate forbids any member or former member from converting contributions to personal use. An investigation of Senate slush funds from campaign contributions, however, reported the following in the *New Republic*:

- Senator Daniel Inouye of Hawaii spent more than $168,322 in campaign funds in 1981 and 1982, a period during which he had no campaign headquarters, no workers, and no telephones. Campaign funds were used for payments to his wife totaling $4,270, two cars ($17,034), insurance ($5,582), and gasoline ($1,954). More than $40,000 was spent on airline tickets; thousands were spent at Washington restaurants and additional hundreds for such items as rented plants and tropical fish and aquarium supplies.
- Senator Spark M. Matsunaga, also of Hawaii, spent $29,330 in campaign funds in the Senate restaurant in 1981 and 1982.
- Senator Alfonse M. D'Amato of New York spent $24,516 in 1981 and 1982 to lease, maintain, insure, and operate two Buicks.
- Senator Alan Cranston of California transferred $66,000 in unused campaign funds to a private checking account.
- Senator Harrison Williams, Jr., of New Jersey took $65,781 in leftover campaign funds with him when he resigned following his Abscam conviction.[4]

The article continued: "In dozens of cases, Senate incumbents have ignored I.R.S. regulations, violated federal election law, and evaded standards for public disclosure and accountability."[5] Members of Congress seem to be thriving on campaign contributions, some of which come from advocacy groups supported by taxpayers. Our explanation of the process of tax-funded advocacy can be summarized as follows:

1. Politicians allocate taxpayer funds for programs under the guise of alleviating the plight of the poor, the sick, the elderly, the unemployed, or others in need, and serving the "public interest."

2. The bureaucrats who administer the programs provide grants and contracts to political advocacy groups ostensibly to carry out program objectives.

3. Much of the money received by political activists is used to lobby, campaign, and organize support for new programs, additional funding for existing programs, and the election or reelection of politicians who favor the appropriations that fund the political advocacy.

4. The political advocacy groups try to persuade the public through the media that greater spending is essential to deal with a pressing social problem; sympathetic politicians receive campaign contributions and assistance in their election or reelection efforts; these politicians appropriate more funds for existing programs and initiate new programs; the bureaucracy awards more taxpayers' funds to the advocacy groups, and the process recycles from step 1.

Taxpayers' funds are used by political activists to promote their views, by public employees who want to finance the expansion of their bureaus, and by politicans who want funds for reelection campaigns and for conversion to their personal use.

There are politicians who criticize tax-funded politics, but, typically, the criticism is rare and muted. The critics fear that opposition to the programs and organizations that receive funding or that voiced suspicion of the motives of political activists will cause them to be labeled racist, antilabor, antipoor, and so forth. In the case of the Legal Services Corporation, Sen. Orrin Hatch (R-Utah) explained: "To question the activities of the [Legal Services] Corporation . . . is, of course, politically disadvantageous. One is led to believe that the nobility of the Corporation's purpose makes any question as to the propriety of some of its activities nothing less than a vicious attack on the poor themselves. This . . . presumption has scared away much needed review and has provided the Corporation with a congressional carte blanche to operate without oversight, without review, and without criticism."[6]

The effect is that the average voter has been misled about many political organizations and their goals. As Gordon Tullock has argued: "Special interest groups normally have an interest in diminishing the information of the average voter. If they can sell him some false tale which supports their particular effort to rob the treasury, it pays. They have resources and normally make efforts to produce this kind of misinformation. But that would not work if the voter had a strong motive to learn the truth. There is not much point in trying to convince housewives that the canned tomatoes you are selling are much better quality than they are. She may buy one can but as soon as she opens it she finds it is of low quality and doesn't go back. In politics, unfortunately, this rule does not exist, because the voter never has the opportunity to open the can."[7] Voters have little incentive to investigate the activities of government or of organizations that receive government grants and contracts. The marginal costs of doing so usually outweigh the marginal benefits; in this case, ignorance is rational.

Most of the examples of tax-funded politics discussed above involved political organizations generally on the Left of the political spectrum. Groups on the Right have also used tax revenues for political activism, but on a much smaller scale. Thus, both sides of the political spectrum engage in tax-funded politics, although organizations on the Right receive only a small percentage of funds from the U.S. Treasury compared with groups on the Left. There are several reasons for this conclusion. First, listings of grants and contracts obtained under the Freedom of Information Act from many agencies contain few entries for conservative political groups. Second, exposés of conservative organizations and movements that investigate their funding sources rarely if ever reveal the receipt of taxpayers' funds. Third, the media have given considerable attention to the grants and contracts that have been directed to conservative groups, and these have been very small relative to the amounts that flow to liberal organizations. This asymmetry in funding patterns can be explained by the ideology of conservative groups, which discourages seeking government support, and by the resistance of public employees to awarding grants and contracts to organizations that criticize their programs and attempt to shrink the size and scope of government.

Tax-Funded Politics and the Governmental Process

One indication of the importance of tax-funded politics to the political process is the creation of the Washington, D. C.-based "OMB Watch." In the early 1980s the Office of Management and Budget (OMB) made an effort to enforce Federal laws against tax-funded politics. The network of publicly financed lobbying organizations responded with intense opposition, which pressured OMB to abandon its enforcement efforts. As the *Washington Post* reported: "OMB Watch was . . . started by a coalition of anxiety-ridden nonprofit groups concerned about an OMB proposal to ensure that government-funded organizations did not lobby with government funds."[8] OMB Watch claimed to have over 1,000 member organizations. And one of its directors asserted: "If not 100 percent, at least 90 percent of our members are federal grantees."[9]

Even though the sums involved in tax-funded politics may seem small when viewed in comparison to a trillion-dollar Federal budget, they are an important element of the political process, not because of their absolute magnitude but because of the political and economic effects they engender. In the 1984 congressional elections, total campaign spending by all House and Senate candidates, incumbents and challengers, was about $375 million. This amount is only a fraction of the amounts spent on tax-funded politics in recent years. If $375 million in campaign spending has an effect on political outcomes and, ultimately, on public policy, several times that amount spent on tax-funded politics is also likely to have an effect.

One likely economic effect of tax-funded politics is that it makes it quicker and easier for special interests to secure wealth transfers through the aegis of the state. Another implication is that tax-funded politics renders government more monopolistic, as it helps protect incumbents. Congressional incumbents are ultimately responsible for all expenditures, and they benefit politically from illegal tax-funded politics. By aiding their interest-group allies, they help ensure their own reelection. This is one factor that explains why there is so little turnover in Congress. In the 1984 congressional elections, for instance, 95 percent of all incumbents in the House and Senate were reelected. Tax-funded politics, along with the proliferation of subcommittees and congressional staff and the franking privilege, makes challenging an incumbent very costly and risky.

Tax-funded politics can also shed some light on why privatization attempts at the Federal level of government have had very limited success. A case in point is the Reagan administration's attempt to privatize some Federal lands in 1981 and 1982. Although there is much evidence that land (as well as other forms of property) is better managed and preserved under private ownership, privatization proposals were successssfully opposed by a coalition of tax-funded environmentalist pressure groups. For instance, the Sierra Club, which received at least $790,746 from the Federal government from 1978 through 1981 and which was recently described by the *New York Times* as "the most influential environmentalist group in the nation" and "the strongest of the environmental groups which lobby,"[10] claimed that "at present, federal lands are protected from overexploitation and abuse by a great number of regulations and a set of key land-use policies. . . . Privatization would remove such restrictions — and would make lands vulnerable to the sort of short-term profit making that many corporations practice in time of economic stress."[11] The Sierra Club, with the help of tax dollars, not only opposed privatization but lobbied for just the opposite: greater nationalization of land. The club's 1982–83 *Annual Report* stated: "Club activists, staff and allies have been involved in ongoing efforts to include new areas in the National Wilderness Preservation System."[12]

Other members of the tax-funded environmentalist coalition joined in these efforts. Friends of the Earth, for instance, lobbied against privatization because it believed government ownership of land is desirable so that "wealth [can] be passed from generation to generation, each using what it needs and prudently conserving resources for future generations."[13] Similarly, the National Wildlife Federation boasted that one of its major accomplishments in 1982 was the passage of major funding reductions for the Reagan administration's proposals to privatize portions of previously nationalized lands. Similar efforts were made by other environment advocacy groups, such as Environmental Action, Natural Resources Defense Council, and the Environmental Defense Fund.

Another example of tax-funded opposition to privatization involves the senior-citizens lobby, which includes such organizations as the National Council of Senior Citizens, the Gray Panthers, the National Retired Teachers Association, and the National Council on Aging. Together these groups received more than $200 million in Federal funds from 1978 through 1981. Although these groups ostensibly exist to promote the interests of senior citizens, there is evidence that they are union "front" organizations. Their boards of directors are dominated by union officials, and their political activities, consequently, do not deviate from those of organized labor. And labor unions — especially public-employee unions — are among the foremost opponents of privatization. The Gray Panthers, for instance, use some of their resources to create political opposition to privatization of hospitals and nursing homes. They do so as a means of protesting private hospitals' profits, which "are enormous," and they "doubt very much that corporations can be trusted."[14] Opposition to privatization is clearly in the interest of unions representing public employees in the health-care industry; both union dues and members' income would be threatened otherwise.

The senior-citizens lobby has also voiced disapproval of privatization schemes in the housing industry. Selling off some public-housing units to tenants has been proposed by the Reagan administration. Such policies, however, would limit opportunities for further construction of public-housing projects, a source of employment for unionized construction workers and of dues revenues for their unions. Consequently, the senior-citizens lobby, as a voice of organized labor, strongly opposes privatization of the "public" housing industry.

These examples of tax-funded opposition to privatization are suggestive, but by no means exhaustive. They indicate that because privatization threatens to reduce the power, influence, and income of politicians, bureaucrats, and political activists, these groups will devote taxpayers' resources to opposing privatization. Although it is illegal for government employees to engage in partisan politics, the law can be evaded by giving government grants and contracts to sympathetic political lobbying organizations. Thus, privatization initiatives are not likely to succeed as long as opponents have access to tax revenues to finance their political activities.

Conclusion

Privatization promotes both efficiency and equity. It is economically efficient because private-property rights provide incentives for cost effectiveness; it is equitable to the extent that government enterprises are almost always granted monopoly power by fiat. Permitting services to be provided by private, competitive enterprises eliminates monopoly power and thereby benefits consumers and taxpayers. The beneficiaries of government monopoly are politicians, bureaucrats, and special-interest groups who vigorously oppose privatization with the taxpayers' dollars. Tax-funded politics is especially insidious, since it compels taxpayers to pay for political activities that are not in their own best interests, namely, opposition to privatization. Taxpayers are being compelled to pay for the promotion of harmful policies.

One means of diluting the power of the tax-funded political network is, at least for many welfare programs, an expanded use of vouchers — cash grants given directly to the intended beneficiaries of the programs rather than channeled through political organizations that ostensibly promote the interests of the poor, the consumer, the environment, and so on. In short, eliminating the political middleman might help eliminate some of the abuses of tax-funded politics and improve the prospects for privatization. Indeed, privatization is one of the most effective ways to reduce tax-funded politics and the undesirable consequences that result from this type of advocacy. By reducing, if not eliminating, the role of politicians in providing public services, the opportunities for political support of advocacy groups with taxpayers' dollars are also restricted. Thus, a major argument in favor of privatization is that it limits tax-funded advocacy.

Tax-funded politics is illegal, but the laws are rarely enforced. Ultimately, then, politicians themselves must be pressured, through greater public awareness, to enforce the existing laws against tax-funded politics and to promote policies that further the taxpayers' interests, including privatization. These actions may seem rather unlikely, since they require politicians to abandon numerous active, well-organized, special-interest groups. It is not inconceivable, however, that political popularity can be gained through "taking on" the special interests by withdrawing their taxpayer subsidies, thereby promoting privatization and providing benefits to the taxpayers.

NOTES

1. 18 USC Sec. 1913. The law provides for termination of employment or removal from office, as well as fines and imprisonment.

2. *Galda v. Bloustein*, 686 F.2d. 159 (3d Cir. 1982).

3. Thomas B. Edsall, "Unspent Funds for Campaign Lift Eyebrows: Defeated Lawmaker Can Pocket $270,000," *Washington Post*, 19 Dec. 1984.

4. Bill Hogan, Diane Kiesel, and Alan Green, "The Senate's Secret Slush Funds," *New Republic*, 20 June 1983, 13-20.

5. Ibid., 13.

6. Orrin Hatch, "Opening Statement," in *Legal Services Corporation Act Amendments of 1983* (Washington, D.C.: U. S. Government Printing Office, 1983), I.

7. Gordon Tullock, *Welfare for the Well-To-Do* (Dallas: The Fisher Institute, 1983), 86.

8. Felicity Barringer, "Keeping Track of Budgeteers," *Washington Post*, 21 Dec. 1984.

9. Ibid.

10. Cited in William Poole, "The Environmental Complex," Heritage Foundation Institution Analysis No. 19 (Washington, D.C.: The Heritage Foundation, 1982), 2.

11. John Hooper, "Privatization: Master Plan for Government Giveaways," *Sierra*, Nov./Dec. 1982.

12. Sierra Club, 1982-83 *Annual Report*, 6.

13. Friends of the Earth fund-raising letter, 1983.

14. Gray Panthers, *Age and Youth in Action*, April/May 1985.

Property Rights and Privatization

LOUIS DE ALESSI

The term *privatization* is typically used to describe the transfer of activities from the public sector to the private sector and includes contracting out as well as reducing or discontinuing the provision of some goods and services by government. More accurately, privatization entails a move toward private property and away from not only government and common ownership but also from government regulations that limit individual rights to the use of resources.

Privatization has drawn support on both ideological and pragmatic grounds. Ideologically, liberals (in the traditional meaning of the word) favor privatization because it reassigns decisions from government employees to private individuals, buttressing individual liberties and fostering a more democratic society. Much of the current support for privatization, however, arises more pragmatically from the expectations that it will reduce costs and release resources for other purposes. From this perspective, privatization is also favored by those who see it as a means of reducing government deficits while maintaining expenditures on social programs and advancing distributive objectives through higher real wages and employment.

Current appreciation of the economic advantages of privatization has been encouraged by two related phenomena. First, it has become increasingly obvious and politically embarrassing that the government provision and production of many goods and services, including the regulation of market activities, generates substantial deadweight losses. For example, Yale Brozen has estimated that current income would be at least 25 percent higher if some postwar programs had not been adopted.[1] Second, recent theoretical and empirical research has helped to scuttle the belief that government employees are public-interest maximizers.[2] It is now clear that government employees, like other economic agents, respond to the opportunities for gain provided by the structure of property rights embedded in the institutions used to control their choices. Economic theory supplies the tools for analyzing the economic consequences of alternative ownership arrangements, and the evidence to date can be used to support the privatization of a broad range of government activities.

Theoretical Framework

Economic theory, although quite complex in its more rigorous formulations, rests on a few simple but far-reaching propositions. Briefly, these are that each individual desires many goods; that these goods are substitutable; and that as the individual substitutes one good for another, keeping the level of satisfaction unchanged, the subjective value of an additional unit of the good being acquired falls relative to that of the good being given up. In the economist's jargon, each individual maximizes a strictly increasing, concave utility function. For each individual, of course, at least some goods are scarce; obviously, without scarcity there is no economic problem.

These propositions apply to all individuals, regardless of the economic system in which they live and their role as decision makers. In practice, they simply recognize that different individuals may attach different weights to different goals (e.g., power, health, the welfare of others) and to different means (e.g., persuasion, compulsion) of achieving them, and that each individual has the incentive to further those goals that he or she prefers. Accordingly, group decisions are best analyzed as the outcome of choices made by individual members of the group in pursuit of their own self-interests, including their view of what is best for the group as a whole. The individual is used as the basic unit of analysis not because of any ethical preferences but because doing so yields better predictions.

The ability of individuals to satisfy their wants is limited by the quantity of resources available, their allocation, their productivity, and the system of property rights. The typical postulates characterizing production functions are that inputs are substitutable; that, for proportionate increases in inputs, total output eventually increases at a decreasing rate; and that, at the margin, the productivity of any input eventually decreases. These propositions apply to all productive activities, including those undertaken by households, privately owned firms, and government bureaus.

Economic theory implies that the lower the cost (whatever has to be forgone) of any good (whatever is a source of utility to the chooser) or any input (whatever is used in production), the more the user will acquire: demand curves for both outputs and inputs are negatively sloped. Moreover, individuals typically respond to an increase in income by consuming more of all goods. And because inputs are costly and production functions have the characteristics that they do, additional units of output can typically be obtained only at a higher cost: supply curves are positively sloped. An individual's income is determined by the assets owned, including one's own labor, and their prices. How prices, including incomes, are set is determined by the system of property rights.[3]

In a world of scarcity, individuals can increase their welfare through specialization and exchange. Specialization allows individuals to engage in those activities in which they have a comparative advantage, including joint production within a firm, and to obtain a preferred combination of goods and services through exchange. Trade, even if there were no production, expands consumption opportunities beyond those that would have existed without it and allows each individual to enjoy a higher standard of living.

Property rights are the rights of individuals to the use of resources. These rights are established and enforced not only by formal legal rules and the power of the state but also by the social conventions that characterize society. Thus one's decisions on how to dress, eat, and talk are constrained by rules of etiquette and custom enforced by social ostracism.

The property rights adopted within a community provide a mechanism for assigning to particular individuals the authority to select how resources may be used, given a class of permissible uses. In particular, it specifies the nature of the rights that an individual may hold to the use, the income, and the transferability of resources. Thus, property rights in some goods may be exclusive and transferable (e.g., private), exclusive but nontransferable (e.g., usufruct), or nonexclusive and nontransferable (e.g., common ownership with open access). For example, a government employee may have the right to use a particular typewriter during office hours but may not take it home or transfer it to a government employee in a different division in exchange for a desk computer. On the other hand, the private owner of a typewriter may use it at home or elsewhere and may rent it or sell it to others at any mutually agreeable price. Similarly, an individual may be allowed to harm (reduce the wealth of) competitors by producing a superior product but not by shooting them, while the same person may be allowed to shoot an intruder but not to sell goods above a price ceiling.

Moreover, property rights in a particular resource may be partitioned, so that different individuals may concurrently hold different rights to its use. For example, the owner of a bundle of (private) rights to the use of a parcel of land may retain some of these rights while assigning the usufruct of others to a lessee. At the same time, a neighbor may own the (usufruct) right to walk across the land, everyone in the community may own the (common) right to dump smoke on it or fly over it, and the government may have the right to build a road through it.

The system of property rights determines, via actual or imputed prices, how the benefits and the harms resulting from a choice are allocated between the decision maker and everyone else. Different institutions typically embody different systems of property rights and thus present decision makers with different constraints, that is, with different opportunities for gain. Economic theory implies that individuals respond to a change in constraints by acquiring more of those sources of utility that have become relatively cheaper. To understand the economic consequences of alternative institutions, therefore, it is necessary to identify how the property rights that they embody affect the relative cost of alternative sources of utility and the resulting opportunities for gain.

Private property means that individuals' rights to the use of (and income from) the resources they own are exclusive and transferable to others at whatever prices are mutually agreeable. The stronger the private property rights are—that is, the more carefully defined, allocated, and enforced they are—the closer is the relationship between the welfare of the owners and the economic or social consequences of their decisions and the greater is the owners' incentive to take account of the harms and benefits that their decisions visit on others. Indeed, in the limit (i.e., transaction costs are zero and property rights are fully defined, allocated, and enforced) there are no external effects; decision makers bear, and therefore take into account, all harms and benefits flowing from their decisions. Future consequences are fully capitalized into current transfer prices, thus taking full account of the expected wants and circumstances of future generations.

Under these conditions, the rights to the use of resources are priced at their opportunity cost and flow to their highest-valued use. Thus the initial distribution of the rights does not affect their subsequent realignment, except indirectly through the effect on the distribution of income.[4] Indeed, the outcome is Pareto optimal: it is impossible to reallocate resources and make someone better off without making someone else worse off.

Common ownership with open access means that individuals lack exclusive, transferable rights to the use of resources. Because they cannot capture the full gains from any investment they might undertake to improve the resources held in common, they have less incentive to conserve them (e.g., postpone grazing or fishing) and to increase their productivity (e.g., build irrigation ditches, improve the habitat), whereas they have more incentive to invest on the privately owned resources (e.g., sheep, fishing vessels) used jointly in production. If private property is economically feasible, common ownership implies that resources are less likely to be allocated to their highest-valued use and output is smaller.

In a world of zero transaction costs, the solution of the economic problem is trivial. All individual and market demand and supply conditions are known instantaneously to everyone, and the rules of the game specified by the system of property rights are enforced instantaneously and costlessly, yielding the appropriate general equilibrium solution. Among other things, each individual would be an independent contractor and firms would not exist.

The fundamental economic problem, however, arises precisely because in the real world knowledge of the continually changing individual circumstances of time and place is costly to obtain, because contracts are costly to form, monitor, and enforce, and because property rights are costly to define, allocate, and enforce. As emphasized elsewhere, the existence of positive transaction costs introduces a new constraint and yields new, efficient solutions.[5] For example, it implies the queuing of resources (e.g., commodity inventories, resource unemployment) and of customers (e.g., backorders). It also implies that some rights are not fully assigned (e.g., some fisheries are owned in common), enforced (e.g., theft is not reduced to zero), or priced (e.g., parking space in some suburban shopping centers are assigned on a first-come, first-served basis), thereby reducing individuals' incentives to take fully into account the harms and benefits occasioned by their decisions.

Opportunities for gain also arise from developing and adopting institutions that economize on transaction costs. One of the most ubiquitous institutions for this purpose is the market, which is simply a low-cost arrangement for facilitating specialization and exchange. Market prices provide both users and producers with the information and the incentive to respond to changes in their individual circumstances and lower the cost to owners of allocating resources to their highest-valued use. Thus the effectiveness of the market in relieving scarcity is closely tied to the extent to which property rights are privately held. Indeed, private property rights provide individuals with the incentive and the opportunity to develop and adopt new contractual and institutional arrangements designed to economize on transaction costs and cope more successfully with a continually changing environment.

The Organization of Production

Business firms are simply contractual coalitions among owners of rights to the use of resources. The problem, then, is why firms arise, why they take different forms (e.g., single proprietorship, partnership, corporation, cooperative, nonprofit, worker-managed, government-owned), and what the consequences are of these alternative ways of organizing production.

Current research suggests that firms arise to solve the shirking-information problem of team production by lowering the cost of monitoring exchanges (including effort) and of directing the allocation of jointly cooperating units.[6] In a private-property system, the dual problem of choosing the monitors and providing them with the incentive to monitor effectively is solved simultaneously by assigning to the owners of the assets most specific to the firm (those assets whose value in the next-best use is considerably below their value in the present coalition) both ultimate control and the right to the coalition's residual earnings. Shirking within the firm is further inhibited by competition among actual and prospective members of the coalition (including managers) and by the market for control of the firm.

As additional transactions are brought within the firm, including a degree of vertical integration to inhibit opportunistic behavior among firms in the same production-distribution chain, the costs of monitoring and coordinating joint production eventually exceed the benefits, setting a limit to the size of the coalition. Moreover, differences in the availability and quality of entrepreneurial skills and in the success of choosing the appropriate contractual agreements imply that firms within an industry differ in size and technology used as well as in the range and quality of output produced.

Transaction costs are crucial in explaining the choice of business form. Thus, if monitoring costs are high relative to benefits, profit-sharing arrangements evolve to decrease shirking. Examples are partnerships in professional or intellectual work and share contracts in mining or agriculture.

Similarly, the modern corporation with transferable shares reduces the cost of raising large sums of capital when team size can be relatively large and the investment in firm-specific assets is substantial.[7] The transferability of shares lowers the transaction costs of revising individual investment portfolios, simultaneously facilitating the realignment of ownership and the formation of coalitions to replace management. Limited liability lowers the cost of exchanging shares by reducing the demand for information regarding actual and prospective shareholders.

Resource owners who join a business coalition typically specialize. Within a corporation, shareholders own the assets that are specific to the firm, bearing the value consequences of exogenous events and of decisions made within the firm. Bondholders specialize in the ownership of assets that are not firm-specific or, at least, are not open to opportunistic behavior by the shareholders. Managers specialize in making day-to-day decisions regarding the operation of the firm and act as agents for the shareholders. Other resource owners (e.g., employees) are typically paid their opportunity cost. To the extent that managers and other employees have invested in firm-specific assets (e.g., human capital), they have the incentive to share in the ultimate control of the firm. Some investment, however, in firm-specific assets by managers and other employees represents a bond to ensure performance, a bond that is forfeited for failure to fulfill the employment contract.

To survive in the competitive environment of a private enterprise system, firms must adapt to changes in circumstances by taking full advantage of opportunities for gains. The prospect of economic profits (returns above the competitive rate) provides firms with the incentive to produce the chosen level of output using the least-cost combination of inputs, thereby minimizing costs, and to choose the wealth-maximizing combination of price, quality, and quantity of output. Firms that fail to adapt, whether by evolving their own responses or by imitating successful firms, die. Competition to exploit the opportunities for gain quickly reduces returns to the competitive rate.

The success of competition in eliminating economic profits does not require the existence of many firms.[8] The threat of entry may be sufficient to inhibit firms from earning monopoly rents. Even more important, recent research suggests that many so-called barriers to entry merely reflect investments in information costs that are equally available to new entrants.

Why some business choices are solved through political rather than market processes is unclear. Several hypotheses, not mutually exclusive, enjoy various degrees of credibility.[9]

One hypothesis is taste. If the nature of the economic system itself is a source of utility, individuals would be willing to give up other goods (e.g., food, medical care) in order to have more government ownership. The evidence, however, suggests that the political choice of one ownership form over another generally rests on the belief that the organization will behave in a different, preferred way. For example, the political choice of whether a transit system is to be privately or municipally owned can be explained by such variables as the method of funding the service, such as user fees, and the voting strength of riders without taking taste into account.

A second hypothesis is wealth redistribution. On the demand side, individuals with a comparative advantage in the use of political power have the incentive to use the state to redistribute wealth toward themselves. On the supply side, politicians have the incentive to provide services to gain votes and other benefits, while government employees have the incentive to enhance their income, power, and prestige by expanding the activities that they control. Under these conditions, political firms may be used to facilitate or mask wealth transfers to selected groups. As noted elsewhere, the evidence supports this hypothesis.

A third possibility relates to the costs of excluding nonpayers. In the case of public goods (i.e., goods whose consumption by one individual does not detract from anyone else's consumption), people have little incentive to reveal their preferences. If the costs of excluding nonpayers are high enough, therefore, some public goods will be produced in smaller quantities than consumers would have been willing to buy. To justify government entry into the business, however, it is not sufficient to point out the drawbacks of the market solution. It is also necessary to show that the government solution in practice would be better. Moreover, the public-good argument can at best be used to support the political *provision* of some goods. Their production, like the production of other goods and services used by government, can typically be contracted out to private firms.

A fourth hypothesis is that some government ownership of business enterprises occurs to solve the shirking-monitoring problem of joint production. Government in principle can contract with private firms to produce the goods desired. As the costs of monitoring whether the output meets contract specifications increase relative to the costs of monitoring inputs when production is vertically integrated, however, the opportunities for shirking by independent contraction increase. Indeed, in many cases, drafting a contract specific enough to permit effective monitoring is simply impossible. Accordingly, there is incentive to integrate some business activities within government.

This hypothesis, particularly relevant to the privatization issue, is worth pursuing further. For example, it is relatively inexpensive to determine whether such physical entities as office supplies, buildings, and roads meet the specifications provided in their procurement contracts. Other considerations aside, government would be expected to purchase rather than produce these goods. As the cost of monitoring some of the output characteristics increases, government may be expected to include a clause in the purchase contract allowing it to place some of its own employees along the production process to monitor inputs. These arrangements are common in government procurement contracts for complex goods like ships and missiles. As the costs of monitoring outputs rise still higher relative to the costs of monitoring inputs, there is increased incentive to integrate the activity within government. For example, from the thirteenth to the sixteenth century, many European states purchased military defense from Swiss and German firms (mercenaries). As military weapons and tactics became progressively more complex, it also became costlier to monitor output as a means of ensuring that the services purchased are indeed available and of inhibiting opportunistic behavior (e.g., taking over the country). Accordingly, production of national defense was vertically integrated within government.

This discussion has suggested two main explanations for government owner-ship of business enterprises: redistribute wealth and solve the shirking-information problem of joint production. These considerations may therefore be used to iden-tify possible candidates for privatization.

The actual or fancied reasons for the existence of political firms affect behavior only to the extent that they are reflected in binding constraints on the firms' deci-sion makers. Accordingly, the next problem is to analyze the behavior of political firms.

The distinguishing characteristic of political firms is the high cost of transfer-ring ownership rights in their specialized assets. Taxpayers who wish to change their portfolio of these shares must typically change the political jurisdiction in which they work and live or change the operation of the political enterprises, both relatively costly activities. Because property rights in the firm-specific assets of political enterprises effectively are nontransferable, specialization in their owner-ship is ruled out, inhibiting the capitalization of future consequences into current transfer prices and reducing the incentive of taxpayers, who bear such consequences, to monitor managers.

This analysis implies that managers of political firms have greater opportuni-ties for discretionary behavior, as judged by market standards, than the managers of comparable privately owned firms, and their choices will exhibit greater vari-ance. Private enterprises must respond to market signals in order to survive. Managers of political firms, on the other hand, are less constrained by market considerations, finding it easier to obtain subsidies and mask their utility-maxi-mizing behavior under the guise of fulfilling other social goals. Indeed, public en-terprises, especially those endowed with politically influential clients, can survive for long periods, and their managers can prosper, even in the presence of persis-tent losses.

The evidence regarding the consequences of government ownership is rich and varied.[10] The industries studied include electric power, water, urban transit, airlines, banks, hospitals, fire prevention, and refuse collection.

Relative to private firms, even those subject to government regulation, managers of political firms have less incentive to tailor output prices to the demand and supply conditions that they face. The evidence from various industries indicates that political firms typically charge lower prices; engage in less revenue-increasing price discrimination, adopting fewer service categories and peak-related charges; relate prices less closely to the cost of supplying different groups of consumers; change prices less frequently and in response to larger changes in the relevant eco-nomic variables; and have rate structures that favor politically active groups. In-deed, government-owned electric utilities buy wholesale electric power at higher prices, and sell it at lower prices, than privately owned firms.

The managers of political firms have less incentive to minimize the cost of producing the output level chosen. The evidence suggests that political firms are less likely to use cost-minimizing input combinations, have higher operating costs, spend more on plant construction, have greater capacity, use more capital-intensive production techniques, are slower at adopting cost-reducing innovation, are more likely to give across-the-board than selective wage increases, have higher costs, and are generally less efficient.

The managers of political firms also have less incentive to take consumer wants into account. The evidence suggests that their firms offer a smaller variety of output, are less successful in satisfying consumer wants, emphasize the production of those service characteristics that are monitored more easily by the political authorities with control over the firm's budget, and make less use of market information in reaching their decisions.

Moreover, managers of political firms have more opportunity to use the firm's resources to enhance their survival in office, thereby increasing the present value of all their job-related, pecuniary and nonpecuniary sources of utility. The evidence indicates that they enjoy longer tenure in office than their counterparts in the private sector.

Some of the evidence may be regarded as tentative, pending further tests. As other essays in this volume document in more detail, however, the evidence overwhelmingly supports the hypothesis that differences in the structure of property rights distinguishing private and political firms affect their behavior systematically and predictably. By market standards, political firms are less efficient and less responsive to consumer wants.

The market is a low-cost, generally effective mechanism for regulating business activity. It uses prices to transmit information and simultaneously to provide the appropriate incentives to owners and users of resources. Within a market system, the role of government regulation is to help define, allocate, and enforce private property rights. In practice, of course, government regulation spreads far beyond these limits.

The problem of specifying the role of government regulation is part of the problem of specifying the system of property rights. Property rights determine whether a firm has the right to compete with a rival by charging a lower price, manufacturing a better product, providing more information to consumers, building a plant of more appropriate size, or setting fire to the rival's facilities. It also determines the contractual agreements that may be used to bind business coalitions and to control relations among independent firms. Thus, a firm may be allowed to establish retail outlets and sell its output at whatever prices it chooses, but it may not be allowed to contract with other firms to set prices or share markets. Some firms like public utilities may not have the right to set the prices of their outputs, and the owners of their specific assets may not be allowed full rights to the firms' residual income.

The nature of the supply-and-demand conditions for government regulation has not been adequately explored. There is widespread recognition, however, that such regulation is frequently established and operated for the benefit of the industries and occupations to be controlled. Owners of the rights to the use of resources have the incentive to seek state support for restricting the entry of competitors, burdening those competitors that manage to enter, affecting the price and availability of substitutes and complements to their own advantage, and enforcing collusive arrangements at taxpayers' expense. Correspondingly, politicians and government employees have the incentive to cater to special-interest groups and expand their own activities.[11]

Although a firm or group of firms may be able to influence regulation to their own benefit, the transfer of conflict resolution from the marketplace to the political arena admits other rent-seeking parties to the decision-making process, and these will work to exact their own tributes. As a result, the regulated entities are typically unable to reap full monopoly profits, and much of the possible gains are dissipated in rent-seeking activities.

The way in which regulation is organized also matters. Information and enforcement costs are positive, while regulators' budgets and wisdom are limited. More important, the property rights that characterize alternative regulatory arrangements exert a powerful influence on regulators' behavior.

Consider, for example, some of the economic consequences of using independent agencies relative to government bureaus to control the behavior of firms in specific industries. Independent agencies are typically headed by politically appointed commissioners whose job-related, contractual sources of pecuniary income are set by statute and can be changed only by legislation. Moreover, the statutes apply equally to all members of a commission; as a result, they are not responsive to individual performance. Government bureaus, on the other hand, are headed by career civil servants whose salaries can normally be increased through promotion to the next higher rank. Because the salary of a civil servant varies with the size of the staff, budget, or case load administered, it is more responsive than a commissioner's to individual performance. It follows that the cost of an easier workload and other nonpecuniary sources of utility is lower for commissioners, who will acquire more of them and thus will have less incentive to engage in regulatory activity.

The evidence supports the hypothesis that, relative to managers of regulatory bureaus, commissioners favor arrangements that ease their workload. For example, a study of the taxicab industry shows that, relative to bureaus, commissions favor single monopolies and various market divisions (e.g., exclusive taxi stands); they are also more likely to establish single tariffs and prohibit rental-driver operations.[12]

Regulators depend on politicians for their appointment and for approval of their budgets. Accordingly, given similar institutional arrangements, regulators at the local level may be expected to be more responsive than state regulators to the voting strength of local users. The evidence supports this hypothesis.[13] Under state jurisdiction, local transit firms charge higher prices, earn a higher rate of return, and are less likely to be converted to public ownership than if they were under municipal control. Moreover, in cities where the proportion of nonusers has increased, profit margins decrease less over time and the probability of conversion to public ownership is smaller. Indeed, there is evidence that state regulation of electric utilities developed primarily to preempt more stringent local regulation.

Focusing more directly on the behavior of regulated firms, a binding profit constraint implies that owners' wealth may be increased by using relatively more capital (thereby increasing the rate base) to produce the level of output chosen. More important for present purposes, however, an active profit constraint also implies an attenuation of owners' property rights and an increase in managers' discretionary authority.

The available evidence indicates that, relative to privately owned firms, regulation by government employees is associated with greater job discrimination, higher costs, more fixed capital, higher prices, lower output, and less research and development.[14]

Government regulation includes antitrust policy, and the cost-reward structure embedded in the responsible agencies has had a fundamental impact on the nature and conduct of that policy. There is evidence that the antitrust activities of the Department of Justice and the Federal Trade Commission have been dominated by bureaucratic and political considerations, with the result that both enforcement and deterrent effects have been capricious and perverse.[15] Moreover, antitrust laws are routinely used in private suits to hold up competitors and prospective buyers in a merger. Even more unfortunately, antitrust laws frequently proscribe contractual arrangements and business practices that in fact enhance competition.[16]

Conclusion

The system of property rights adopted within a society establishes the kinds of competition that may be used to resolve the conflict of interests occasioned by scarcity. Under private property, people bear the value consequences of their decisions. Market prices provide information and incentive to both users and producers, thereby relieving scarcity by facilitating specialization and exchange. Although the existence of positive transaction costs may inhibit the exhaustion of all mutually beneficial trade, market processes offer a flexible means of responding to change in a world of widely dispersed knowledge.

Government involvement in the provision and production of goods and services as well as in the regulation of business activity has been justified to rectify a variety of allocative (e.g., monopoly, public goods, externalities) and distributive problems. Individuals, however, have the incentive to manipulate the power of the state to their own advantage, and alleged limitations of the market frequently provide the rhetoric for groups seeking protection from competitive forces. Moreover, government employees are not public-interest maximizers, even if they knew what the public interest is.

The extension of government activities beyond those concerned with the definition, allocation, and enforcement of private property rights limits the ability and incentive of individuals to respond to changes in circumstances and weakens the effectiveness of the market in reducing scarcity.

The system of property rights established by government ownership and regulation of some business activities reduce the extent to which individuals bear the value consequences of their decisions. Both regulators and regulated have increased discretionary authority as judged by market standards and thus enjoy increased opportunity to pursue their own goals, such as more leisure, power, and wealth. The evidence and the analysis presented in this essay suggest that government ownership and regulation result in output that is smaller and less responsive to individual wants. Thus a careful program of privatization would result in higher output and increased welfare.

NOTES

1. Yale Brozen, "The Economic Impact of Government Policy" (Paper presented at the symposium, "Economic Policy in the Market Process: Success or Failure," Slot Zeist, The Netherlands, 29 Jan. 1986).

2. Louis De Alessi, "The Economics of Property Rights: A Review of the Evidence," *Research in Law and Economics* 2 (1980): 1–47.

3. Armen A. Alchian, "How Should Prices Be Set?" *Il Politico* 32 (June 1967): 369–82; and idem., "Some Economics of Property Rights," *Il Politico* 30 (December 1965): 816–29.

4. Ronald H. Coase, "The Problem of Social Cost," *Journal of Law and Economics* 3 (October 1960): 1–44.

5. Louis De Alessi, "Property Rights, Transaction Costs, and X-Efficiency: An Essay in Economic Theory," *American Economic Review* 73 (March 1983): 64–81.

6. Armen A. Alchian and Harold Demsetz, "Production, Information Costs, and Economic Organization," *American Economic Review* 62 (December 1972): 777–95; and Eugene F. Fama, "Agency Problems and the Theory of the Firm," *Journal of Political Economy* 88 (April 1980): 288–307.

7. Louis De Alessi and Raymond P. H. Fishe, "Why Do Corporations Distribute Assets? An Analysis of Dividends and Capital Structure," *Journal of Institutional and Theoretical Economics* 143 (March 1987): 34–51.

8. William J. Baumol, "Contestable Markets: An Uprising in the Theory of Industry Structure," *American Economic Review* 72 (March 1982): 1–15; and Harold Demsetz, "Barriers to Entry," *American Economic Review* 72 (March 1982): 47–57.

9. Louis De Alessi, "On the Nature and Consequences of Private and Public Enterprises," *Minnesota Law Review* 67 (October 1982): 191–209.

10. Steve H. Hanke, "The Literature on Privatization," in *The Privatization Option*, ed. Stuart M. Butler (Washington, D.C.: The Heritage Foundation, 1985): 83–97; and De Alessi, "Review of the Evidence."

11. Thomas E. Borcherding, ed., *Budgets and Bureaucrats: The Sources of Government Growth* (Durham, N.C.: Duke University Press, 1977).

12. Ross D. Eckert, "On the Incentives of Regulators: The Case of Taxicabs," *Public Choice* 14 (Spring 1973): 83–100.

13. De Alessi, "Review of the Evidence."

14. Ibid.

15. William F. Long, Richard Schramm, and Robert Tollison, "The Economic Determinants of Antitrust Activity," *Journal of Law and Economics* 16 (October 1973): 351–64; and John J. Siegfried, "The Determinants of Antitrust Activity" and Peter Asch, "The Determinants and Effects of Antitrust Activity," *Journal of Law and Economics* 18 (October 1975): 559–81.

16. Yale Brozen, *Concentration, Mergers, and Public Policy* (New York: Macmillan Publishing Co., 1982), and David D. Haddock, "Basing-Point Pricing: Competitive vs. Collusive Theories," *American Economic Review* 72 (June 1982): 289–306.

Privatizing the Welfare State

JOHN C. GOODMAN

That there is a problem with the United States welfare system is confirmed by evidence from many sources, including anecdotal reports, scholarly analyses, and statistical tests. All told, the evidence of a problem is clear, unmistakable, undeniable, and overwhelming.

Beginning in the mid-1960s a number of studies of the welfare system were conducted by scholars with impeccable academic credentials. None of these studies actually proved that welfare was causing poverty. Yet each provided a penetrating analysis of particular dimensions of the problem and did so in powerful and persuasive ways.

The Moynihan study. Now a classic in the field, *The Negro Family* was published in 1965.[1] Its author, Daniel Patrick Moynihan, then a professor at Harvard University, expressed alarm over the fact that 20 percent of all black children were living in single-parent households. (Today the figure is more than 60 percent.) The book touched off a storm of controversy, as did his later advice to the Nixon administration: Quit pouring money into the black community and instead follow a policy of "benign neglect."

The Anderson study. Martin Anderson, a senior fellow at Stanford University's Hoover Institution and former chief of the Office of Policy Development in the Reagan administration, wrote the pathbreaking book *Welfare* in the late 1970s. In it he calculated how much a poor family in California would lose (in terms of new taxes and lost welfare benefits) if the breadwinner went into the marketplace and earned an extra dollar of income. Astonishingly, Anderson discovered that at almost every level of income, low-income families faced the highest effective tax rates of any group in the country; poor families could lose as much as 80 cents for earning one more dollar from productive work; and welfare recipients who earned an extra dollar of income lost considerably more than one dollar in certain in-kind benefits, such as Medicaid.[2] Anderson concluded that the welfare system was designed from top to bottom to encourage dependency and to discourage self-reliance.

The Gilder studies. George Gilder, a sociologist, spent several years in the mid-

1970s living among poor families who were receiving welfare. Gilder's study, *Visible Man*,[3] and his best seller, *Wealth and Poverty*,[4] analyzed in great detail how the welfare system was destroying the family, especially the black family, in low-income communities.

The NCPA study. "Welfare and Poverty" was the first study to document how the welfare establishment has managed to spend increasingly larger sums of money while maximizing the poverty count.[5] Official measurements of poverty count only money income and ignore in-kind benefits, such as medical care, food stamps, and public housing. By spending ever-increasing amounts of money on in-kind (noncash) benefits, instead of cash benefits, the welfare establishment has managed to make welfare increasingly attractive without disqualifying recipients by endangering their status as "poor." Between 1965 and 1981, cash transfers to the poor barely changed at all in real terms while noncash benefits increased 5,238 percent.

The Murray study. More than any other single study, Charles Murray's *Losing Ground* shocked liberals and conservatives alike into realizing that something was wrong with the United States welfare system.[6] Murray argued that in central cities the black family had been all but destroyed, and he made a forceful case that the welfare system bore chief responsibility for this shocking development.

One of the criticisms of the studies by Gilder, Murray, and others is that they did not perform rigorous statistical tests to support their positions. Social scientists, by nature, like controlled experiments and rigorously developed econometric tests of important propositions. As it turns out, this kind of evidence is now in hand.

The negative income-tax experiments. In controlled experiments performed by the U.S. Department of Health and Human Services, the effects of a guaranteed income on families were observed over several years in large cities. In the Seattle and Denver income-maintenance experiments, families were given a minimum level of income by the Federal government. Compared with similarly situated families not on welfare, families who were given the income changed their behavior substantially.[7] The number of hours worked by husbands dropped 9 percent; by wives, 20 percent; and by young male adults, an incredible 43 percent. The length of unemployment among husbands increased 27 percent; among wives it increased 42 percent, and for single female household heads it increased 60 percent. Divorce increased 36 percent among whites and 42 percent among blacks.

The Gallaway-Vedder study.[8] This study, produced for the National Center for Policy Analysis by Lowell Gallaway and Richard Vedder of Ohio University, was a first-of-its-kind statistical analysis that attempted to document the number of people who were living in poverty by choice because of the attractiveness of the welfare system. The study found that at least 5.7 million people — about one-sixth of the poverty population — are living in poverty by choice as a result of the generosity of public welfare and that each additional $1 billion in welfare spending increases the poverty population by 250,000.

Since 1972, there has been a strong, positive relationship between the amount of welfare spending and the amount of poverty, after adjusting for other important factors, including the unemployment rate and the rate of economic growth. Put simply, more poverty has resulted from the increased amount the government pays people to be poor.

One of the greatest tragedies of the welfare system is its effects on children. The statistical evidence shows that the increasing attractiveness of welfare benefits throughout the 1970s increased poverty among children by more than 20 percent. Almost 2.5 million more children are living in poverty today as a direct result of the expanded welfare state.

The states that have paid the most generous benefits to welfare mothers have experienced the greatest increases in child poverty. By contrast, states that have been the least generous have seen major reductions in child poverty. Between 1969 and 1979, the child poverty rate rose 27.9 percent in the ten states with the highest welfare benefits while the rate fell by 17.4 percent in the ten states with the lowest welfare benefits.

The General Accounting Office report.[9] In the previous studies, the focus was on the harmful effects of increased welfare benefits on the behavior of people. What made the study by the General Accounting Office (GAO) unique was that it focused on the opposite phenomenon: What happens to the behavior of people when welfare benefits are reduced?

The GAO study focused mainly on welfare mothers who were earning a private income before and after losing their Aid to Families with Dependent Children (AFDC) benefits. It showed that, approximately two years after losing AFDC benefits, welfare mothers, on the average, had increased the number of hours they worked, were commanding a higher hourly wage, and had increased their real income from working significantly. In Boston, 43 percent of the welfare mothers had at least as much or more total income after they lost their welfare benefits as they had before. (Their average real income from working increased 25 percent.) Not only did the welfare mothers who lost AFDC benefits respond by changing their work behavior; they also reacted to the loss of welfare benefits by making important changes in their family lives. Two years after losing their AFDC benefits, a significant number of welfare mothers had increased their family size by at least one adult. In Syracuse, 19 percent did so, and in Dallas, 22 percent.

Two Views of Poverty and Welfare

When welfare policy is set by the government (whether at the national, state, or local level), politicians invariably search for a single, all-encompassing explanation of what the welfare program is all about. What usually follows is a single set of rules that applies to all beneficiaries, regardless of individual attitudes or circumstances.

In this context, two opposing views of the problem of poverty persistently clash. The first view sees the problem of poverty as a lack of income — caused by conditions over which low-income people have no control. The other view sees the problem as largely one of individual behavior that people, in principle, can control. Today the former view is forcefully expressed by scholars like Michael Harrington, Sar A. Levitan, Clifford M. Johnson, and John E. Schwartz. The latter is expressed with equal vigor by Warren Brookes, George Gilder, and Charles Murray.

The argument that poverty is caused by conditions over which low-income people have no control is not a new one. Nineteenth-century critics of the Elizabethan Poor Laws, such as Charles Dickens, Arnold Bennett, and George Landsbury, repeatedly emphasized this view and attacked the Poor Laws as inhumane. For example, of a visit to a workhouse for the poor, Landsbury wrote: "Going down the narrow road, ringing the bell, waiting while an official with a not-too-pleasant face looked through a grating to see who was there, and hearing his unpleasant voice . . . made it easy for me to understand why the poor dreaded and hated these places. . . . It was not necessary to write the words 'Abandon hope all ye who enter here.' . . . Everything possible was done to inflict mental and moral degradation. . . . Of goodwill, kindliness, there was none."[10]

Other prominent people, however, devoted their lives to improving the plight of the poor and concluded that poverty was mainly the result of individual behavior. Charles S. Loch, secretary of the Charity Organization Society, one of the most important private charities in England at the turn of the century, wrote: "Want of employment in nine cases out of ten in which the plea is used is not the cause of distress. It is, as often as not, drink."[11] In Loch's view, it was important that the conditions under which relief was given never be perceived as more desirable than the least appealing job opportunities in the labor market.

These two opposing views — poverty as the result of conditions over which people have no control and poverty as the result of individual choice and behavior — have important implications for public policy.

In modern times, those who take the bureaucratic approach to the problem tend to define it in terms of people's financial condition. Accordingly, the magnitude of the problem is "measured" by Federal statisticians who attempt to count how many families have incomes that fall below the official poverty level. The solution to the problem is to give families living in poverty enough money to raise their income levels above the poverty line.

It follows that the purpose of welfare is quite simple: to give away money. And, indeed, this is an apt way of describing AFDC, the Food Stamp Program, and other entitlement programs. The bureaucrats who run these programs are literally in the business of giving away money. By and large, the program administrators give little thought to making positive changes in the behavior of their clientele. And defenders of the programs either minimize or ignore the negative behavioral consequences these programs create. Thus, scholars like Greg Duncan and Richard Coe argue that the United States welfare system serves as a social safety net, which gives relief to people in need without encouraging long-term dependency. By contrast, those who take a behavioral approach to the problem of poverty see the United States welfare system as one that increasingly rewards bad behavior. Why has poverty increased in America? To Charles Murray, the answer is straightforward: the government is paying people to be poor.

Which view is correct? Neither completely nor accurately describes the welfare-poverty crisis. It is true that some people are poor because of conditions over which they have little or no control. It is also true that other people are poor by choice. The correct way to depict the United States welfare system is by recognizing that it gives relief to people in need while encouraging perverse behavior. Even if one does not accept the precise estimates of the Gallaway-Vedder study, the evidence is overwhelming that the United States welfare system does both harm and good at the same time.

Boston and Dallas: A Case Study

There are striking differences among poor people as to why they become poor, how long they remain poor, and how and why they cease being poor. The difficulties in generalizing about the effects of welfare — even the effects of a fairly well-structured program like AFDC — can be appreciated by comparing welfare mothers in Dallas and Boston who lost their AFDC benefits as a result of program changes in 1981.

As for welfare benefits, Massachusetts is one of the most liberal states in the country. Texas, by contrast, ranks near the bottom of the fifty states in AFDC payments per recipient and has a record that many would regard as stingy. The standard AFDC payment to a family of three in Boston in 1981 was more than three times greater than the payment in Dallas ($379 a month versus $116). In addition, the Boston AFDC mother had many more opportunities to exploit the entire welfare system.

To see how lucrative welfare benefits in Boston are, consider the case of a welfare mother as described by a reporter writing in the *Boston Globe* in 1975:

> The mother is well-organized. She buys food stamps twice a month, refuses to live in a housing project, is a member of a community women's group at Catholic charities, and is studying for her high school diploma. Her bi-monthly cash grant is $466; she gets a flat grant every three months of $142; and her monthly savings from food stamps amount to $86. Her cash income may be given as $599 monthly, or $7,188 a year. If she and her family spent the average amount paid personally for health care in this country (and the mother gets some psychiatric care), this would amount at full cost to an additional $1,750 in health care expenses. Since there are no financial restrictions for the family on the use of health care, and the mother is intelligent and knowledgeable, one may assume that full use of this opportunity is taken. The three older children go free of charge to an alternative school which costs paying pupils $2,000 a year, and another child goes to a day care center whose cost for a paying child would be $1,000 a year. Cash income and free health and education services to this family thus amount to $16,028. The other children work summers, and I will not cost that out. The family pays no taxes, and need put nothing aside for savings, as the welfare department is committed to meeting its needs. A working head of family would have to earn at least $20,000 to match this standard of living.[12]

The characteristics of welfare mothers who lost their AFDC benefits in Dallas and Boston are quite different. Clearly, the welfare mother in Dallas was in greater need. She had more children and younger children than her Boston counterpart. After AFDC payments were discontinued, the Boston mother was three times more likely than the Dallas mother to be above the poverty level, three times more likely to have private health insurance, and 38 percent less likely to turn to private charity for food. There were also clear differences in their abilities to compete in the labor market. Twenty-nine percent of the Boston mothers had some college education, compared with only 11 percent in Dallas. Surprisingly, 2.5 percent of the Boston mothers who lost AFDC payments had a college degree and 1.7 percent had a graduate degree. Furthermore, the Boston mother showed greater ability to hold down a job for a longer period of time. Length of time with the current employer was twice as long in Boston as it was in Dallas. Interestingly, the Boston AFDC mother showed a greater propensity to accept welfare and take advantage of the welfare system. She went on AFDC more quickly, stayed on it longer, and was more likely to have received other welfare benefits, such as housing subsidies. She was also more likely than the Dallas mother to have received AFDC as a child.

Among AFDC mothers who lost their benefits in 1981, the loss in Boston was more than twice the loss in Dallas. In addition, about 85 percent of the Boston women also lost food stamps, compared with only 42 percent in Dallas. Yet, despite the greater loss of benefits in Boston, the welfare mothers there suffered much less economic dislocation than those in Dallas. Total income for Boston mothers declined only 12 percent, while for Dallas mothers it declined 31 percent.

This difference stems from the fact that Boston mothers were more likely to recoup in the private marketplace income that they had lost from AFDC and food stamps. They increased the hours they worked, earned more per hour, and, on average, increased their monthly earnings by 25 percent. Thirty-five percent of Boston mothers actually had more total income after they lost their AFDC benefits than they had before. By contrast, in Dallas (with a lower unemployment rate than Boston) there was, on the average, virtually no increase in hours worked and only a 6 percent increase in monthly earnings.

It appears, then, that Boston's liberal welfare benefits, doled out to people who were not necessarily very needy, were discouraging productive work and that removing these benefits spurred recipients to increase their work effort. By contrast, in Dallas, where AFDC mothers had a greater need and less ability to compete in the marketplace, welfare benefits had only a moderately discouraging effect. A very different story emerges when one looks at the effects of welfare on the family. In Boston, 5 percent of welfare mothers increased their households by at least one adult, compared with 22 percent in Dallas. The effect of welfare on the family is apparently greatest where it makes the greatest financial difference.

Finally, when given the choice between working and receiving no welfare or not working and becoming dependent on the dole, recipients responded differently in the two cities. In Boston, 11 percent returned to AFDC (usually after ceasing employment), but in Dallas the percentage was twice as high. Moreover, of those who returned to AFDC, the length of time on welfare was much shorter in Boston than in Dallas. It appears that the more lucrative the private marketplace options, the more likely that work will be chosen over welfare.

The comparison of these two cities, then, underscores the difficulty in making generalizations about the nation's welfare system. Even generalizations about a single city are hazardous. Yet this is precisely how the Federal government runs the welfare state.

Public-Sector Failure and Private-Sector Success

Although volumes have been written about the failures of government welfare programs, the academic community has paid surprisingly little attention to private-sector charity, which is playing an extremely important role. In 1984, total charitable contributions reached $74.25 billion, with contributions by individuals accounting for 83 percent, or $61.55 billion, of that total. More than 85 percent of all adult Americans make some charitable contribution each year, and 47 percent of all adults volunteer their time to charitable causes — an average of three hours a week per person. The dollar value of these contributions of time is at least $65 billion; if this value of volunteer labor is included, private-sector contributions to charitable causes exceed the poverty budgets of Federal, state, and local governments combined.[13]

Entitlement programs for welfare are structured so that benefits are granted solely on the basis of personal circumstances. Applicants do not have to give the reasons for their circumstances, nor are thy required to explain how they plan to change them in the future. They do not even have to show a willingness to change. In the AFDC program, for example, there are essentially four requirements for eligibility: (1) low income; (2) very few assets; (3) dependent children; and (4) no man in the household. Anyone satisfying these requirements is entitled to benefits. And the word *entitlement* means "right"— benefits cannot be withdrawn simply because the recipient refuses to modify his or her behavior.

The philosophy of the private sector is quite different. Because of the emphasis on a behavioral approach to the problem of poverty, the best private charities do not view the giving of assistance as a "duty" or the receipt of assistance as a "right." Instead, charitable assistance is viewed as a tool that can be used intelligently, not only to provide relief but also to change behavior. At many private charities, for example, the level of assistance varies considerably from individual to individual. Private agencies usually reserve the right to reduce the level of assistance or withdraw assistance altogether if recipients do not show behavioral changes.

Many private charities require that a caseworker and a recipient of aid establish a plan designed to move the recipient to a condition of self-sufficiency. For example, at Jessie's House, a transitional home for the homeless in Hampton, Massachusetts, shelter beyond a week's stay is contingent on positive evidence of individual improvement. At the Dallas Salvation Army, caseworkers are not significantly bound to grant a minimum or a maximum level of assistance. Aid varies according to the caseworker's evaluation of the recipient's condition and record of behavioral improvement.

Whether receipt of welfare is a "right" or a "privilege" is on one level an ethical and philosophical question. On another level, the question has profound implications for how society is going to function. Under entitlement programs, recipients and potential recipients of aid have full freedom to exercise their preferences at will. In many cases, they can choose poverty over nonpoverty. Once this choice is made, the rest of society is presented with a welfare bill that it is obligated to pay. Thus, in a sense, under entitlement programs the preferences of the recipients determine the behavior (through the tax burden) of those who pay the bills.

The philosophy of the private sector is quite different. In general, private agencies view the preferences of those who pay the bills as the standard, and the recipients are expected to change their behavior to satisfy the givers. In other words, under the private-sector approach, welfare recipients must adjust their behavior to the preferences of the rest of society, not the other way around.

If one accepts the view that people should take responsibility for supporting themselves and their families and that welfare assistance should be administered in a way that encourages rather than discourages this behavioral ideal, it follows that the approach of the best private charities is far superior to the approach of entitlement programs. Because people and their circumstances differ, it is only through a program of "hands-on-management" of charitable giving that relief can be given without at the same time encouraging antisocial behavior. "Hands-on-management" means tailoring aid to meet individual needs and circumstances.

One basic principle of the American philosophy of government is that people turn to government only as a last resort. In other words, it is generally assumed that the government provides socially desirable services that the private sector will not or cannot perform.

Ironically, in the field of social welfare this philosophy has been turned on its head. In the early years of the War on Poverty, it was thought that Federal welfare programs were designed to provide a social safety net—to provide services that the private sector, for one reason or another, had failed to offer. Yet it is becoming obvious that just the opposite has become the case—increasingly, the private sector is providing the social safety net by reaching people whom government fails to reach and by providing the essential services that government welfare programs fail to offer.

If a humane welfare system means anything at all, it means getting aid first to people who need it most. One of the most astonishing and little-known facts about the welfare state is what a miserable job it does in pursuing this goal. Consider that only 41 percent of all poverty families receive food stamps, although 28 percent of food-stamp families have incomes above the poverty level. Only 23 percent of all poverty families live in public housing or receive subsidized housing benefits, but almost half of the families receiving housing benefits are not poor. Only 40 percent of all poverty families are covered by Medicaid, and yet 40 percent of all Medicaid beneficiaries are not poor. *Amazingly, 41 percent of all poverty families receive no means-tested benefit of any kind from government.* Yet more than half of all families who do receive at least one means-tested benefit are not poor.

Where do people in need turn for help when they are not getting government assistance? They turn to private charities. Of all the shelters for the homeless in the United States, 94 percent are operated by churches, synagogues, nonreligious groups, and other voluntary organizations. The private sector is also very heavily involved in emergency food distribution. The Second Harvest network, which operates 79 of more than 300 food banks in the United States, distributes about 118 million pounds of food each year, worth about $78 million. This food is donated by the food industry and by private donors; about 40 percent of it goes to food centers patronized by the homeless.

Several studies of low-income families confirm that when people get in trouble, they turn to the private sector first. A study in Detroit found that when faced with a crisis, 80 percent of low-income people turned to other people or agencies within their own neighborhood rather than to government agencies for help. Similar findings were reported in a study conducted by the University of Southern California.

A major issue in the welfare-poverty industry is whether the recipient of aid should have to "do anything" in order to qualify for continued receipt of welfare benefits. Nowhere is the controversy more evident than with respect to the issue of workfare.

Throughout the 1970s there was a continuous political battle at the national level over whether workfare should be tied to welfare. A fascinating account of the politics of this battle has been written by Lawrence M. Mead, who has documented the great lengths to which the welfare bureaucracy lobbied against any workfare requirements.[14] The welfare bureaucracy apparently lost the battle when Congress passed the Work Incentive (WIN) program and the Community Work Experience Program (CWEP), which were designed to encourage work. However, because it administers these two programs, the bureaucracy that lost the battle won the war. In the WIN program, only 20 percent of adult AFDC recipients were found by the welfare bureaucracy to be suitable for workfare. Most of these adults went into training or school activities rather than into job positions. Only 2 percent actually got jobs. In CWEP, only 39 percent of adult AFDC recipients were found by the welfare bureaucracy to be suitable for workfare, and only 7 percent participated regularly.

As previously noted, the attitude of the best private charities is quite the opposite. These agencies see independence and self-sufficiency on the part of their "clients" as one of their primary goals. Often this goal is accomplished either by encouraging or requiring the recipients of aid to contribute their labor to the agency itself.

The attitude toward family on the part of private-sector charities also stands in stark contrast to the incentives built into Federal programs. AFDC eligibility rules in nearly half of the states do not allow families with an employed father to receive assistance, regardless of how low the family income is. In the other states, the family is ineligible if the father is present at all, regardless of employment. By contrast, at the Dallas Salvation Army shelter for battered and abused women, the mothers of young children are required to either work with professionals to repair their relationship with their husbands or find employment in order to receive continued assistance.

Private-sector charitable activities are diverse and widespread in cities and counties throughout the country. Knowledge of these activities is scanty, but as more research is done the evidence mounts that the private sector outperforms the government in areas such as foster care and job training for teenagers and the mentally and physically handicapped. Moreover, public housing placed in the hands of tenants costs less and is of higher quality than when owned and maintained by government. Private-sector crime-prevention programs, alcohol and drug abuse programs, and neighborhood preservation programs have also proved to be superior to public-sector programs.

Despite the success of private charities, there is growing evidence they are being "crowded out." The private sector's willingness to contribute to social-welfare activities is influenced by what the Federal government is doing, or at least by what the private sector perceives it to be doing.

Since 1955, charitable contributions by individuals have ranged between 2.5 and 3.0 percent of disposable income, yet the percent of income contributed to social-welfare activities in 1980 was less than half of what it was in 1955. A similar trend exists for all sources of private giving, including corporations and foundations. Twenty-two percent of all private charitable contributions went to social welfare activities in 1955, but by 1983, that figure had dropped to 11 percent.

This decline in private contributions to social-welfare agencies appears to be in response to a marked increase in government welfare spending. In other words, the more the government became involved in antipoverty activities, the more the private sector retrenched. As the welfare state has expanded, the public has responded by giving a larger percent of its charitable contributions to other activities — schools, hospitals, art and cultural activities, and various other civic and public programs.

The expanding welfare state is crowding the private sector out of the market. According to one study, a 10 percent increase in social-welfare spending by the government leads to a reduction of $27, on the average, in private contributions by taxpayers who itemize their deductions. Overall, each additional dollar of social welfare spending by the government leads to a thirty-cent reduction in private contributions.

Why should the government be involved in the business of charity in the first place? The traditional economic argument is that spending money for the relief of poverty has social effects that extend beyond the interest of the individual giver. Thus, giving to charity is different in principle from the act of buying a loaf of bread. The purchaser of the bread enjoys the full benefits of his purchase when he consumes the product. Yet a gift to charity benefits not only the giver but also everyone else who has an interest in (and gets personal satisfaction from) the charitable objective. As a result, given complete freedom of choice, people will give too little to charity. They will do so because they will consider only their individual, private benefit from the gift and ignore the social benefits created for others. Put another way, given freedom of choice, people will try to become "free riders" on the charitable gifts of others and fail to contribute their "fair share."

These are the theoretical arguments behind government coercion — requiring people to give a certain portion of their incomes for the relief of poverty. Most people accept these arguments, in one form or another.

It does not follow, however, that because of these arguments the government should nationalize the charity industry. The government requires licensed drivers to carry automobile liability insurance, but few would argue that it is necessary or desirable for the government to nationalize the automobile liability insurance industry. But the government has become a public monopoly in the welfare industry. It has put itself in the position of being the exclusive recipient of charitable contributions taken by coercion (through the tax system) and of having sole discretion over how these dollars are spent.

The most serious defects of the American system of public charity all stem from the unfortunate fact that the government has monopolized it. In the first place, under this monopoly the dollars almost never go where the givers would have preferred them to go. Although voluntary gifts totaling $74 billion are made each year by the private sector, no one ever gives money voluntarily to the AFDC or food-stamp programs. Furthermore, when spending decisions are made through the political process, it is inevitable that powerfully organized special interests have considerable influence over how the dollars are spent. Thus it is no accident that more than two-thirds of all Federal welfare spending ultimately ends up in the pockets of people who are distinctly not poor. Medicaid dollars go to doctors and hospitals; food-stamp dollars go to the agricultural industry; housing subsidies go to landlords; and legal-service dollars go to lawyers. Finally, precisely because it faces no competition in the marketplace, the public charity monopoly can continue to spend money in wasteful and inefficient ways, to fail miserably in achieving its objectives, and to misbehave in other ways without fear of losing customers to a competitor. To remedy these defects, public-sector charity must be denationalized.

Privatizing Welfare: Three Proposals

The basic idea of privatizing public charity is a simple one. The government would continue to force people to give their "fair share" through the vehicle of the income-tax system. But individual taxpayers, rather than politicians, would decide how their share of the welfare bill would be spent. In other words, taxpayers would be free to allocate their welfare tax dollars to any qualified private charity. In this way, private charities would compete on an equal footing with government welfare programs for the portion of the Federal budget allocated to poverty programs.

Furthermore, there would be free and open entry into the market; anyone could start a private charity and be eligible for "tax dollar contributions," provided the charity had a social-welfare purpose and satisfied certain other minimal requirements.

One proposal involves partial privatization of public charity. Under this proposal, individuals could allocate up to 10 percent of their personal Federal income taxes to qualified private charities. These gifts could be made directly to the private charities and then deducted from taxes owed on their income-tax returns. Alternatively, taxpayers would have the opportunity on their returns to instruct the U.S. Treasury to pay up to 10 percent of their taxes to specific private charitable organizations. Any amount allocated to private charities under this proposal would have to be deducted from the Federal government's poverty budget. In other words, for each tax dollar allocated to private-sector charity, public-sector charity would be reduced by a dollar.

In 1984, total Federal personal income taxes amounted to $296.2 billion. Ten percent of this amount, about $30 billion, is a little less than one-third of all Federal welfare spending. Had this proposal been in effect in 1984, individual taxpayers would have had the opportunity to allocate one-third of the Federal welfare budget away from government programs to private-sector programs. If the public took full advantage of this opportunity, Congress would be required to cut $30 billion out of public-sector programs. How the cuts would be made would be left up to Congress.

A second proposal is a natural extension of the first. It broadens the choice of the individual taxpayers by allowing them to allocate their entire share of the social-welfare budget among all public- and private-sector agencies and programs involved in the "business" of welfare. Every social-welfare agency—public and private—would compete against every other agency for welfare tax dollars. In principle, this proposal allows the public to make all of the decisions on how the social-welfare budget is allocated, although taxpayers would be free to forgo this responsibility by indicating on their returns that they would like to relinquish to Congress the right to decide how their welfare tax dollars are spent.

In 1984, total means-tested welfare spending by the Federal government was $100.5 billion—about one-third of all personal income taxes paid that year. This proposal would therefore give people direct control over how one-third of their tax dollars would be spent.

These two proposals are confined to a range of activities that fall under the designation of "welfare." They specifically exclude educational, cultural, medical, and other human-service activities that are not directly related to the problems of poverty. Yet, because these activities also have a public nature to them, it seems desirable to expand the range of taxpayer choice to include them as well.

A third proposal would do just that. Under this proposal, Congress would define a "human-services budget," which would include, in addition to poverty programs, spending on education, medical research, arts, and cultural programs. (It would exclude spending on religious and political activities, as would the other proposals.) Under this proposal, all public- and private-sector agencies with a human-services purpose would compete with one another for taxpayer dollars, and individual taxpayers would have the option of allocating their individual shares of the human-services budget.

These three proposals have obvious advantages that should lead to a more humane and desirable welfare system. The proposals would replace monopoly with competition and would allow freedom of entry into the marketplace. Charitable organizations would be able to attract contributions only by making a persuasive case to the public. No longer could inefficient, wasteful Federal programs count on uncontested access to taxpayer dollars. No longer could special interest groups count on political largess as a result of their special influence. Most important, the people giving the money would have direct control over how their "tax dollar contributions" are spent.

Notes

1. Daniel P. Moynihan, *The Negro Family: The Case for National Action* (Washington, D.C.: U. S. Department of Labor, March 1965).

2. Martin Anderson, *Welfare* (Stanford: Hoover Institution Press, 1978), chap. 2.

3. George Gilder, *Visible Man: A True Story of Post-Racist America* (New York: Basic Books, 1981).

4. George Gilder, *Wealth and Poverty* (New York: Basic Books, 1981).

5. John C. Goodman, "Welfare and Poverty," Policy Report #107, National Center for Policy Analysis, Dallas, Texas, 1985.

6. Charles Murray, *Losing Ground* (New York: Basic Books, 1984). See also Charles Murray, "White Welfare, White Families, White Trash," in *National Review*, 28 March 1986, 30–34.

7. Summarized in Murray, *Losing Ground*, 151–52. See also *Overview of the Seattle-Denver Income Maintenance Experiment Final Report*, U. S. Department of Health and Human Services, May 1983.

8. Lowell Gallaway and Richard Vedder, "Paying People to be Poor," Policy Report #121, National Center for Policy Analysis, Dallas, Texas, 1986.

9. *An Evaluation of the 1981 AFDC Changes: Initial Analyses*, General Accounting Office, 2 April 1984.

10. Quoted in Maurice Bruce, *The Coming of the Welfare State* (London: B. T. Batsford, 1961), 41.

11. Quoted in Bentley B. Gilbert, *The Evolution of National Insurance in Great Britain: The Origins of the Welfare State* (London: Michael Joseph, 1966), 51–52.

12. Cited in Anderson, *Welfare*, 36.

13. This is total spending on means-tested programs. See Vee Burke, "Cash and Non-Cash Benefits for Persons with Limited Income: Eligibility Rules, Recipient and Expenditure Data, FY 1982–84," Congressional Research Source Report No. 85-194 EPW, 30 Sept. 1985.

14. Lawrence M. Mead, *Beyond Entitlement* (New York: The Free Press, 1986).

Social Security and the Private Sector

PETER J. FERRARA

Social Security began in 1937 as a modest required investment in public-sector pension and insurance coverage. The maximum annual Social Security tax on both employer and employee for an individual worker was just $60 for the first thirteen years of the program, through 1949. In 1958, the maximum annual tax was only $189. Even as late as 1965, the maximum tax was only $348.

But in 1986 the maximum annual employer-employee payroll tax for an individual worker was $6,006. By the end of the decade, it will be almost $8,000 and will continue to grow thereafter. Why must we require today's workers to invest so heavily for their retirement and insurance needs only through Social Security? Of all Federal government activities, Social Security (defined broadly as the entire social insurance system, including Medicare) has the most widely utilized and broadly recognized private-sector alternatives. Pensions, Individual Retirement Accounts (IRAs), 401(K) plans, Keoughs, and other plans perform basically the same function in the private sector as Social Security retirement benefits and supplement those benefits. Private life insurance performs the same basic function as Social Security survivors insurance. Private disability insurance serves the same purpose as Social Security disability insurance. Private health insurance provides the same basic service as Medicare. The private alternatives to Social Security are not imaginative theories devised by free-market libertarians. They are major American industries that serve the public well.

Requiring such a huge investment only in Social Security rather than allowing workers to choose from the broad spectrum of private alternatives can be seen as perhaps the foremost restriction on economic freedom in American life today. Such a restriction deprives workers of control over major portions of their own incomes.

This restriction has also become enormously costly for the Federal government. Social Security, including Medicare, accounts for more than half of Federal domestic spending and almost one-third of total Federal outlays. National defense and debt interest together with Social Security account for about 70 percent of total Federal spending. Given the extent of Social Security spending, it is no wonder that the

Federal government is huge. The program requires virtually all Americans to be dependent on the government for the bulk of their income during a major portion of their lives — their retirement.

The Changing Face of Social Security

Mandating such a huge investment only in Social Security is making less and less sense, because while the program has provided a good deal to today's elderly, it is outdated from the perspective of today's young workers and will not serve them well. Indeed, given the enormous tax burdens today's young workers now face over their working years, even if they receive all of the Social Security benefits offered under current law, they will still receive low, below-market — often negative — returns on their taxes.

This problem is not a chance development but an inevitable result of Social Security's fundamental structure and method of operation. Social Security operates on a "pay-as-you-go" basis, which means the taxes paid into the program today are not saved and invested to finance the future benefits of today's workers but are immediately paid out to finance the benefits of current beneficiaries. The taxes of future generations of workers are to be used to finance the benefits of today's workers.

This pay-as-you-go method of operation favored workers who retired on Social Security in the past. Workers retiring in the early years of the program had to pay only the quite low taxes along with their employers for a few years before retirement. But these early retirees were paid full benefits out of the taxes of those still working. Such benefits consequently represented high returns on the taxes that they and their employer did pay.

As each year went by, however, this return fell steadily as the workers who were retiring had paid, along with their employers, higher taxes for more of their working careers. For most of today's retirees, the benefits still represent above-market returns on the taxes that they and their employers paid into the system. But today's young workers and their employers will pay taxes of several thousand dollars a year into the program for their entire careers. These workers no longer enjoy any of the beneficial aspects of the start-up phase of the pay-as-you-go system. Instead, since no investments are made through this system, today's young workers will lose the full market returns they would have earned if their funds had been privately invested. The pay-as-you-go system can pay returns only to the extent that tax revenues are increased over time, and such returns cannot keep up with private capital market returns.

A study published by the National Chamber Foundation calculated the real rates of return that would be paid by Social Security under current law to young workers entering the work force.[1] The study focused on a number of hypothetical families composed of workers who entered the work force in 1985 at ages ranging from eighteen to twenty-four and earned a wide range of different career income levels. These families included married and single workers, two-earner and single-earner couples, and families with and without children. The study takes into account all Social Security benefits — including retirement benefits, survivors benefits, disability benefits, and hospital benefits.

The study found that the great majority of workers in two-earner families would receive real returns under Social Security of around 1 percent or less, and some would receive returns below zero. Single workers would receive even lower returns, with most significantly below 1 percent, and many suffering below-zero returns. Given predominant social and cultural trends, most young workers entering the work force today would be in one of these two groups. While families with only one working spouse would have higher returns, reflecting the bias within Social Security against two-earner couples and single workers, most of these families would still receive real returns only at around 2 percent. Overall, the data show that for most young workers entering the work force today the real rate of return would be less than 1 percent to 1.5 percent, with the returns to many workers virtually zero or even below zero.

The study also calculated that if these young workers could invest the Social Security taxes to be paid by them and their employers over their careers in private investments yielding the average return earned in the stock market over the last sixty years, most of them would receive three to six times the retirement benefits offered by Social Security while still matching the pre–age sixty-five survivors and disability benefits promised by the program. Calculations in the study made at lower assumed private-investment returns still left the workers with much higher benefits than offered by Social Security. Besides these higher benefits, the system of private market investments would also generate substantial additional tax revenues to finance other government goods and services or general tax reduction. Social Security generates no revenue available for these purposes.

It makes no sense to require today's young workers to invest so heavily only in Social Security in the face of low returns now offered them. Indeed, some workers are required to invest $6,000 a year in a system that offers them basically zero or below-zero returns.

Moreover, whether Social Security can pay even the inadequate returns and benefits promised to these young workers under current law remains questionable. Under the Social Security Administration's own intermediate projections, if all of the program's trust funds are added together and any can draw from the others as needed, the entire combined program will run short of funds to pay promised benefits by 2026, just before those entering the work force today will be retiring. By 2035, the program's total expenditures will be running almost 50 percent greater than total revenues every year. Paying all the benefits promised to today's young workers under these projections will require a total Social Security payroll tax rate, including both employee and employer shares, of over 23 percent, compared with 14.3 percent in 1986.

These "intermediate" projections, moreover, may be overoptimistic. Fertility is assumed to increase substantially and permanently from current levels, providing more workers to pay taxes into the system. The rate of growth in life expectancy over the past forty years is assumed to slow down considerably, leaving fewer retirees to collect benefits. Unemployment is assumed to stabilize at 6 percent and inflation at 4 percent each year through 2060. The most important economic factor for Social Security, the rate of growth in real wages, is assumed to stabilize at 1.6 percent until 2010 and then remain at 1.5 percent every year for the following fifty years. Yet real wages over the past thirty years have grown less than 1 percent, and over the past fifteen years real wage growth has been negative.

Many independent observers, including former Social Security Chief Actuary A. Haeworth Robertson, think that more realistic assumptions may be found in the Social Security Administration's "pessimistic" projections. These projections assume that fertility declines to a degree consistent with long-standing trends, and life expectancy increases at about the rate of recent decades. Real wage growth is assumed to stabilize permanently at 1 percent, unemployment at 7 percent, and inflation at 5 percent. These assumptions are at least quite plausible. In the past, the so-called pessimistic projections have generally turned out to be the closest to reality.

Under these projections, the entire combined program will run short of funds to pay full benefits by 2002. By 2035, when those entering the work force today will be in retirement, the program's expenditures will be well over two times as high as total revenues each year. Paying all the benefits promised to today's young workers would require an astounding total Social Security payroll tax rate of 37 percent. For a worker making $20,000, this would mean a total Social Security annual tax of $7,500, split between employer and employee. At such a rate, the maximum Social Security tax in 1986 would have been $15,540.

The payroll tax is already far too high, seriously hampering economic growth and limiting job opportunities. As noted above, the maximum annual tax will soon be $8,000 a year and will continue to grow every year thereafter. For most workers, the combined employer and employee payroll tax is greater than the worker's income tax liability. In 1985, payroll tax revenue, borne primarily by low- and moderate-income workers, were over 70 percent greater than total Federal corporate and indirect business tax revenues. A married worker with two children earning only $7,700 in 1986 paid about $550 in payroll taxes, with another $550 from his employer that probably came out of his wages as well — a total of $1,100 out of productive capacity of this needy, low-income worker.

The payroll tax is simply a tax on employment, and here as elsewhere the result of taxing something is that there is less of it. One study estimated that the payroll tax increases scheduled from 1985 to 1990 alone will ultimately eliminate almost 1 million jobs and reduce the gross national product by $25 billion a year.[2] In a society supposedly deeply concerned about employment opportunities, the incredible payroll tax burden on employment is ludicrous. Ironically, while today's young workers must bear such a huge tax burden, their own future benefits seem insecure and unlikely to be fully paid.

The Social Security benefit structure is also riddled with inequities that render the program especially unsuited to today's young workers. Workers are not paid equal returns on past taxes paid into the program. In particular, the program pays discriminatorily lower returns to two-earner couples, couples without children, and single workers. The program imposes a rigid, 1930s-oriented benefit structure on everyone, which cannot be flexibly adapted to different and changing needs of different workers and families. Consequently, the program poorly serves today's pluralistic, economically and socially mobile work force.

In addition, blacks and other minorities with below-average life expentancies tend to receive discriminatorily lower returns on this account, because they generally live fewer years in retirement to collect benefits. A white male born today can expect to live 50 percent longer in retirement than a black male and can consequently receive 50 percent more in retirement benefits. Moreover, blacks as a group are significantly younger than whites, and since Social Security offers low returns the younger one is, the program disadvantages blacks on this account as well. Finally, given the huge burden of Social Security spending, those who wish to see a sharply expanded role for the private sector, free markets, and a major reduction in the burden of government must recognize that this cannot be accomplished without addressing Social Security.

Breaking Free

Since Social Security serves today's young workers so poorly, it should be recognized that requiring them to invest so heavily for their retirement and insurance needs only through the program makes no sense. The time has come to allow today's workers the freedom to substitute private-sector alternatives for at least some and eventually all of their Social Security coverage.

It was once routinely suggested that any such private-sector option for workers would destroy the financial foundations of Social Security, leaving inadequate funds to pay the promised benefits to today's elderly. But this contention is demonstrably erroneous. The option can be designed so that it would actually strengthen Social Security financially and ensure benefits for today's elderly while providing an opportunity through the private sector for today's young workers to enjoy a more secure and prosperous retirement.

Under such an option, workers and their employers would be allowed to contribute to private-sector investment accounts up to some reasonable initial limit each year. Workers and employers would continue to pay their Social Security payroll taxes in full, but they would receive a full rebate for their contributions to the private account from their income taxes. In practice, this means each contributor should receive an income tax credit equal to 100 percent of his contributions each year (a full dollar off his income taxes for each dollar contributed to the private account).

To the extent that such contributions were made to a worker's account during his working years, his future Social Security benefits would be reduced under a proportional formula. For example, a worker who contributed an amount equal to 20 percent of his Social Security retirement taxes to his private account every year during his career would have his Social Security retirement benefits reduced by 20 percent. Such a worker, of course, would then have new benefits through his private account that would probably more than make up for these forgone Social Security benefits, leaving him with higher retirement benefits overall. (The tax credit could be reduced to less than 100 percent of contributions as long as the resulting reduction in future Social Security benefits was reduced proportionately).

This private-sector option could then be expanded gradually over time and extended to the full range of Social Security benefits. Workers and their employers could be allowed to contribute additional amounts to their private accounts for the purchase of private life insurance, again in return for income tax credits. To the extent that such contributions were made, the worker would forgo Social Security survivors insurance benefits and rely on the private life-insurance benefits instead. Workers and employers could also be allowed to contribute additional funds for the purchase of private disability insurance, in return for income tax credits. The worker would then forgo Social Security disability benefits and rely on the private disability benefits to the extent of such contributions. Workers could be allowed to contribute additional funds in return for income-tax credits and use the funds to purchase private medical insurance to substitute for Medicare in retirement. Ultimately, each worker would be completely free to choose how much to rely on the private accounts and how much to rely on Social Security.

The purpose of the income tax credits is in effect to return money to workers to the extent that they agree to forgo future Social Security benefits and rely on their private accounts. But it is crucial to recognize that the tax credits are taken against income taxes, not the payroll taxes that exclusively finance Social Security. The program's payroll tax revenues would not be reduced in any way and would continue to flow into the program in full to finance benefits for today's elderly.

Indeed, the private-account option would sharply strengthen Social Security and improve the ability of the program to pay promised benefits. While the program's payroll-tax revenues are maintained in full, expenditures in the future would be reduced substantially as workers relied more and more on the private accounts and less and less on Social Security. The long-term financing problems of the program would be markedly reduced as a result, and if the private-account option is expanded rapidly enough, these financing problems could be eliminated entirely, even under pessimistic assumptions, all without reducing benefits or raising payroll taxes. In fact, with the private-account option eventually expanded to the maximum, Social Security expenditures could be reduced dramatically enough to allow room for sharp reductions in payroll-tax rates.

At all times, workers would be completely free to rely entirely on the strengthened Social Security system without change. There would be no reduction in Social Security benefits for such workers or today's elderly. But workers who did opt for the private accounts could expect much higher retirement benefits. These benefits would also be completely equitable; each worker would receive the actuarial value of what he and his employer paid in plus market-investment returns. The private accounts, moreover, would be financed on a fully funded basis, which would secure them against the financial instability inherent in Social Security's unfounded, pay-as-you-go system.

Workers would also have much greater freedom of choice and control over their incomes through the private accounts. While they would still be required to provide for their retirement and insurance contingencies through some means, the private accounts would enable them to choose and control the investments and insurance purchases to satisfy these requirements. Workers could consequently tailor their individual packages of investments and insurance coverage to suit their personal needs and preferences. Workers relying on the private accounts could be allowed greater freedom to choose their retirement age, after a specificied minimum age, such as the minimum age of fifty-nine and one-half for unpenalized IRA benefits under current law. They could also choose to leave some of their private-account funds to their heirs, an option that Social Security does not allow. The individualized flexibility and enhanced personal freedom of the private-account option along with the Social Security is clearly an overall system far better suited to today's pluralistic, mobile work force than the rigid, 1930s-oriented Social Security system alone.

The reform could also have important benefits for the economy. National savings could be sharply increased through the funds paid into the private accounts, resulting in the creation of new jobs and enhanced economic growth. Eventual payroll-tax reductions would benefit the economy as well.

The reform would also create special new opportunities for the poor, because it would give them control over some capital through the private accounts. The National Chamber Foundation study showed that if a career minimum-wage earner entering the work force today could invest his Social Security taxes, including the employee and employer shares, in a private account over his career, at the average return historically earned in the stock market, he would accumulate almost $300,000 in today's dollars by retirement, even while providing for the preretirement survivors and disability benefits of Social Security. This fund could pay him out of the continuing returns alone more than he is currently offered under Social Security, allowing him to leave the fund as a solid foundation for the economic advancement of his children.

The Supplemental Security Income (SSI) program would continue to provide means-tested, general-revenue financed, welfare benefits to the elderly poor, ensuring that retirement income would not in any event fall below a basic minimum. A substantial portion of benefits paid through Social Security today may be considered welfare benefits, since they are not based on past tax payments into the program but on certain criteria thought to indicate need. Because Social Security benefits are paid without a means test, however, this welfare assistance ends up going to too many who are not in need. But the more workers rely on the private account, the more welfare assistance would be paid only through the means-tested SSI program, channeling welfare benefits only to those who are actually poor and eliminating the current substantial waste of welfare benefits paid through Social Security.

In addition, the more that workers across the whole economy are allowed to accumulate assets in their private accounts in lieu of Social Security, the more equal the national distribution of wealth would become, since the substantial assets in their private accounts would be more equally distributed than the current distribution of wealth. If all workers provided for their needs through such private-investment accounts rather than Social Security, the national concentration of wealth would be reduced by one-third, according to one study.[3] This would be achieved not by redistributing existing wealth but by providing for the creation of equally distributed new wealth. Moreover, through the private-account investments, each worker would develop a substantial ownership stake in American business and industry, and that would likely improve the public attitude toward private business and free markets.

Finally, the reform would sharply reduce Federal spending as workers began relying more and more on their private accounts rather than on Social Security. Total Federal spending could be reduced by more than one-fourth and Federal domestic spending by as much as one-half if workers are allowed the option to rely exclusively on the private accounts. No other reform offers the potential for such a dramatic reduction in Federal spending, all without the pain of benefit cuts but simply through the choices of workers offered the chance of better benefits in the private sector. Such reform is absolutely essential if there is ever to be a major reduction in the heavy burden of Federal spending, given the huge proportion represented by Social Security.

It should be emphasized that the entire Social Security system need not be targeted for reform all at once. Workers could be given an option just to substitute private life insurance for Social Security survivors insurance, for example. Social Security pays $10 billion to $15 billion in benefits each year to the survivors of young workers, performing nothing more than the function of private life insurance. There is no reason for the government to be preempting such a large portion of the private life-insurance market in this way. An option focused only on such survivors benefits would be a major reform in itself that many could support entirely apart from any other option for any other portion of Social Security.

Reform could focus simply on an option to substitute private disability insurance for Social Security disability coverage. The disability program has shown a tendency to allow too many workers on the rolls who are not actually disabled or to continue benefits even after beneficiaries could go back to work. The government bureaucracy lacks real incentives to enforce the program's standards. Periodic attempts to clean up the problem fail in any event because of the heavy politicization surrounding the program, which can preclude rational, objective consideration of disability cases. Disability insurance could be provided in a superior manner through the private sector. Insurers would have concrete incentives to prevent nondisabled claimants from receiving benefits, for if they fail to do so their costs will be too high and they will be unable to compete. The far less politicized private environment would also allow more objective consideration of disability claims. An option focused solely on disability insurance could consequently be quite attractive as a major reform standing alone that many might support independently of consideration of any other option.

Medicare by itself faces a dramatic long-run financing crisis that must be addressed soon. An option for workers to substitute private health insurance coverage for Medicare would allow the long-run financing gap to be reduced without cutting benefits or raising payroll taxes, as discussed above, for the general long-term financing problems of Social Security. An independent option focusing exclusively on Medicare might consequently be highly appealing at this time. An independent option could also be focused on only a small part of Social Security retirement benefits. Many who might not support a complete option may favor such a partial option since workers would still have the majority of their benefits promised under Social Security as a floor of income. Such a partial could still mean a much bigger role for the private sector. Positive experience with any one of these options could then improve the political climate for independent consideration of further options.

The income-tax credits for contributions to the private accounts would result in a loss of income-tax revenue. But this loss could be kept to reasonable levels by focusing the option initially on only one relatively small part of the program and then slowly expanding it. The revenue loss would eventually be offset completely by reduced Social Security expenditures as workers relied more on their private accounts and less on Social Security. For options focused on the program's survivors and disability insurance, these expenditure offsets would occur relatively quickly. In other cases, long before the full expenditure offsets, the revenue loss could be eliminated on net due to new revenues generated from the increased investment through the private accounts.

From the beginning there should be increased savings through the private accounts roughly equal to the amount of temporary net revenue loss, since the tax credits are allowed only for savings made in the private accounts. So, even if the government had to borrow entirely to cover the temporary net revenue loss, there would be no net increase in the government-borrowing drain on private savings. Moreover, such borrowing would in any event amount only to an explicit recognition of the government debt that already exists implicitly in the unfunded liabilities of Social Security.

The Politics of Social Insurance Privatization

Attempts to cut Social Security benefits are routinely defeated. But that should not be surprising. What else could one expect, given a program that pays now or promises in the future cash benefits for virtually everyone in America?

But focusing on a private-sector option for workers should transform the issue politically. Such an approach allows proponents to reject benefit cuts entirely and to guarantee today's elderly their benefits while offering new opportunities for today's young workers through the private sector. Such a private-sector option involves a positive approach that takes nothing from anyone. It simply increases the freedom and opportunities of workers.

Such reform should appeal to young workers, for the current system does not serve them well, and they have much to gain from the change. They do not trust the current system to pay them their future benefits. They can see the burden of the payroll tax and instinctively believe that the system does not offer them adequate returns. They can see that the current system is not well suited to the modern worker.

Such reform should appeal to the elderly as well. It not only leaves their promised benefits completely intact, but it also strengthens the financial ability of the program to pay those benefits. In addition, the elderly themselves are concerned about their legacy to their children and grandchildren. The new opportunities created by the reform for today's young workers should be important to them also.

Indeed, assuring today's elderly their benefits while creating new opportunities for today's young workers probably reflects public opinion among both young and old. It is not the system or institution of Social Security per se that has the devotion of the American public. What both young and old support are the promised benefits for today's elderly. With those benefits assured, both young and old are open to the idea that there is a better way to do it for the future.

For market-oriented policymakers, political risks in this area cannot be avoided in any event. On its present course, Social Security will continue to provide nothing but trouble for such policymakers. It will stand as an uncuttable leviathan in the Federal budget. Expansionists will continue to lobby to provide new benefits through the system, leaving opponents on the defensive. Indeed, even with the huge Federal deficit and the dramatic long-term Medicare financing crisis, welfare-state partisans are lobbying heavily for new benefits through Medicare to pay for catastrophic acute hospital and medical care and long-term nursing-home care. And Social Security inflation adjustments are being changed to provide increases even while inflation is quite low, when increases would not previously be triggered. Moreover, periodic financial crises in the program will leave those favoring the private sector in the position of resisting inexorable payroll-tax increases with nothing to offer as an alternative but politically disastrous benefit cuts.

The private-sector approach offers market-oriented policymakers the opportunity to break out of this defensive posture and the hopeless debate over increasing taxes or cutting benefits, shifting the Social Security debate to entirely new ground. It completely avoids both cuts in benefits for today's elderly and increases in taxes for today's workers and instead allows workers to choose a better deal in the private sector. As suggested above, it consequently offers policymakers a purely positive reform approach that should appeal to both young and old.

The proposed private-sector option can be seen as simply expanding the Social Security framework to bring in a greater role for the private sector. A structure is maintained to enable workers to meet their retirement and insurance needs through either the private or public sectors. The option would merely modernize and liberalize the current system, providing the freedom and flexibility best suited to today's workers. The benefits of such reform should easily outweigh the short-term transition costs. The proposed option consequently offers a politically appealing reform approach, which can be quite popular.

Conclusion

There is no reason to force workers to invest so heavily for their retirement and insurance needs only through Social Security; they should be allowed to provide for some and eventually all of such needs through the private sector, if they prefer. Since Social Security serves today's young workers this poorly, mandating such a heavy investment in the program is unjustifiable. Doing so simply imposes a huge, unnecessary spending burden on the Federal government as well as a heavy, unnecessary restriction on the economic freedom of American workers.

NOTES

1. Peter J. Ferrara, *Social Security Rates of Return For Today's Young Workers* (Washington, D.C.: National Chamber Foundation, 1986).

2. Aldona E. Robbins, "Social Security: At What Price? A Look at Long-Term Deficits and Their Effect on the U. S. Economy" (Washington, D. C.: Institute for Political Economy, March 1986).

3. Martin Feldstein, "Social Security and the Distribution of Wealth," *Journal of the American Statistical Association* 71 (December 1976):800–807.

Contracting Out:
A Painless Alternative
to the Budget Cutter's Knife

STEPHEN MOORE

"Without competition there can be no champions, no records broken, no excellence."

President Ronald Reagan,
State of the Union Message, 1984

During the 1970s, New York City's golf course on City Island gained notoriety for its miserable playing conditions. Residents used the course as a trash dump; teenagers held parties on the fairways at night, building bonfires and littering the course with beer cans; and graffiti was omnipresent. The carcasses of stolen and stripped automobiles were often left in the sand traps for weeks at a time; those who frequented the course were reputed to have invented special rules for playing a ball that came to rest therein. Rats roamed freely in the woods. Worst of all, to maintain the course in this wretched condition cost New York City taxpayers about $200,000 a year.

Today, the course is a moneymaker for the city. The greens and fairways are now mowed regularly; the traps are raked and cleared daily; and graffiti, litter, and rodents have been removed. Despite slightly higher greens fees, play is up 12 percent and expected to continue to rise.

What caused this remarkable turnaround? In 1984 the city contracted out the operations of the course to American Golf Corporation, a private company that leases public golf courses nationwide. The transfer to private operation has been an unparalleled success, popular with both golfers and New York City taxpayers. Now other cities are rushing to follow New York City's lead: in 1986, more than 150 municipal golf courses were run by private firms.

Golf-course operations is just one of hundreds of commercial services that cities and counties have turned over to private providers in the last decade. In local jurisdictions all over the country, private firms have contracted with public agencies to repair streets, fight fires, collect the garbage, clean buildings, recover delinquent debts, and even manage the city's entire government operations. Contracting out has become such an accepted cost-cutting practice that, according to John Goodman, president of the National Center for Policy Analysis, "there is not a single city service that is not being contracted out to a private firm somewhere in the U.S."[1]

When the government contracts out a public service, it retains its funding responsibility but hires a private company to provide the service. The primary motivation for contracting out is to cut government costs by employing more economically efficient private vendors. The injection of competition into the procurement process is the critical feature of contracting out that drives down the expense of government goods and services from 20 to 50 percent. Contracting out also allows public agencies to exploit the efficiency and specialized skills offered by the private sector that may be unavailable within government.

While hundreds of cities and towns have enthusiastically turned to private contractors, the Federal government has displayed ambivalence toward contracting out as a means of pruning government spending. Though the limited experience with private contractors on the Federal level has been almost universally positive and though expanded reliance on contracting out has been endorsed by the General Accounting Office, the Congressional Budget Office, and the President's Private Sector Survey on Cost Control (the Grace Commission), few functions have been converted to contract since 1980. In fact, during Ronald Reagan's presidency, more than 120,000 Federal employees engaged in commercial activities have been *added* to the Federal payrolls.

If an aggressive contracting-out campaign is to be waged on the Federal level, it is clear that a new strategy is required — one that mobilizes support from taxpayers and the business community while neutralizing public-employee opposition to the reform. Washington policymakers would do well to imitate the privatization methods that have proved successful in city hall.

The Local Experience with Contracting Out

Mario Cuomo, the Democratic governor of New York, recently affirmed: "It is not government's obligation to provide services but to see that they're provided."[2] This philosophy seems to be the new rallying cry for hundreds of cities across the country that have made budget reforms a top priority.

The states and cities have demonstrated during the 1980s a remarkable willingness to experiment with innovative public management techniques in their efforts to cut agency costs without cutting service benefits. The long list of alternative approaches to government service delivery adopted by the cities and states in recent years includes issuing vouchers for education and health care, relying on volunteers and nonprofit groups to provide certain social services, enacting work for welfare programs, coordinating procurement policies with neighboring communities to take advantage of quantity discounts (a practice known as "piggy backing"), and hiring outside management consultants to advise city officials on cutting costs.

But of all the management and procurement reforms that cities have implemented, none have been as sweeping as contracting out. A 1984 survey of cities by the National Center for Policy Analysis documented the remarkable growth in contracting out since the early 1970s. Over the period 1973–82, the number of cities contracting out legal services increased from 187 to 788. The number of cities contracting out data processing rose from 9 to 337. Only 5 cities contracted out park maintenance in 1973; by 1982, 142 cities did. Meanwhile, the dollar amount of service contracts joining municipal governments with private firms tripled, from $22 billion in 1972 to $66 billion in 1980.

So comprehensive has this privatization revolution been that many commercial activities once performed almost exclusively by public employees are now predominantly contracted out. Street repair and vehicle towing, for instance, are now contracted out by eight out of every ten cities. According to recent surveys, about 55 percent of all cities contract out for at least part of their ambulance services. And this privatization movement is expected to continue to engulf an ever-growing list of cities and a widening variety of services. Touche Ross & Co., a Big Eight accounting firm, has predicted that government contracts with private firms will total $3 trillion by the year 2000 if the current expansion continues.

An exciting recent development in privatization on the local level has been the trend toward contracting out social services with nonprofit organizations. Between 1970 and 1980 the number of government contracts with private firms to provide social and human services doubled. In 1983 more than $1 billion in public services were provided by voluntary nonprofit groups. Day care, drug treatment, and public health centers are among the list of social services that cities have found to be readily convertible to contracting out.

In 1981, chief executives of fifty-seven public agencies that contract out social services in the San Francisco Bay Area were asked to identify the major advantages to contracting out. Contracting with nonprofit groups was seen as superior in five areas: flexibility in initiating and terminating services, reduced cost, specialized competence of the contractor, effectiveness in reaching clientele, and less bureaucracy.

How Much Have Cities Saved by Contracting Out?

Over the past five years at least a dozen studies have been conducted, quantifying the cost savings generated on the local and county levels from contracting out public services. Researchers have almost universally concluded that contracting out is more economical than paying city employees to perform the commercial service. The real issue seems to be not whether the city will save money but *how much* it will save by contracting out.

Table 1 shows the cost-savings estimates from five recent studies for a variety

TABLE 1

Cost Savings Estimates From Contracting Out Studies Conducted Since 1981

Author of Study	Type of Service	Percentage Savings
Ecodata, under contract with HUD	Municipal street cleaning	43
Ecodata, under contract with HUD	Municipal janitorial services	73
Ecodata, under contract with HUD	Municipal tree trimming	37
Ecodata, under contract with HUD	Municipal overlay construction	96
Ecodata, under contract with HUD	Municipal traffic light maintenance	56
American Public Works Association	Wide range of municipal services	39
U. S. Department of Transportation	Municipal contraction of urban mass transit	35–50
E. S. Savas	Municipal refuse collection	30
Steve H. Hanke	Municipal wastewater treatment	20–50

Sources: Barbara J. Stevens, ed., "Comparative Study of Municipal Service Delivery," Ecodata, Inc., 1984, iv; American Public Works Association findings cited in Stuart M. Butler, "The Privatization Option," Heritage Foundation, *The Heritage Lectures No. 42*, 1985; U. S. Department of Transportation, Urban Mass Transportation Administration, *New Directions in Urban Transportation: Private/Public Partnerships*, June 1984; E. S. Savas, "Policy Analysis for Local Government: Public Versus Private Refuse Collection," *Policy Analysis* (Winter 1977): 49–74; Steve H. Hanke, "Privatization: Theory, Evidence, and Implementation," in *Control of Federal Spending*, ed. C. Lowell Harriss (New York: The Academy of Political Science, 1985), 101–13.

of contracted public services, ranging from street repair to the operation of local transit systems. Savings range from 25 to 94 percent.

In addition to these studies comparing the cost of public versus private service delivery, a number of cities have recorded astonishing dollar savings from contracting out:

• Phoenix has saved $5.3 million each year by contracting out seventeen city services, according to the city's auditors.

• The Southern California Association of Governments reported that townships in the Southern California area have reduced public transit subsidies from $5 million to $500,000 annually, by contracting out twenty-two bus lines.

• The city of Los Angeles estimated that it has saved $200 million annually out of its $7 billion budget through its extensive contracting-out program. Over 200 contracts have been issued since the passage of Proposition 13 in 1978.

• Elk Grove, Illinois, one of the first cities to contract out its fire-fighting service, has saved $200,000 from the switch to private fire fighters.

There are two reasons why contracting out is capable of generating such impressive budgetary savings. First, the private sector is more efficient than government in performing commercial activities. For instance, a study by economist William Orzechowski found that productivity rates are generally higher among private-sector employees than public employees.[3] Further, because private firms are driven by the profit motive, they have a powerful incentive to seek innovative approaches to reducing service costs. Arthur Bernaccia, president of Liberty Lines, a private transit firm, stated the point succinctly: "If we don't operate efficiently, we don't make any money—it's as simple as that."[4] No such incentive exists in the public sector, where cost increases merely require digging deeper into the taxpayers' pockets and where the "reward" for efficiency improvements is reduced program funding in the next fiscal year.

The second reason that contracting out is less expensive than performing services "in-house" is perhaps even more important — and that is competition. When government services are not subjected to competitive bidding, the agency acts as a monopolist, charging the government whatever it pleases. But in the case of competitive procurement, the contract is awarded to the lowest of perhaps dozens of bidders. To win the contract, each private vendor has an incentive to offer its services at the lowest possible price. In effect, this competitive-bidding process allows the government to "shop around" for the lowest price when purchasing services.

Interestingly enough, injecting competition into the procurement process generates even greater efficiency within the bureaucracy. An analysis of Defense Department cost comparisons won by the Federal work force revealed, for instance, that the agencies' bids were lowered by 17 percent when civil servants were forced to compete with private firms. These lower in-house bids alone have saved the Department of Defense more than $100 million. Similarly, when the city of Phoenix first held competitive bidding contests for its trash collection, the public agency lost four years in a row. In 1984, however, the agency won back the city contract, issuing a bid $1 million below that of any private firm. Robert Jensen, director of Phoenix Public Works, explained the agency's rebound by noting: "Our people are really in a competitive mode. We have cut our costs way back because we have learned from . . . private contractors. We have the unions convinced of the need to improve productivity."[5] This is why E.S. Savas, the author of *Privatizing the Public Sector*, insisted: "The real issue is not so much public versus private; it is monopoly versus competition."[6]

The Federal Experience with Contracting Out

The Federal government now employs nearly 1 million workers, who perform 11,000 separate commercial activities. The Federal work force includes electricians, dentists, janitors, plumbers, caterers, laboratory technicians, and even veterinarians.

As with local successes, the limited Federal experience with contracting out these services has been highly favorable. Defense Secretary Caspar Weinberger, for instance, has called contracting out the Pentagon's "most successful cost saving program." The budget figures support his claim: an exhaustive Defense Department study completed in 1984 reviewing 235 service contracts issued between 1980 and 1982 found that, on average, costs were trimmed by 30 percent. These numbers were confirmed in 1985 when the U.S. Air Force examined the cost of 132 functions contracted out to private firms. The study concluded that contracting out had led to a 33 percent reduction in program costs.

Other agencies have had similar successes, though on a smaller scale. The Federal Aviation Administration (FAA) has discovered that when it contracts out air-traffic control operations to private operators, costs have been cut by 25 to 50 percent. In 1981, private operators ran the control tower in Farmington, New Mexico, for $99,000; the year before the FAA had operated the tower itself at a cost of $287,000. The U.S. Department of Transportation saved $725,000 in 1983 by simply contracting out its computer operations. The Department of Defense (DOD) obtains military uniforms from two sources: private clothing manufacturers and a federally owned garment factory in Philadelphia. In 1985 the General Accounting Office (GAO) compared the two sources and determined: "It cost the [government] factory twice as much as commercial contractors to produce coats."[7] Despite these documented cost savings, the short history of Federal policy governing contracting out has been one of increased regulation and mounting restrictions on the number of government functions that are subject to competitive procurement.

Dwight Eisenhower was the first president to establish a Federal contracting-out policy. In 1955 he signed a historic presidential directive specifying that "the federal government will not start or carry on any commercial activity to provide a service or product for its own use if such a product or service can be procured from private enterprise." Regrettably, this original policy statement was largely repudiated in 1966 when it was replaced by OMB Circular A-76. This new directive requires the Federal agencies to conduct detailed cost comparisons between "in-house government suppliers" and private vendors. The agency must choose the cheapest alternative. Though the circular has been amended at various times since 1966, the cost comparison requirement remains the cornerstone of the contemporary A-76 program. This cost-comparison process is so unfairly tilted against private contractors that it acts as a formidable impediment to moving Federal commercial services into the private sector. Some of the handicaps imposed on commercial firms include:

• The private contractor's bid must beat the in-house estimate by at least 10 percent to cover government "transition costs" or the function remains in house.

• The private bidder must submit a "firm contract" proposal with a fixed price, whereas the agency is only required to submit a cost *estimate*. This places the private bidder at a significant disadvantage; if the private bidder's actual costs exceed its expected costs, it will not receive additional Federal funds and may take a loss on the contract. By contrast, the agency is not penalized for submitting low-cost estimates, as it can simply request additional agency funds midway through the project.

• The commercial firm's bid must include an allowance for indirect costs, while the agency's need not. The U.S. Chamber of Commerce estimated that this alone constitutes a 20 to 30 percent handicap to the private bidder.

• Costs are added to the bid submitted by private providers for government monitoring of contract performance, while no cost for quality assurance is included in the agency cost estimate.

• In negotiated procurement, very low bids may be rejected as being "outside the competitive range." This means that the selected proposal from private bidders is not always the lowest bid and hence more awards are won by the agency provider.

Altogether, these handicaps in the cost-comparison process have placed private bidders at an estimated 35 percent cost handicap. Consequently, many activities that would be less costly if they were contracted out must remain in-house. As unfair as this cost-comparison process is, private vendors nonetheless win the majority of these competitions. A much greater problem than the cost-comparison process itself is that only a small percentage of Federal commercial activities are ever subject to competitive bidding.

Since 1980, Capitol Hill has passed more than twenty separate contracting-out prohibitions. Barriers to contracting out in the Department of Defense have been the most intrusive, since most government commercial functions are performed by this agency. Congress justifies these legislative impediments to contracting out commercial activities by suggesting that "national security" interests might be jeopardized by hiring private firms. One wonders, however, how national security would be compromised by allowing the Department of Defense to contract about 150,000 government positions in the areas of supply, maintenance, and repair of military equipment; data processing; and warehousing, all of which are exempt from A-76 cost comparisons. Nor is there any justification for Congress's ban on using private contractors for the performance of fire fighting or security-guard functions on military bases. If such congressional restrictions were lifted, the secretary of defense would still have the authority to prevent contracting when legitimate security considerations arose.

Congressionally imposed restrictions in civilian agencies are equally insidious. A provision inserted by Congressman Robert W. Edgar (D., Pennsylvania) into the 1984 Continuing Resolution prohibits the General Services Administration from contracting out guard, elevator-operator, messenger, and custodian services. These exemptions cost Federal taxpayers $32 million each year.

Regulations also prohibit the Federal government from using private legal clinics as an alternative to Legal Services Corporation lawyers, privately operated job-training clinics to replace more costly Job Corps centers, or private management firms for managing the national parks (even though 142 state and local governments contract out park management). The Veterans Administration is prohibited from contracting its medical-care activities unless in-house facilities cannot fully handle the patient load. The Grace Commission found that when VA nursing home care was contracted out because of insufficient in-house capacity, the average cost per day was cut in half — $45 per day versus the $109 per day that the VA charges. This VA restriction costs the Federal taxpayers at least $70 million annually.

The net result of all these congressional restrictions has been that only an estimated 30 percent of the government's $20 billion to $30 billion bill for commercial services is even eligible for the cost savings potential of contracting out.

But the blame does not end there. Congressional restrictions in no way explain why the Reagan administration has reviewed fewer than 6,000 civilian agency positions as candidates for contracting out since 1983, in spite of the 1982 recommendation of the president's Grace Commission that 500,000 government positions be contracted to more efficient private firms. A 1986 report by the Office of Management and Budget (OMB) revealed that of twenty-two Federal agencies reviewed for contracting out, eleven had not conducted even a single A-76 cost comparison between fiscal years 1982 and 1985. At the current rate of reviewing Federal programs for contracting out, it will take an estimated 100 years to conduct cost estimates for every Federal commercial activity.

Consider, for example, the contracting-out program at the National Oceanic and Atmospheric Administration (NOAA), which recently unleashed an active A-76 Program with projected annual savings of $30 million by 1988. Jack Coleman, former special assistant at NOAA and now the executive director of the National Council of Technical Service Industries, observed: "The amazing thing is that these achievements have occurred under circumstances where John Byrne [former NOAA administrator] and Anthony Calio [present NOAA administrator] both encouraged footdragging and subversion of the program. It has been no secret in NOAA of their dislike for A-76. The sad thing is that Byrne and Calio reflect the attitudes about A-76 held by most government managers, both political and career."[8] Clearly, program administrators will not voluntarily reduce the size of the work forces under their command.

In sum, contracting out on the Federal level has been impeded by resistance from Congress, the executive branch, and the bureaucracy. It has also been blocked by the public-employee unions' criticisms.

Objections to Contracting Out

There can be little doubt that the reluctance to contract out—not only in Washington but also in many other large cities—stems from politicians' aversion to challenging powerful public-employee unions. These unions have levied a barrage of attacks against contracting out that have turned many policymakers and taxpayers into skeptics as to its benefits. The following are four of the most common objections to contracting out, each as voiced by the public-employee unions. Only the last of these four has merit.

Charge: "Contractors frequently cut corners by hiring inexperienced, transient personnel at low wages, by ignoring contract requirements, or by providing inadequate supervision."[9]

Performance evaluations of contracted activities refute the contention that employing private contractors diminishes service quality. In fact, service performance has often improved after contracting out. A 1984 nationwide study by Ecodata, Inc., prepared for the Department of Housing and Urban Development, investigating a variety of contracted municipal services concluded that "for many of the services, the individual cities with the lowest cost of service delivery also achieved among the highest levels of quality."[10] Similarly, in a 1981 survey of eighty-one local governments by the California Tax Foundation, twice as many cities contracting out indicated that service quality had improved than complained of poorer service.

Nor is there any evidence that the quality of care is compromised by contracting out social services. A 1983 study by the University of California, Berkeley, of contracted municipal hospitals in California found that in none of the hospitals investigated was service quality diminished when hospital operations were turned over to private firms. Kentucky officials stressed that the quality of care markedly improved when the state contracted out the operation of its largest mental-retardation facility.

Cities that are experienced in contracting out have learned to minimize service problems and contract disruptions. Scottsdale, Arizona, for instance, which contracts out 40 percent of its municipal services, takes into consideration the ease with which a service contract can be monitored when it decides which activities it will contract out to private firms. The city's contracts always specify a thirty-day cancellation policy for unsatisfactory service performance, and price increases are limited to one a year. In this way, Scottsdale provides the vendor with an incentive to maintain high quality service and to hold costs down.

> Charge: "Contracting out involves laying off public employees. . . . Laid-off public employees are entitled to unemployment compensation paid by the employer . . . and they may also qualify for various public welfare programs. These are all hidden costs."[11]

Few government workers are permanently displaced when contracting out occurs. A sample of 9,650 government employees affected by DOD contracts found that only 300 — or fewer than 5 percent — were left with no employment after contracting out. The vast majority of affected Federal workers were either reassigned jobs within the government or went to work for private contractors. More important, the cost of providing public assistance to displaced workers is trivial relative to the savings from contracting out. The General Accounting Office interviewed Federal workers who had been separated from the Federal work force as a result of contracting out and found that their public-assistance payments would eventually total about $200,000. The report concluded that these costs "would have little effect on DOD's estimated savings of $65,484,000 from contracting out."[12]

> Charge: "The costs of contracting out are out of control like wildfire. Billions of taxpayer dollars have been wasted to pay for excessive costs over and above original bids."[13]

Recent scandals in Pentagon procurement have cast a dark shadow over Federal contracting-out policy. Ironically, while study after study documenting huge taxpayer savings of 20 to 30 percent and hundreds of millions of dollars from contracting out at the Pentagon have received barely cursory notice from the media, the occasional horror story of Defense Department purchases of $7,600 coffee pots and $400 hammers have commanded headlines throughout the country.

To be sure, these stories have served a useful purpose. Reforms in Defense Department procurement policy — including imposing stiff penalties on contractors for unjustified cost overruns and easing specification requirements to permit contractors to purchase off-the-shelf spare parts when manufacturing weapons and equipment — are long overdue. But the issue is whether these incidents justify tighter restrictions on contracting out as many in Congress are demanding.

Some strong evidence suggests that, despite contractor cost overruns and occasional overpayments, contracting out remains an effective approach to reducing government spending—particularly at the Pentagon. A 1985 General Accounting Office study of DOD contract cost overruns discovered that in seventeen of nineteen cases investigated, even with cost overruns, the final contract price remained below the in-house estimate. The GAO investigation further noted that the cost hikes were generally "justified" because "in 18 of the 19 cases studied . . . price increases resulted from such factors as wage increases required by the Department of Labor and new work requirements."[14]

A subsequent study by the Office of Management and Budget reviewed sixty-six Federal service contracts with cost overruns. In all but three of these incidents, OMB found that the final contract cost was still below the original government-agency estimate. According to the report: "Cost comparison decisions in favor of contractor performance are more cost advantageous to the government 97 percent of the time *even when contract costs increase.*"[15]

Charge: "Contracting out builds a rival government of favored companies . . . .Defense contractors—in competing with career-federal workers—have been given a fast track in their run for big profits."[16]

One of the genuine dangers of contracting out is that by awarding lucrative contracts to the private sector, the government creates a powerful prospending constituency. There is evidence that this has occurred in the Department of Defense, where large defense contractors, whose economic survival depends on congressional approval of big ticket items, are now spending millions of dollars each year lobbying for a continued rise in the Pentagon budget. The same is true on the domestic side of the budget. Too often the provider becomes the most vocal proponent of spending and the most formidable obstacle to reform.

Of course, even when government activities are not contracted out, a prospending constituency still exists: contracting out merely transfers the spending constituency from the public-employee unions to the private-sector provider. The danger is that this new prospending lobby may wield more influence than that it replaced. For this reason, contracting out is often an inferior form of privatization to moving activities out of the public sector entirely.

How to Promote Contracting Out on the Federal Level

What steps can be taken to engineer a rejuvenated contracting-out movement on the Federal level? To answer this question, it is instructive to examine the forces that have prompted cities to privatize services.

Perhaps the most critical factor that pushed cities and states to privatize was prolonged and intense budgetary pressures. The financial condition of most state and local governments during the late 1970s and early 1980s was singularly bleak. Indeed, from about 1977 to 1984, the states and cities experienced all at once almost every conceivable fiscal nightmare: double-digit inflation, the taxpayer revolt that started in California and later spread to many other states, declining Federal aid, and the deepest economic recession since the Great Depression. These combined forces created a simultaneous reduction in government revenues, and a heightened demand for public services rose.

Unlike the Federal government, which recorded unprecedented levels of new debt to weather this fiscal storm, most of the cities and states were not afforded the "luxury" of deficit finance and were required to maintain balanced budgets. Nevertheless, few cities made drastic cutbacks in services and very few passed major tax hikes, as many skeptics claimed they must. Rather, state and local governments, which had once been regarded as the weak little sisters of the Federal government, became both innovative and economical in their spending behavior. They began to contract out services simply because they had no other choice; services had to be performed at a lower cost or not at all.

The city of Imperial Beach, California, serves as an ideal case study in how budgetary stress can provide the impetus to creative public management. Following the passage of Proposition 13, Imperial Beach began contracting out a vast array of services — including its ambulance services, recreation centers, and transit systems. The size of the city work force was cut by 65 percent. Sherman Shenberg, Imperial Beach city manager, recalled the city's rush to privatize services by noting: "It was out of dire necessity. Four years ago we were concerned that Imperial Beach would have to declare bankruptcy."[17]

A second reason that cities have privatized services and the Federal government has not is that taxpayers are much less tolerant of wasteful spending at the local level than at the Federal level. At the local level they see a direct connection between wasteful spending and the size of their local tax bill. Taxpayer scrutiny of local spending behavior compels city managers to adopt cost-cutting procedures. In sharp contrast, because the cost of unnecessary spending on the Federal level is spread thinly among millions of taxpayers, it fails to incite such passionate voter disapproval. Consequently, the Federal budget cutter makes few friends; the big spender earns the endearment of powerful and well-financed interest groups. This is the politics of Federal spending. More than anything else, it explains why contracting out is rare in Washington.

It is critical, therefore, that any Federal approach to contracting out take into account these political dynamics. The following four-step strategy might neutralize the political obstacles to turning over services to private contractors.

1. *Limit Federal aid payments to the states and cities.* One of the implications of the preceding discussion is that moving service funding responsibility to lower levels of government would stimulate an expansion in contracting out. The Federal government now distributes more than $100 billion in Federal grants to state and local governments to pay for projects that almost exclusively benefit local residents. These payments often distort local communities' spending priorities and provide them with a disincentive to contract out. For instance, the Federal Urban Mass Transit Administration distributes about $5 billion annually to pay for local transit systems. The availability of these grant funds has encouraged cities to reject economical private-transit operations in favor of tremendously expensive

public-transit systems — systems that local communities would never consider building if they were to pay for the projects themselves.

Similarly, Federal wastewater-treatment grants, which until recently paid 75 percent of the cost of municipal construction of new water-treatment plants, reward cities for building costly new public plants rather then turning to more economical private systems. When the Federal subsidies were reduced in the early 1980s, many cities were compelled to turn ownership and operations of the plants over to private investors. The message is clear: forcing local residents to finance services with their own tax dollars is the best method of encouraging economical approaches to public service delivery.

2. *Mobilize countervailing constituencies to thwart union objections.* Union opposition to contracting out would be less effective if those who stand to gain from contracting out would lobby for contracting out. As Mark Schultz, former director of Federal procurement policy for the U.S. Chamber of Commerce, complained: "The federal employee unions' tremendous influence has continued unabated because the business community and private sector unions have yet to exert a comparable countervailing influence."[18] These groups must broaden and solidify their support for contracting out.

3. *Move the contracting-out decision out of the hands of the affected agency.* The cost-comparison process initiated by OMB Circular A-76 has been an unmitigated failure. Having the agency itself make the in-house-cost estimate and the determination as to whether contracting out is the more efficient route is like asking the PLO to arbitrate a border dispute between Israel and Syria. The bureaucracy can either skew the process so unfairly against the private bidder or delay the proceedings for so long — often up to three years — that very few contracts are ever awarded.

Local governments have developed innovative approaches to handling the cost-comparison process that could serve as a model for Federal policy. A number of municipalities use independent auditors to review contract bids from private firms and to compare these bids with the public agency's cost estimate. Phoenix has taken the lead in this regard. The city created a separate auditing department that not only evaluates outside bids but also verifies the accuracy of the in-house estimate. It computes the proper allocation of overhead and whatever indirect costs could be eliminated by contracting out — costs that the agencies themselves are notorious for overlooking. The auditor awards the contract and monitors its performance, whether it is won by private firms or public workers.

The Federal government should experiment with such an approach by creating an auditing office in the Office of Management and Budget or the General Accounting Office. The reform would offer three improvements over the present system. First, bureaucratic foot-dragging would no longer act as a restraint, since the agency's failure to make a cost estimate would simply result in functions being contracted out by default. Second, in-house-cost estimates would be more accurately measured, thereby transferring a greater number of contracts to more economical private vendors. Third, service quality would improve, since performance standards would apply equally to contractors and the agencies.

In fact, there is no reason why the independent agency would have to be a government entity. Eventually, the Federal government should contract out the contracting-out process. A private auditor could be made responsible for calculating cost estimates, awarding decisions, and monitoring performance problems. The auditor would then receive payment based on savings to the government and satisfactory performance of the contracts it awarded and managed. This would give the auditor an incentive to solicit bids, because the more money it saved the government through contracting out, the more profit it would earn.

4. *Turn certain contracted services over to Federal-employee-owned businesses.* One means of overcoming union resistance to privatization is to turn Federal employees into private contractors by encouraging worker buy-outs. Great Britain has privatized many of its government activities with this approach. In certain instances, the Thatcher government has gained organized labor's support of contracting out. In 1986 the U.S. Office of Personnel Management proposed legislation that would allow Federal employees and private contractors to form joint partnerships for performing contracted services. Peter Young, director of the Adam Smith Institute, noted that such an arrangement would be ideal for contracting out a wide range of activities, including Coast Guard towing, bus services, air-traffic control operations, and military health-care facilities.

Conclusion

The primary and perhaps sole objective in government procurement was set down by the 1972 Commission on Federal Procurement: to acquire "products and services of the needed quantity at the lowest reasonable price available." Few taxpayers would object to this criterion. Yet, because of congressionally imposed restrictions on contracting out and the "civil disobedience" that characterizes bureaucratic responses to administrative contracting initiatives, the A-76 program has proceeded slowly during Ronald Reagan's presidency. In 1985 there were more Federal workers performing commercial activities than there have ever been. In short, the privatization revolution that is taking place on the state and local levels is passing the Federal government by.

Budget pressures seem to have acted as the springboard for moving state- and local-government services into the private sector. While the Federal government is in the initial stages of the Gramm-Rudman era of deficit reduction, a unique opportunity exists for similar budgetary reforms in Washington. As the cities and states have learned, it makes political sense to seize every opportunity to cut spending in relatively painless ways before having to confront the tough spending trade-off decisions. And since contracting out does not reduce the level of services that program beneficiaries receive and in many cases improves the quality of service delivery, special-interest group opposition to contracting out is typically much less pronounced than it is to budget cuts. As such, there is some reason to be optimistic that Federal contracting out—with potential budget savings of $3 billion annually, according to the Office of Management and Budget—will constitute a vital element to any realistic deficit-reduction strategy.

NOTES

1. National Center for Policy Analysis, "Cities Can Cut Costs by Using Private Firms," press release, 23 June 1985.

2. *New York Times*, 28 May 1985.

3. William Orzechowski, "Economic Models of Bureaucracy," in *Budgets and Bureaucrats: The Sources of Government Growth*, ed. Thomas E. Borcherding (Durham, N.C.: Duke University Press, 1977).

4. *Wall Street Journal*, 27 Nov. 1984.

5. "Taking Public Services Private," *Nation's Business*, August, 1985, 20.

6. E.S. Savas, "The Efficiency of the Private Sector," in *The Heritage Lectures No. 42*, ed. Stuart Butler, Heritage Foundation, pp. 15–31.

7. *Philadelphia Inquirer*, 20 April 1986.

8. William Jackson Coleman, "James W. Winchester's Experience at NOAA as a Presidential Appointee," draft, 1985, pp. 4–5.

9. American Federation of State, County and Municipal Employees, *Passing the Bucks*, 1983, pp. 14–15.

10. Barbara J. Stevens, ed., "Comparative Study of Municipal Service Delivery," Ecodata, Inc., 1984. iv.

11. American Federation of State, County and Municipal Employees, 21.

12. U.S. General Accounting Office, "DOD Functions Contracted Out Under OMB Circular A-76: Costs and Status of Certain Displaced Employees," 12 July 1985, executive summary.

13. American Federation of Government Employees, "AFGE Launches Campaign Against Contracting-Out," press release, 12 May 1986.

14. U.S. General Accounting Office, "Review of DOD Contracts Awarded Under OMB Circular A-76," 26 Aug. 1981.

15. U.S. Office of Management and Budget, 1986, 4.

16. American Federation of Government Employees, 1986.

17. "Taking Public Services Private," 1985, 21.

18. Mark Schultz, statement before the U.S. Senate Committee on Small Business, 27 Aug. 1981, 8.

Airport Privatization

GABRIEL ROTH

"The market does not solve all our problems; but it takes a special kind
of idiocy to refuse to let it do jobs it obviously can do. . . . The FAA has
consistently demonstrated its manifest preference for thoroughly regulatory remedies."

Alfred E. Kahn
Washington Post, 18 September 1984

Students of political economy can find in the debates on the future of National Airport—the local airport of the District of Columbia—a rich
source of information about the borderline between the public and private sectors
of the United States economy and about how it is treated under a Republican administration that was elected to push back this frontier toward the private sector.

The Washington metropolitan area enjoys the services of three airports: National Airport, which is closest to downtown Washington, D.C., particularly to
the Capitol Hill area that is dominated by Congress; Dulles International Airport,
about thirty miles away from Capitol Hill, to the west; and Baltimore-Washington
International (BWI), about the same distance to the north. Of the three airports,
National is the smallest and the most congested; indeed, it has been "saturated"
since the 1960s, in the sense that demand for landing and takeoff "slots" far exceeds the supply. Except to the extent that these slots may be sold by the airlines
to one another, they are allocated by the Federal Aviation Administration in accordance with its administrative procedures. The operations at National also engender complaints about noise, but this issue, though important, will not be considered here. Both Dulles and BWI airports, on the other hand, are uncongested
in the sense that additional landing and takeoff slots can be made available at
most hours. Although commercial traffic at National could be increased by more

Thanks are due to Paul Feldman, vice president for transporation of the Services Group, and to Roy
Pulsifer, of Roy Pulsifer Associates, for their help in the preparation of this essay.

advanced ground equipment or by cutting down "general aviation" (aircraft that do not carry fare-paying passengers), the consensus in the Washington, D.C., area is that it would be desirable for the growth in air traffic to take place at Dulles and BWI rather than at National. But there is no agreement on how to decide who is to use National and who the other airports.

Both National and Dulles airports are owned and operated by the Federal government through the Federal Aviation Administration (FAA), which is part of the Department of Transportation. BWI is owned and operated by the state of Maryland.

The Department of Transportation, which is responsible for no other major airports, is eager to divest the Federal government of National and Dulles airports because of the acute problems associated with their administration and the congressional budgetary procedures that have to be followed before any funds can be spent on their improvement. While most people agree that Federal ownership of the airports is undesirable, there is no general agreement on the preferred alternative, and at least eight attempts to transfer the airports to local control have failed. This essay will consider some of the issues that would be involved in a transfer to the private sector.

Preliminary Considerations

Airport planners distinguish between "landside" capacity (the capacity to handle passengers in terminals, automobiles in car parks, and so on) and "airside" capacity (the capacity to accommodate aircraft landings and departures). References to "congestion" (excess demand at peak periods) and "saturation" (excess demand at all permitted periods) generally refer to "airside," which is governed by runway capacity.

Of the some 600 United States airports that received FAA grants, only four — Kennedy and La Guardia in New York, National in Washington, and O'Hare in Chicago — are considered to be saturated. While airport planners predict that, if present trends continue, the busiest twenty airports (which handle some 60 percent of passengers) will be saturated within the next ten years unless substantially expanded, there will be hundreds of other airports with capacity to spare. Additionally, at least 4,000 small airports will be used only by general aviation. When all airports are taken into account, the percentage of those suffering from severe congestion is less than 1 percent.

The second preliminary point is that airport landing and departure fees are determined by administrative rather than commercial criteria and are generally nominal. They bear no relationship to the economic costs involved. A private aircraft carrying one or two people might pay $4 to land at National Airport without regard to the delays the operation might cause to other users. Charges are generally the same at all times of the year and at all times of the day and do not vary much from airport to airport. Thus the financial incentives are insufficient to encourage those in control of aircraft to avoid congested airports and patronize those that have spare capacity.

Transport economists have suggested for at least twenty years that the economic pricing of congested airport facilities would yield substantial benefits and revenues.[1] They stress that remedying the shortage of airport capacity is unwise before existing facilities are priced in accordance with the general principles of allocating scarce resources, namely, that prices be raised to the point at which the costs of accommodating additional traffic are covered by the revenues generated by that traffic. Although market-clearing prices (designed to equate demand to supply) are taken for granted in most sectors of the economies of private-enterprise societies, including of course the allocation of aircraft seats, such pricing is not used for the allocation of landing capacity at airports where this capacity is in short supply. One result of this unwillingness to price the use of landing and takeoff "slots" is that passengers arrive at some airports on time and then have to wait an hour or more for the departure of their planes because of the unavailability of runway capacity.

A third preliminary point is that nothing in the nature of airports requires them to be operated or owned by a public authority. Burbank Airport was owned and operated by Lockheed when it was the main airport for Los Angeles. Lockheed sold the airport to raise money but still operates it. AVCO Textron operates airports in Saudi Arabia, and Pan Am turned Westchester County Airport in New York State from a liability into a profitable asset. Thus a number of substantial firms—including the United Kingdom's International Aeradio Ltd.—operate airports, and there are also many privately owned airports. While most major airports worldwide are owned by the public sector (the one at Grand Bahamas is a notable exception), it is not a sufficient reason for assuming that they cannot be privately owned. After all, most airlines in the world are owned by the public sector, as are most railroads and telephone systems, but one cannot conclude from this that United States airlines, railroads, and telephones should be nationalized.

It may be objected that the externalities associated with airports, both positive and negative, require them to be subject to public control. But public control of permitted noise levels, safety standards, location, and so on is entirely consistent with private ownership.

Why Privatize Airports?

Because of the general perception that airports should be owned and operated by government agencies, the case for their privatization needs to be stated. This case does not depend on the suggestion that private operators are wiser, kinder, or harder working than people in government service but on the proposition that scarce resources are more likely to be allocated to their most urgent uses if operated by profit-seeking owners than if administered "in the public interest" by political bodies. How does this proposition apply to airports?

It applies most strikingly in the charges levied for aircraft landings. The public sector, which has been known to incur losses, is surprisingly reluctant to make profits. Landing fees at National Airport, for example, are 48.17 cents for each 1,000 pounds of authorized landing weight (ALW). Thus a Boeing 727 with an ALW of 150,000 pounds would be charged about $72, while a Metro 2, with an ALW of 12,500 pounds would be charged $6. Aircraft in the general aviation category are charged less, only 30 cents per 1,000 pounds of ALW, though these planes are subject to a minimum charge of $4. These rates are designed to cover the historic and current costs of the landing facilities, such as runways and lighting; they bear no relation to the demand for scarce landing facilities or to the use of prices to balance demand with the available supply. The result is that similar prices are charged throughout the system, irrespective of demand, and prices are not used — as in market systems — to allocate scarce resources among alternative uses or to signal the need for new investment.

Since the use of publicly owned airports is not rationed by price, other methods have to be used to allocate capacity when airports get "congested" or "saturated." The methods range from waiting in line on the ground until a "slot" becomes available to blanket restrictions, such as the one at National Airport prohibiting direct connections to points farther than 1,000 miles away (to overcome this restriction, planes to Dallas and Denver stop at Dulles Airport, twenty-five miles away, from which direct flights are permitted). National Airport also has a rule that twenty-seven out of every sixty hourly operations are reserved for general aviation. Slots that are available to commercial airlines were once allocated by a committee of existing users, a restrictive cartel that is generally illegal for the private sector to operate. Recently, members of the cartels have been allowed to "sell" slots.

The absence of pricing mechanisms to balance supply and demand in public airport facilities leads to another critical advantage of the private sector: the presence of surpluses or deficits to indicate an excess or shortage of capacity. The citizens of Denver have been told that Stapleton Airport will be saturated in the 1990s and that a new airport has to be built, which will cost $2 billion and could require a landing fee of $600 for cost recovery. But, as present landing fees are around $40, there is no reliable way of estimating the intensity of the demand, that is, the extent to which users of the airport would be prepared to pay its costs. Since most airport users do not belong to the poorest segments of society, it is not at all obvious that airports should be built for their use without a clear willingness to pay.

One important source of revenue for airport improvement is the Airports and Aviation Trust Fund, which is financed by a tax amounting to 8 percent of the sale of tickets. But the allocations from that fund to individual airports do not appear to depend on the willingness of the providers or users of airports to meet any proportion of the cost.

Some Recent History

In 1984 the Heritage Foundation's "Mandate for Leadership II" recommended that National and Dulles airports be privatized by being "auctioned to the highest bidder." A similar recommendation was made by Robert W. Poole, Jr., president of the Reason Foundation, who developed the argument in "Privatizing Washington's Airports," a paper published in May 1985 by Citizens for a Sound Economy of Washington, D.C. Poole attempted to calculate the approximate value of National Airport to a private-sector operator. Assuming that many of the 16 million passengers going through National each year would be prepared to pay $20 extra to land there rather than at Dulles or BWI (because of the lower cost in time and taxi fares to reach the commercial and governmental centers), Poole calculated that an operator charging market-clearing landing fees at National Airport could increase current revenues by $250 million a year. Using an estimate of a capital value equal to ten times annual revenues, Poole calculated the capital value of National to be around $2.5 billion. At about the same time that Robert Poole's paper appeared, the secretary of transportation received a report from a blue-ribbon panel headed by Linwood Holton, a former governor of Virginia, suggesting that both National and Dulles airports be transferred to that state. A price of $47 million, based on historic costs, was suggested as appropriate; market value was not considered to be a proper criterion for pricing the properties. The Holton report also recommended that a regional commission assume responsibility for both airports. The commission would include representatives of the local authorities concerned.

One might have thought that an administration committed to economic efficiency in the use of public resources, to reduction of Federal deficits, and to the encouragement of private enterprise would not hesitate to explore the idea of transferring the airports to the private sector. One would have been mistaken. The Reagan administration ignored Robert Poole's paper and drafted a bill in early 1986 for Congress to implement the recommendations of the Holton commission.

An Offer from Rothschild

In February 1986 John Redwood, head of the international privatization operations of the London merchant bank of N. M. Rothschild and Sons, Ltd., arrived in Washington, D.C., to attend and address the international conference on privatization arranged by the U.S. Agency for International Development. It is not known what opportunities for investment in Third World countries were identified by John Redwood during his stay in Washington but, having developed a sensitivity for such matters, and being interested in airports, he noticed the opportunity presented by an asset that had been valued in the billions of dollars and that the Federal government was proposing to transfer to a local authority for less than $100 million. After his return to London, John Redwood announced that if the United States government would accept a bid from the private sector for one or both airports, N. M. Rothschild would be ready to assist the government, either by advising it directly or by attempting to organize a consortium that would bid for these facilities. Redwood's announcement received considerable attention in the Washington press and provoked Holton to declare that he would also be prepared to buy the airports if he were allowed to convert their land use to condominium construction. Some of the newspaper reports incorrectly indicated that the bank was actually prepared to bid for the airports, and some mentioned figures of around $1 billion.

Some members of Congress were unhappy over the administration's proposal and, on 24 March 1986, Senator Gordon Humphrey (R., New Hampshire) arranged a press conference to publicize the subject and to allow the bank to clarify its position. The following statement was presented at that conference on the bank's behalf:

PRIVATISING WASHINGTON'S AIRPORTS

N. M. Rothschild & Sons, Ltd. (NMR) is encouraged by the recent interest shown in privatising National and Dulles Airports, but wishes to clarify several points.

1. The airports would be kept as airports.
NMR would not be interested in developing the airports for residential purposes nor in seeking major changes in currently permitted land uses. The purposes of a privatisation designed by NMR would be to upgrade both airports, especially National, and improve their financial viability and their contribution to regional economic development. Several opportunities for improvement can already be identified:
—improvement of car parking facilities at both airports;
—improvement of the connection to the Metro station at National;
—expansion of the North Terminal at National; and
—development of mid-field terminals at Dulles.
If any changes in land use were sought, they would be for purposes complementary to airport operation.

2. NMR will not try to organize or participate in a consortium to purchase the airports until the legislative or executive branch of the U.S. Government indicates that it would welcome offers from private investors. N. M. Rothschild & Sons would be happy to advise the Federal Government on regulation and organization of the sale, if that was preferred, rather than acting for prospective buyers.
As clearly stated previously, NMR would work on assembling a group of investors only after receiving an indication that the Administration would be willing to consider airport privatisation. The amount of the bid would depend on investor response and on the conditions set down by the U. S. authorities for the use of the airports.

3. NMR's interest in Washington's airports is an outgrowth of its successful participation in other privatisation ventures, both inside and outside the United Kingdom.
The experience of N. M. Rothschild & Sons in privatisation is described in the accompanying materials. NMR has worked on privatisation in Europe and the Far East, and is currently retained by the British Government to sell the British Gas Corporation, the largest privatisation ever attempted anywhere in the world.

4. Privatisation of the airports could bring early benefits to the U. S. taxpayer.
N. M. Rothschild & Sons understands that, as part of the plan to transfer the airports to the State of Virginia, the airlines using them would be allowed to sell their landing rights ("slots") to other airlines. Thus, these landing rights would in effect be given to the airlines without charge. Under an NMR privatisation plan, on the other hand, these

valuable assets could be bought by the private sector from the Federal Government, and the amounts paid to the Government would accrue to the taxpayers through reduction of the budget deficit. Furthermore, under private ownership, property and other taxes would be payable by the private sector to the State of Virginia and relevant government authorities.

Giving the Landing Slots to the Airlines

The final section of the Rothschild statement refers to the FAA's decision that airlines using the four airports with imposed service restrictions — Kennedy, La Guardia, National, and O'Hare — would be allowed to sell their landing rights at will after March 1986. These "sales" are not absolute, since those who "buy" landing slots do not have total rights to them; the FAA can rescind the rights to land and take off at any time. Nevertheless, these rights will have some value, and some have been transferred. In September 1986, for example, Pan American Airlines bought from Texas Air a sizable number of slots at National and La Guardia to provide additional service on the crowded Washington-New York route.

Early in 1986 Thomas Donlan wrote that "the total value of the landing slots at the four airports could be $680 million."[2] While this estimate is considerably lower than Robert Poole's, it is still enormous and represents a gain for the airlines that they did not earn. Some members of Congress objected to the gift of these facilities to the airlines, and Senator Nancy Kassebaum (R., Kansas) introduced a Senate resolution canceling this arrangement. However, her amendment was designed to restore the allocation of these slots to their previous situation in which "little cartels at each airport, called scheduling committees, worked out landing and departure slot times by consensus, enjoying an exemption from antitrust rules."[3]

The bill to transfer National and Dulles airports to Virginia was presented in the Senate in April 1986. An amendment by Senator Gordon Humphrey requiring the airports to be sold to the highest bidder was presented but withdrawn for lack of support. It was strenuously opposed by lobbyists for the FAA, who circulated the following document to explain why the airports should not be sold to the private sector:

WHY A PRIVATE SALE OF DULLES AND NATIONAL MAKES NO SENSE

Under present circumstances, a sale of Dulles and National to a private operator would raise serious problems:

• A private operator's costs for running the airports, and charges to the users, would be substantially higher than an independent authority's.
• A private operator would have to raise rates to recover its capital investment, as well as the $530-$700 million costs of capital improvements.
• A private operator would not be eligible for formula grants under the Airport and Airway Improvement Program.
• A private operator would not be eligible for tax-exempt revenue bond financing (assuming it continues after enactment of the tax bill).
• Public airport operators are subject to a comprehensive set of regulations imposed

to assure equal access to all, to guarantee nondiscrimination, and to provide for environmental concerns, among other. They are enforced through FAA grant agreements. A private operator would not be subject to any of them.

• Nothing would keep a private operator from excluding general aviation aircraft, or from operating National all night.

• All in all, it would make as much sense to sell the Interstate Highway System, which, like the airports, is paid for with user fees, and permit a private operator to charge tolls.

These objections are trivial and mostly incorrect, since the conditions that govern the use of the airports by "regional commissions" can also be imposed on private owners. The reference to the interstate highways suggests that the FAA does not understand that the revenues from road-use charges can be paid to private road owners as easily as to public ones.

The main opposition to the bill in the Senate was mounted by Senator Paul S. Sarbanes (R., Maryland), who thought that the transfer of both airports to Virginia would enable the profits from National to subsidize the costs of Dulles, which could then compete unfairly with Maryland's BWI. The bill eventually passed the Senate but met with further objections in the House of Representatives. An amendment that would have required the Department of Transportation (DOT) to offer the airports for sale to the private sector was prepared by Representative Beau Boulter (R., Texas) but withdrawn after the personal intervention of Elizabeth Dole, secretary of transportation. Some members did not like giving up control of the airports; their agreement was secured by an amendment that would require the Regional Commission to be subject to a "Congressional Review Board." Others wished to extend the permitted flying distance from National Airport to 1,250 miles to allow direct flights from Dallas/Fort Worth and Houston. Yet others wished to attach the Kassebaum amendment to the bill to prohibit the sale of slots by airlines.

Finally, in the last hectic days of the 1986 session, the bill cleared the house, and a version agreed upon with the Senate was signed by the president. The price tag was raised to $187 million for a fifty-year lease, to meet the objection that the airports were being disposed of too cheaply. To placate the Maryland interests, the DOT promised to expedite the release of funds to increase runway capacity at BWI. The permitted flying distance from National was increased to 1,250 miles; the Kassebaum amendment was lost. Dulles and National Airports will therefore be transferred to the state of Virginia, which is unlikely to favor their privatization.

Conclusion

The Reagan administration's determination to keep Dulles and National airports in the public sector raises a number of issues. One issue is the priorities of the FAA, which lobbied against the privatization of the airports on the ground that private ownership would result in higher landing charges to aircraft and therefore in higher ticket prices. Yet, as shown earlier, the imposition of higher landing charges at congested airports is a necessary component of any arrangement that would provide an efficient allocation of air traffic in the United States.

An outside observer has to wonder whether the FAA receives any economic advice, because the premise that private ownership of congested airports would result in higher landing fees is a dubious one. Following the deregulation of air fares and schedules, the scarcity of these slots already allows airlines to charge higher fares to airports that are saturated. People flying from Washington, D.C., to La Guardia, for example, pay $75 for a weekday flight from National but can fly for $49 from Dulles or BWI. Under deregulation, the absence of economic landing fees at congested airports does not lead to lower ticket prices but merely transfers to the airlines the "scarcity rent" that is collectible for the use of these scarce facilities. The FAA's attitude can be compared to that of a trustee who declines to charge a market rent for land held in trust and used by a hotel, on the ground that he does not wish the hotel guests to pay high room rates. But the room rates in a hotel are determined by the supply of and demand for rooms, not by the rent that the hotel owner pays for his land. If he is allowed to pay a low land rent, he will make more money from renting out rooms.

A second issue concerns the relationship between the FAA, Congress, and the airlines. That the FAA should choose to give away landing rights worth hundreds of millions of dollars to airline companies seems extraordinary. One can only assume that the FAA thinks, as does the writer of this essay, that slot trading by airlines is better than the Kassebaum position of no trading at all. Allowing the airports to sell the slots would be even more beneficial to the public, but that does not seem to have been advocated by the FAA, or even by the Office of Management and Budget, which gets the best economic advice and understands the issues involved.

One of the curious paradoxes that comes out of this story is that it is through privatization — selling the airport landing rights to the highest bidder — that the taxpayer can get the value of the landing rights that are inherent in congested airports. While the airports remain in the public sector, these rights — which may be worth billions of dollars — are either wasted or given to airline companies that have done nothing to earn them.

Notes

1. E.g., Paul Feldman, "On the Optimal Use of Airports in Washington, D.C.," *Socio-Economic Planning Sciences*, vol. 1 (Oxford, England: Pergamon Press Ltd., 1967), 43–49; and Ross D. Eckert, *Airports and Congestion: A Problem of Misplaced Subsidies* (Washington, D.C.: American Enterprise Institute for Public Policy Research, 1972), 72.

2. Thomas Donlan, "Golden Gates: Landing Slots a Windfall for the Airlines," *Barron's*, 24 Feb. 1986.

3. Ibid.

Ownership and Efficiency in Urban Buses

A. A. WALTERS

One of the characteristic features of urban bus systems is creeping, if not galloping, municipalization or nationalization of services. The rationalizations for public ownership vary in detail, but all have a common theme: the need to integrate and coordinate services and to avoid the wastes of competition. This objective does not require public ownership; suitably regulated private bus companies could perform as well as those of a nationalized concern. But public ownership is thought to make it easier to coordinate activities and, in particular, to ensure that certain unprofitable but "socially necessary" services are provided. Claims that nationalization would reduce costs are the corollary of the elimination of alleged wasteful competition. Route rationalization, such as eliminating duplicate routes, and the introduction of efficient maintenance procedures for large fleets are meant to produce significant reductions in cost for the publicly owned concern.

Apparently, there have been no scholarly evaluations of the extent to which nationalization has achieved the aims of integration, coordination, and rationalization. This may well be because these concepts are difficult to define. But analysts of public transport must investigate the costs of transport and how such costs vary with respect to the institutional form. The main purpose of this essay is to compare the costs of services of privately owned buses with those of the nationalized companies. This discussion does not consider the range through which increasing size brings lower cost per unit of service (economies of scale) and the conditions under which differences in size lead to increasing unit cost (diseconomies of scale). If there are economies of scale, above the 300- to 400-bus concern, these should operate in favor of the nationalized corporation; and if there are diseconomies, the contention of the "nationalizers" or "integrators" is discredited. Nor are the

This essay was prepared while the author was a staff member of the World Bank. The views and interpretations, however, are those of the author and should not be attributed to the World Bank, to its affiliated organizations, or to any individual acting on its behalf.

sources of the differences in cost of the public and private sectors rigorously identified—although some general explanation of the differences observed in, for example, wage costs are tentatively suggested.

One main drawback of this study is the limitation of the sample. The data of three cities in developing countries and two cities in developed countries with similar bus operations in the private and public sectors have been examined. The choice of cities was limited, since there are few examples of public buses and substantial numbers of private buses operating under similar conditions with similar routes and in the same factor markets. This selectivity is important, because it might be suggested that the existence of a large number of privately owned buses attests to the failure of nationalization. The opposite charge, that the private sector has ruined the nationalized corporation, cannot be substantiated in the sample cities. The nationalized corporation had the authority to grow; it lacked financial, operational, and administrative means. The private sector has been tolerated, not encouraged, because of the failure of the public sector. Thus it may be alleged that only hopeless situations were selected. The evidence presented here suggests that this is not the case, but the issue can be settled only by the accumulation of more evidence.

Data on Costs

Evidence on relative costs comes in two basic forms. First, there are the results of experts' cost investigations or inquiries. In some cases the accounts can be examined, but in most cases the records are inadequate and the experts substitute vigorous inquiries directed at operators and direct observation. What emerges is a comparison of unit costs. The second form of evidence is to infer the relative costs from one fact, the amount of money needed to cover the deficit of the municipalized or nationalized bus company, and from one axiom—that if private operators persist in offering their services, they will be making at least normal profits. If for example, a publicly owned bus company covers half of its cost with a subsidy and if private operators run virtually identical services in the same city at the same fare, the costs of the public operation may be twice those of the private operator.

Of the two forms of evidence, the latter is preferred. The subsidy is normally a matter of public record and is thus open for all to see. Similarly, the level of fares is not difficult to observe and cannot easily be obfuscated. Service conditions are also issues on which the outsider can make judgments. On the other hand, the cost evidence is more subjective and open to interpretation. Many investigators have substantial experience only in the public sector, and they quite naturally apply the standards that they think are appropriate, especially with respect to maintenance, depreciation, amortization, and perhaps also labor costs. It is not unusual for such experts to suggest that the private operators cannot possibly be covering their true costs and that they will eventually go bankrupt. The classic statement of this position with respect to the trucker but equally applicable to bus operators is the Salter report of 1933, which states that the trucker "is able to purchase his vehicle on the installment system and is often tempted to force his way in by offering rates which are completely unremunerative and which necessarily lead to bankruptcy which, nevertheless, does not discourage others – or perhaps even himself – from following the same course in perpetual succession. . . ." This strange description was found to be quite inconsistent with the facts. Indeed, unregulated truckers had lower bankruptcy rates than virtually all other industries in the period of 1920-33.[1] It is also troublesome to estimate "normal profits" as a constituent of cost.

Another generic problem with these comparisons is that the extent of regulation, both overt and covert, as well as the political direction varies considerably and sometimes to an unknown extent. Although private operators may be legally free to pursue their own policies, the threat of nationalization often compels them to conform to what is thought to be in the interests of the political regime then in power. The nature and extent of this political or bureaucratic control has been elicited as much as possible, but there is no doubt much was not uncovered.

Subsidies and Fares

A comparison of the costs of a publicly owned bus company with those of private concerns can be useful only when the two are operating in virtually the same environment and under the same conditions. Calcutta, Istanbul, and Bangkok are three cities in developing countries in which such parallel companies and private operators were identified. One is naturally cautious about drawing conclusions from a self-selected sample of this kind. Is it not true, for example, that the very fact that private operators are tolerated attests to the failure of these public companies? In other cities it may be suggested that public competition has been a "success" and that the worst cases have been selected. There is much circumstantial evidence against this argument. In many low-income countries public bus companies have large and increasing deficits. Sabastien Thiriez found this sample to include the public bus companies in Bangkok, Calcutta, Istanbul, Madras, Jakarta, Karachi, and Cairo.[2] Table 1 shows data on these deficits. Furthermore, a study of countries in the Organization for Economic Cooperation and Development (OECD) in 1975 showed that subsidies were ubiquitous, ranging from 11 to 70 percent of operating cost (i.e., excluding large capital costs) with an average of 37 percent.[3]

In 1985, public bus companies covered about 56 percent of their total costs with their revenue in Calcutta; 88 percent, in Istanbul; and 74 percent, in Bangkok. Calcutta deficits began in fiscal year 1962-63 and have increased every year except 1982 (doubling between 1972 and 1977). Istanbul's deficits increased fourfold from 1973 to 1978, although they have decreased in real terms since then. In Bangkok the public operator has had a deficit since 1976 when the nationalized company was formed, and the deficit is expected to increase substantially.

But in each of these three cities private operators also ply with the same fare,

TABLE 1

Deficits of Operators of Publicly Owned Buses in Developing Countries

City (Company)	Year	Deficit (U.S. $ million)	Deficit per Bus on the Road	Total Revenue/ Total Cost
Abidjan (SOTRA)	1985	$ 27.00	$28,500	0.71
Accra (OSA)	1984	0.25	23,800	0.51
Ankara (EGO)	1984	10.50	18,000	0.67
Bangkok (BMTA)	1985	43.50	12,000	0.74
Cairo (CTA)	1985	94.00	52,000	0.42
Calcutta (CSTC)	1985	11.60	16,700	0.46
Casablanca (RATC)	1982	4.60	10,200	0.82
Delhi (DTC)	1984	92.00	21,300	0.39
Istanbul (IETT)	1984	4.50	5,000	0.88
Jakarta (PPD)	1985	33.00	28,700	0.50
Karachi (KTC)	1983	6.90	8,300	0.49
Khartoum (KPPTC)	1985	0.40	8,300	0.80
Madras (PTC)	1986	1.80	1,000	0.96
Mexico City (R100)	1985	164.80	23,000	0.12

Source: Sabastien Thiriez, Bus Services: Criteria for Profitability, World Bank Technical Paper (1986).

carrying a substantial proportion of bus ridership (75 percent in both Calcutta and Istanbul and around 45 percent in Bangkok). They earn a profit sufficient at least to induce them to stay in business while also paying taxes. The most rapid growth in private operators' share of ridership and the total bus fleet in Calcutta and Istanbul has occurred after some years of public ownership. These data do not discredit the tentative hypotheses that private operators provide similar bus services at lower costs. The differences can be impressive; in Istanbul, with the same fares and large buses, the public operator loses 12 percent a year while private operators make a profit of up to 20 percent. Private minibus operators' profits are higher, ranging from 20 to 40 percent of total costs.[4] A study of Australian public transport in high-income countries stated: "For a typical suburban route now run by a public operator and subsidized at the 60 percent level, transfer to a private operator might be expected to reduce the subsidy required by some two-thirds, assuming no change in fare level."[5] The use of these data on subsidies to adduce the relative costs of private and public bus operations involves the assumption that the private operators are making only normal profits. Since there is, in all cities, a persistent pressure on the authorities and others by prospective private operators for a license or some other "authorization" to run a bus, one may suspect that profits are above normal. Thus the ratio of revenue to cost in publicly owned enterprises is an underestimate of the ratio of the costs of the private firms to the costs of the publicly owned concern. The ratio of private costs to public costs is therefore likely to be lower than the range of 0.37 to 0.72 observed in the sample cities. These are, of course, indirect estimates and need to be checked against other studies of cost.

Cost Comparisons

Some evidence is available on the costs of private and public concerns in the following cities:

Calcutta. Calcutta State Transport Corporation (CSTC) had a monopoly on service within the corporate limits before 1966. Because of an inability to meet the growth in demand, CSTC lost its monopoly, and by 1978 Calcutta was served by about 940 publicly owned CSTC buses, 1,500 private (usually owner-operated) buses, and a large fleet of smaller paratransit vehicles that will not be considered here.

According to figures quoted by private operators to the Indian government's Taxation Equity Board, the cost of operation in 1978 was about Rs 3.35 a kilometer or Rs 0.096 a seat-kilometer. Considering the nature of the forum, these figures are possibly overestimates. Based on CSTC accounts, public buses in 1978 cost about Rs 6.32 a kilometer or Rs 0.113 a seat-kilometer.

Since buses in Calcutta are almost always full — often with more than three times as many passengers as seats during peak periods — cost as a function of capacity, seated and standing, better reflects vehicle utilization and is more meaningful. Based on gross capacity, private buses are even less expensive, with a cost of Rs 0.051 per capacity-kilometer for private buses and Rs 0.78 per capacity-kilometer for public ones. These figures show private buses to cost 53 percent of public bus costs on a kilometer basis, 85 percent on a seat-kilometer basis, and 65 percent on a capacity-kilometer basis. Recent estimates show private bus costs as only 37 percent of public costs on a passenger-kilometer basis.[6] Evidence to counter the argument of selectivity bias may be adduced by comparing the cost of private bus operation in Calcutta with the Bombay Electric Supply and Transit (BEST), which is considered to be the most efficient public company in India. Even so, the private operators' cost is lower per kilometer.

Bangkok. The city is served by some 4,400 publicly owned Bangkok Mass Transit Authority (BMTA) buses, about 13,000 private buses and minibuses, and a large number of smaller private vehicles. Reliable financial statistics are unavailable for public and private operators. Therefore, in this case, one can only look at the losses. BMTA was created in 1976 through the consolidation of twenty-two private companies and two public companies. Although some of these companies were profitable, in 1985 BMTA covered only 74 percent of its costs.

In fiscal year 1977-78 BMTA lost B 350 million (U.S. $17 million), and in 1979-80 lost about B 950 million (U.S. $47 million). In July 1979 the fare was raised to B 1.5; however, deficits still persist: in 1985 it was still a high U.S. $43.5 million.

Istanbul. The city is served by about 1,500 publicly owned Istanbul Electric Tramways and Tunnel (IETT) buses, about 4,800 privately owned minibuses and midibuses (one-half of which are owner operated), a large fleet of *dolmus* (exclusive and shared-ride taxis), and some 100 IETT trolley buses that will not be considered here.

In 1977 the cost of operation for an IETT bus was about Lt 20-23 effective kilometer or Lt 0.5-0.55 a seat-kilometer. In the same year minibuses cost Lt 2.7 a kilometer or Lt 0.27 a seat-kilometer. Minibuses, even on a seat-kilometer basis, cost less than half as much to operate and without subsidy provided service to almost twice as many passengers as the stage bus. Since 1977, however, IETT has streamlined its operations, dramatically improving cost recovery to 88 percent in 1985.[7]

Australia. In 1975, Australian cities with a population of more than 10,000 had a total of 9,120 buses, of which 4,168 (46 percent) were owned by private companies. The average costs for a sample of public and private operations in fiscal year 1972-73 are indicated in table 2. The far-right column shows the unit cost of the bus system as a proportion of the figure for MTT in Hobart (a fairly typical public operator in terms of its average cost). Average unit costs of private buses were estimated to be between 50 and 65 percent of those of the typical public operator.

New York metropolitan area. A 1974-75 study estimated the average cost of public bus operation to be about 11 to 15 percent higher per hour than private bus operations. The weighted-average private bus costs per vehicle-hour were $19.76 in 1974 and 1975, while the costs per vehicle-hour for the public operator were $22.14 in 1974 and $23.82 in 1975. The relatively small difference in cost may be a result of the stringent regulation of private operators and the extensive unionization in the New York City area. In the study, average cost rose with the size of the company. The two largest operators (with 2,400 and 1,400 buses) had a mean cost of $24.40 per vehicle hour. Nine smaller bus companies with a maximum of 310 buses had an average aggregate cost of $18.05. This is interesting in that public operators tend to be large while private bus firms tend to be small with the owner-operator common in low-income countries.

Table 3 summarizes the results for the five cities. Because of the imprecise nature of operating-cost data and the limited scope for interpretation, the cost comparisons should be taken as a tentative corroboration of the implications of the data on subsidies. It seems that private operators with a substantial subsidy can provide about the same service as public operators.

TABLE 2

Average Costs for Various Bus Operators in Australia, 1972-73 (Australian dollars)

			(Average Cost)	
	Operating Costs (A$'000 p.a.)	Bus Km p.a. (million)	c/km	% of MTT Hobart
MMTB Melbourne	6,394	11.9	53.7	104
MTT Hobart	3,184	6.2	51.4	100
MTT Adelaide	8,270	17.5	47.3	92
MTT Perth	13,777	37.7	36.5	71
Brisbane CC	12,048	20.1	60.2	117
Victorian private	13,754	45.9	30.0	58
Various private	4,899	17.3	28.3	55

Source: I. Wallis, *Private Bus Operation in Urban Areas: Their Economics and Roles* (Sydney, Australia: R. Travers Morgan, Pty., Ltd., 1979).

TABLE 3

Summary of Cost Comparisons

	Year	Private (1)	Public (2)	Ratio (1):(2)
Calcutta	1978	Bus	Bus	
		(Rs)	(Rs)	
Per kilometer		3.350	6.320	0.53
Seat kilometer		0.096	0.113	0.85
Capacity kilometer		0.051	0.078	0.65
Per passenger kilometer	1985			0.37
Istanbul	1977	Minibus	Bus	
		(Lt)	(Lt)	
Per kilometer		2.740	20–23	0.13
Seat kilometer		0.270	0.5–0.55	0.51
Australia	1979	Bus	Bus	
		(U.S.$)	(U.S.$)	
Per kilometer		0.270	0.270	0.58
New York City—Metropolitan Area	1974–75	Bus	Bus	
		(U.S.$)	(U.S.$)	
Per vehicle hour		21.400	23.82	0.90
Bangkok[a] (maximum)		–	–	0.70

[a] Based on implied costs, not on cost study.

Private Operators — Exploitation and Quality

Table 4 lists most of the charges made against private bus operations. The four main criticisms are that private operators exploit labor, have poor financial practices, contribute to traffic anarchy, and bring about declining levels of service.

One concern shared by many observers from high-income countries is that private operators may pay low wages for long hours. In all cases examined, employees of the private companies were paid lower wages with fewer benefits than their counterparts in the public sector. However, private-bus employees seemed to be earning normal or above-normal wages. In Istanbul and Calcutta private-bus workers earn more than the average bus rider. Because of the greater flexibility of labor contracts in the private sector (for example, the driver may do simple maintenance and repairs, and part-time workers may be employed), the wage cost per bus hour is likely to be much lower than the wage costs in the public sector. Wage costs of the private sector are not inflated by the absenteeism characteristic of public operators. And by maintaining market wage rates and nonrestrictive labor practices the private operators maintain appropriate capital-labor ratios and ensure that there is no inefficient substitution of capital for labor.

It is often alleged that private bus operators make inadequate financial and insurance provisions and do not allow for depreciation and maintenance of their vehicle. In some cases, such as Bangkok and the early days of the minibus in Hong Kong, it has been suggested that, through the operation of the loan-shark and

TABLE 4

Criticisms of Private Operators

Job environment
  No benefits or pensions
  No job security
  Long hours
  Low wages
  Child labor

Financial concerns
  Owners do not account for amortization
  Default on loans
  Buy vehicles and spare parts on black market
  Support loan sharking/protection rackets/gangsterism
  Lack insurance

Service concerns
  Cause congestion (inefficient use of road space)
  Contribute to traffic anarchy (poor driving habits)
  Stopping in street to load or unload
  Lack inspection
  Cruising (waste fuel)
  Overcrowding
  Cause and have more accidents
  Overcharge in peak and evening hours
  Vanish in rain and when in low demand
  Fear of cartelization
  Creaming of riders

protection rackets, they fell into the hands of gangsters and racketeers.

It is difficult to test all these assertions, but some are clearly not true. In Calcutta and Istanbul, private companies have maintained buses much better than the public concerns. Observers in Bangkok claim that private minibuses are often overloaded and unsafe—but it is not clear that they are generally worse maintained than the public buses. One would expect that the standard of maintenance and passenger safety in the private sector would correspond to passenger demand. The customer gets as much safety as he wants at the going rate. It would be patronizing to impose Western standards (and costs) of road safety on people outside the industrial countries. One might expect owner-operators to drive more carefully to protect their investment and generally to take better care of their vehicles than would hired drivers. Kenneth Huddart, in an unpublished study of accidents in Mombasa, Kenya, where common wisdom attributes most accidents to the minibuses (*mutatus*), found no significant increase in accident rates between the introduction of *mutatus* in 1972 and 1978, when some 1,270 *mutatus* were in operation. H. I. Sanli, discussing Istanbul, suggested that differential financial constraints, such as high interest rates and high taxes, on private bus operations contribute to overloading, poor driving habits, and long hours of driving. But no concrete evidence supports the allegation of "higher accident rates."

The most common fault attributed to private bus operators, particularly in low-income countries, is that they contribute to congestion. Such allegations need to be put in perspective. In Bangkok, for example, about 12,000 paratransit vehicles are in operation as compared to some 220,000 private cars. The paratransit vehicles operate almost fully occupied during peak periods of demand, but the cars are rarely occupied by more than two people. The fault lies with the car, not the bus.

Traffic-rule enforcement, priority lanes for buses and private minibuses, separate and distinct minibus stops, and a host of traffic management techniques for all traffic can be used to improve traffic flow to reduce congestion. The private sector has contributed some ingenious systems of its own as well. To maintain equal intervals between buses in Calcutta, a private bus driver who runs late must pay a fine to the driver behind him.

The most persistent charge against private operators is that they serve only profitable routes and that the levels of service deteriorate where they operate. In Calcutta and Istanbul, however, the public operators have first choice of routes. Evidently, they choose the most desirable routes and leave the less desirable ones to the private operators. In Calcutta, the private operators are also generally restricted to areas outside the center of the city with much poorer road conditions. In Bangkok, the minibuses serve the *sois* (usually narrow and sometimes unpaved side roads), which cannot accommodate large buses. In Istanbul, minibuses have profitably served routes dropped by IETT. The *dolmus* and especially the minibus provide transport service to the squatter areas (settlements declared illegal by the municipality) where municipal bus transport has been withheld. This evidence seems to counter the charges that private operators only serve the "best" or most profitable routes.

Another charge is that the private-bus operators take only the "cream" of the traffic peak. But such "creaming" may benefit public buses, because it reduces ridership during peak hours. It has been estimated, for example, that the public bus service in Bangkok would need 40 percent more buses to serve during peak hours, and this would increase its deficit substantially.

Empirical evidence has discredited other arguments suggesting that levels of service deteriorate when private operators compete. In Calcutta, private buses were found to be more evenly spaced, more comfortable, and less subject to breakdown, and they have "better general appearance and performance" than publicly owned buses.[8] In Istanbul, in Chiengmai, Thailand, and in most other cities, minibuses operated faster than the public buses. Since private operators often find it profitable to use minibuses, levels of service improve through increased frequencies of transport services. Thus it appears that many of the problems described in table 4 are figments of the imagination. Some involve the imposition of Western standards on developing countries, and some have much cheaper alternative solutions.

Conclusion

While public and private operators may charge the same fare, private operators provide equivalent if not better services at no subsidy in most countries, and public operators require massive subsidy support. Private operators generally appear to be 50 to 65 percent less expensive than public buses, and in addition they usually pay large sums of money into government treasuries. Obviously, cost is only one consideration; the level of service is just as important. The charges against private operators are not supported by the data; and, even if they were, there are much more cost effective solutions than banning them. Because of restrictions on fares, the demand far exceeds the supply in many cities, and if the private operators disappeared the public operators could carry the total traffic only with greatly increased subsidy. In addition, these private operators have cropped up locally, respond quickly and efficiently to the market, often provide a myriad of other services (such as works buses, freight, and delivery services), use local expertise and materials, and adapt easily to the needs of the area.

Finally, one may even reflect that the disparities between public and private ownership are so large that there is a prima facie case for opening up all nationalized bus monopolies to private operators of either buses or minibuses. The implications of such a policy, however, are far beyond the objectives of this essay.

NOTES

1. William McLeod and A. A. Walters, "A Note on Bankruptcy Rates in Road Haulage Industry," *Journal of Industrial Economics* (1956): 71–80.

2. Sebastien Thiriez, *Bus Services: Criteria for Profitability,* World Bank Technical Paper (1986).

3. Organization for Economic Cooperation and Development, *Subsidies and Costs in Urban Buses* (1975).

4. Thiriez.

5. I. Wallis, *Private Bus Operators in Urban Areas: Their Economics and Roles* (Sydney, Australia: R. Travers Morgan, 1979), 9.

6. Thiriez.

7. Thiriez. This improvement was probably associated with threats of privatization.

8. T. Thomas et al., "Travel and Public Transport in Calcutta," Urban Transport Research Group, Warwick University, United Kingdom, 1977.

Selling the New York City Subway: Wild-eyed Radicalism or the Only Feasible Solution?

JAMES B. RAMSEY

The *New York Times* often publishes letters to the editor complaining about subway conditions (bad and getting worse) or subway finances (ever-greater deficits owing to inadequate subsidies from nonriders). The only solution ever suggested is that non-New Yorkers ought to pay more for support of the subway; but, of course, the phrase usually employed is "more support by the state and Federal governments." More than one-half of the total costs are already subsidized.

The New York City subway system is one of the oldest and largest in the world, rivaling in miles of track and number of passengers served the Moscow, Tokyo, and London systems. The maintenance of the capital equipment, track, and buildings has been below economically efficient levels since the 1920s, but only in recent years has the level of neglect escalated to irretrievable proportions. Virtually no train is without substantial maintenance defects. No station can be said to be in a reasonable state of repair, although a few stations have had a welcome face-lift.

Many trains and stations are so completely covered with graffiti that no maps can be deciphered, and vision through the windows is impossible. In sum, the entire subway is a decaying, filthy mess. What else can one call a dimly lit, littered tunnel that drips water and smells?

Nevertheless, the New York City subway system does have one outstanding potential advantage. The distribution of people, places of work, and entertainment in the city is such that the traditional complaint that almost all traffic is only one way at each rush hour is not heard. On many lines the trains have empty cars only during the period from well after midnight until the early morning rush hour, about four hours. In addition, especially in Manhattan, trains are crowded in both directions simultaneously most of the day and evening.

The New York City subway problem is of general interest, for New York City's current problems will emerge in other cities for the same reasons. The suggestion of selling the New York subway is therefore merely an illustration of a general approach to the revitalization of a service of broad interest—"public" transportation. But how and why the current state of affairs came about cannot be understood without considering the history of the New York City subway system. This discussion will provide the background for an analysis of the economic and political aspects of the situation. That analysis in turn will set the stage for what is the only remaining financially viable solution, the sale of the system to private firms. The advantages and disadvantages of the proposal will be discussed and the argument summarized in the last section.

A Brief History of the New York City Subway

The very beginnings of the subway set the pattern to be followed for the subsequent seventy-five years—New York public transportation was to be a political football. As early as 1860, Hugh B. Wilson raised $5 million from private sources for a subway line in Manhattan and the state assembly approved the measure, but Boss Tweed, the Tammany Hall Democratic leader, persuaded the governor to veto the bill in behalf of the horsecar companies. By 1900, a change in the economic realities enabled work to begin on the Interborough Rapid Transit (IRT) line. Private money was raised for equipment, but public money was used for the construction and right-of-way in exchange for an agreement on a fixed fare of 5 cents. The IRT was a financial and operating success, and it was soon extended. Again, public financing was used for construction, mainly because the fare was held to 5 cents, the lease was for only forty-nine years with no right of renewal, and the city had the right to recapture all of the facilities after ten years at the original cost plus 15 percent.

The financial backers of the Brooklyn-Manhattan Transit System (BMT), originally called the Brooklyn Rapid Transit Company, obtained a lease for new lines in Brooklyn in 1911 and began operations in 1918. The financial arrangements were similar to those for the IRT. Both lines were essentially complete by 1920.

After the initial success of the subways, the city had wanted to increase its control and ownership, but its own difficult financial position coupled with certain restrictions on its debt limits prevented the city from gaining full control. An intermediate step was the creation of the Independent (IND) subway system, which opened in 1932 and had no private involvement in its operation. By 1940, the city was able to buy out the two private lines. The IRT had been forced into receivership, and the BMT had been under audit by the city for breach of contract. The intent of the unification was cogently expressed by Nathan L. Miller, governor of New York, in 1921: "The profitable parts of the system must maintain the unprofitable," i.e., internal cross-subsidization for political benefits. And the second universal slogan was: "The passenger fare shall be five cents." The legal change that facilitated the move was a 1938 amendment to the city's charter that excluded from the city's debt limit the cost of the unification. The IRT and the BMT were bought on the basis of the city's credit, not transit earnings, which even then met only part of the carrying charges on the debt.

The 5-cent fare was maintained until 1948, when it was raised to 10 cents, and then a more rapid escalation began—15 cents in 1954, 20 cents in 1966, 30 cents in 1970, 35 cents in 1972, 50 cents in 1975, 60 cents in 1980, 75 cents in 1981, 90 cents in 1984, and $1 in 1986. Notwithstanding the fare increases, the "deficits" rose dramatically during the late 1960s. In 1974, the state began to provide direct operating assistance, and in 1975 the Federal government also began to support the system. Between 1960 and 1975, fuel and power increases accounted for 12.1 percent of increased costs, declining ridership an estimated 18.4 percent, and increases in wages and benefits 56.7 percent.

What is clear from this discussion is that the subways' malaise did not begin recently, and the problems are still not being addressed. Public control has gradually but inevitably led to the deterioration of the system.

Analysis of the Problem

The financial reason for the subways' difficulty is easy to state: labor costs per passenger mile have risen faster than the sum of revenues and subsidies per passenger mile. The difficult question is why. The near impossible question is what to do about it. Moreover, the problem has a puzzling aspect when one examines the situation in more detail. As labor costs rose relative to other costs, capital equipment was not substituted for labor, as would be the case in any normal profit-maximizing industry. The reason, of course, is political; the degree of pressure that a municipal union can bring to bear on a city government and the arrangements that the government can make because of its rule-making ability inevitably force bodies like the Transit Authority into trying to pay for wage increases that projected revenues do not justify by reducing maintenance and repair of capital equipment—in short, by disinvesting in capital.

A private firm's response to a higher wage rate is to substitute capital and technology for labor. Thus the full impact of the wage increment is muted through the more extensive use of capital and relatively less use of high-priced labor. In even more difficult circumstances, the private firm will reduce output, sell off nonprofitable portions of the firm, or in extremis declare bankruptcy. For purely political reasons, municipal transit authorities are not allowed these options. The ultimate response that mitigates excessive union demands—unemployment and the closing of the firm—is not available to them; worse, before the ultimate collapse of the system, labor productivity falls as the existing capital stock is depreciated so that the problem is compounded at each round of labor negotiations. Unfortunately, despite what municipal authorities seem to think, deferred maintenance is not an interest-free loan; the real interest rate of such loans is very high.

Between 1968 and 1979 total full-time employees fell from 34,649 to 34,007, a reduction of less than 2 percent. But labor costs per passenger rose from 20 cents to 63 cents over the same period. These figures do not include pay for transit police, capital engineers, and CETA (Comprehensive Employment and Training Act) employees. Between 1965 and 1980 total labor remuneration of transit employees rose 222.6 percent, while the Consumer Price Index rose by only 127 percent. Of the 222.6 percent increase, salaries and wages rose by only 176 percent, while pension and retirement expenses rose 556 percent. Stated another way, between 1965 and 1978 transit employees' weekly earnings rose 148 percent, while increases in other fields were much lower: manufacturing, 119 percent; construction, 101 percent; trade, 108 percent; service workers, 112 percent; and local and suburban transport and public utilities, 115 percent. It is only fair to note, however, that water and air transportation workers obtained 214 percent and 170 percent increases respectively between 1965 and 1978.

Looking at increases in wages and other benefits is only one side of the coin; the other is the productivity of the labor force. Thus, if productivity grew at a faster rate than the rate of increase in wages, labor costs per unit of output could fall. An initial view of the situation is provided by the observation that in the 1960s the number of passengers per employee was between 170 and 180, but by the beginning of the 1970s that figure had fallen to 128. An optimistic estimate of the national average transit-productivity gain as a percent per year is positive, but it is as likely to be negative. Perhaps the best guess is that the national average transit-productivity gains are zero. It is reasonable to surmise that the MTA's contribution to the national average is negative. Further, while the ratio of capital to labor for the United States domestic economy has been growing at about 2.5 percent a year since 1948 and that for transit has grown at only 0.52 percent a year, and this figure does not adequately allow for the long-term deterioration of capital equipment through neglected maintenance. On balance, the change in the capital-labor ratio for the New York City Transit Authority (NYCTA) is probably negative.

Unfortunately, it is impossible to compare directly public-employee performance on subways with that of private-sector employees in similar firms. However, such comparisons can be made with the bus drivers and bus mechanics, or "maintainers," as the NYCTA calls them. The comparison is especially instructive in New York City, because the Transport Worker's Union has a virtual monopoly on the labor supply in the entire area. The union negotiates a single wage rate for most drivers, public and private, throughout the New York City and suburban areas. However, there are wide differences in fringe and retirement benefits, as well as in other pay-related areas. In 1979, the last year for which comparative figures are available, NYCTA bus drivers earned a representative salary of $29,705, including fringe and retirement benefits, whereas comparable drivers for the Green Bus Line, the most expensive alternative, earned $26,881. The NYCTA drivers, however, generated an average revenue of $23,303, that is, the revenues did not even pay the bus driver's salary, whereas the private bus companies averaged $40,115 per driver. Passenger revenues per employee are $16,694 for NYCTA and $26,279 for the private companies.

For bus mechanics the NYCTA total pay package is approximately equal to the average private bus company's total pay. But an audit by the state comptroller found that the NYCTA required nearly 50 percent more maintenance hours to service each bus than the average private firm.

The initial explanation for this dismal record is the power of the unions. Federal, state, and local legislation provides transportation unions with strong powers, both economic and political. In New York City and its suburbs the Transport Worker's Union (TWU) is a monopoly whose degree of control is unmatched by any firm or even trio of firms in any industry in the country. Local 100 of the TWU bargains for eight out of ten private labor contracts and covers 93 percent of the buses and 95 percent of the bus operators. Of course, the subways are completely unionized. This gives the union enormous economic power — whether or not it has the "legal right to strike"; indeed, the legal prohibition does not seem to be much of a barrier to strikes and has been no barrier to higher wage agreements.

If the economic power of the union is combined with political leverage, the union's ability to tax the rest of society is impeded only by political reluctance to raise fares and the length of debates on tax increases. Once a municipality has taken on direct responsibility for providing a service, even through the device of an "authority," the pressure to politicize most issues is overwhelming. An ostensible strike against the TA on economic issues becomes a political battle involving the political gains and losses to the incumbent politician. In this situation, well-organized blocs of voters, like those provided by the TWU, provide a degree of political influence matched by few other groups. Better still from the union's viewpoint, settlements now have direct access to the public purse; settlements that would immediately bankrupt a private firm can be financed indefinitely by taxing the general public. While the public purse is not unlimited, a politically influential group's ability to extract large sums at the expense of anonymous taxpayers is high and is obviously in the self-interest of the politician supported by a well-organized union cadre.

One important lesson not lost on the subway riders is that the fare is only a small part of the actual cost of riding the subway. In truth, the fare is become even more irrelevant; the real total cost is already high and rising rapidly.

The economist recognizes the importance of distinguishing between nominal prices (the current $1 fare) and real prices, which include all other costs to the rider. The best way of evaluating the cost of a subway ride to a prospective rider is to ask what is the cost of the best alternative. Take for example a rider from Sheepshead Bay in Brooklyn. There are three viable choices — subway, car, or commuter express bus. The car is already expensive to use in terms of the money outlay for parking, up to $30.00 a day, and the operating expense of about $4.00 a day. The advantage of a car, however, is that it is available when it is wanted, the service is door-to-door or nearly so, the ride is comfortable, and the riding conditions are far superior to the subway. The monetary costs can be lowered in exchange for some loss of convenience by car pooling. When conditions on the subway are considered, it is no wonder that many travel by automobile.

The second choice is to ride an express bus, an option that is growing in popularity, particularly from the outermost areas of Brooklyn, Queens, and Staten Island. Once again the monetary cost of $3.00 to $5.00 a trip is far higher than for the subway, but the comfort, cleanliness, safety, and social acceptability of one's traveling companions more than offset the loss of convenience of being able to travel at any time.

The subway fare is cheap for journeys from the outer boroughs but not for short trips. The subway, when it runs as scheduled, can provide a quick trip. And that is about all one can say for the subway. The real cost is measured in lack of safety, uncertainty as to the time of travel, filthy surroundings, overcrowding, and often some disturbing riders. One dollar is a very small part of the cost, and each time people experiment with alternative modes of getting to work, for example, during a subway strike, they discover that the real costs of the subway are greater than the use of a private car or a charter bus. In fact, ridership on the express buses is rising rapidly as commuters leave the subways—a clear indication that the riding public is willing to pay more, far more, for a quality ride. The main lesson from this discussion is that if the fare were raised and the quality of the service significantly improved, one could easily generate an increase in ridership resulting from an overall reduction in the total price to the rider. The mere substitution of clean, well-lit stations and clean, quiet trains would greatly improve the desirability of subway travel.

No mention has yet been made of management's role in the half-century decline of the subway system. Ironically, especially within the last few years, senior management has been notable for its drive, knowledge, and concern to create a useful public service. Traditionally, the first group to be blamed for poor performance is management, and in a private firm that view is quite correct. But in an organization that is highly subject to political influence, the charge is not necessarily true. By and large the senior management knows what must be done to improve the system, but for political reasons it cannot do it.

The political power of the unions has already been mentioned. But pressures for inefficiency come from the riders as well. Political pressure keeps the fare down, and when there is an allowed increase the amount is too little and too late. Subway lines and stations that economically should be closed or have their service reduced because of lack of ridership are kept open through political intervention at an enormous cost.

The reader may imagine the difficulties to be faced if he or she had to cope with a work force that cannot be effectively disciplined (MTA workers' lack of commitment to their jobs is notorious), service that cannot be changed to meet changing demands, capital projects that are a political battle, the exhausting prospect that even routine decisions face potential political intervention, and, finally, revenues that are held down until a crisis is precipitated.

Political control of a firm leads to gross economic inefficiency. The differences between alternative situations lie in how the inefficiencies are manifested. For some operations — for example, the Washington, D.C., system — the plant and equipment are modern and clean, but the subsidies are enormous. In New York, the subsidies are relatively modest by public-transportation standards, but the employee-pension burden is so egregious (it is possible to retire at nearly full pay after only twenty years of service) and work-force discipline is so negligible that the outcome is a decaying system. As the subsidies for other transportation systems decline, they will also begin to depreciate capital in order to pay for intemperate wage and pension increments.

The Only Feasible Solution

There should be one simple but outstandingly clear lesson from the above discussion. The current system is not viable; there is no sum of money, no subsidy so great, that cannot be eaten up by union demands and political intervention. Indeed, the more the system is subsidized and the more management and the unions recognize that fact, the more inefficient the entire system will become and the higher the costs will be. Some device is needed that will limit union demands to the bounds of reason and concentrate the minds of management on trying to generate an efficient system that serves the public. The following suggestion, which is politically feasible, could produce this necessary miracle.

The proposal is to sell off the subway system line by line over a period of about five years. The fundamental elements of the scheme are that there are to be no price controls, no entry barriers to new subway firms other than those dictated by safety, and no political intervention in behalf of the unions, and the city is to share in the profits of the system. The last element is crucial to the political feasibility of the proposal.

A team of evaluators chosen in part by the city and in part by the potential bidders for the subway will evaluate the net "market value" of the current capital stock of that part of the system to be sold. This capital price must be paid in order for the bidding firm to acquire the right to provide subway service in the city. The choice of which firm is to rebuild and run the subway will be by competitive bids on net profit share to the city; that is, the highest bid share of gross profits (net of all capital costs) to be paid to the city wins the right to provide subway service on the line or lines bought. But it must be expressly agreed that no price controls and no mandated service requirements will be imposed. In a California oil lease sale where this bidding scheme was tried, the net profit share was 94.77 percent.

The city can use its profit share in any way it chooses — for example, to finance subway rides for the poor by giving them an income subsidy paid from the profit shares. Alternatively, it can pay for the provision of uneconomical service. One objective of the scheme is to separate the need for an efficient transportation system from the politically understandable wish to subsidize certain segments of the electorate.

By moving to a privately funded and operated system wherein any gains or losses are the direct responsibility of the owners, the minds of management will be concentrated on providing the service demanded by the public. Only when managers' jobs depend on their efforts and efficiency will there be a serious effort to control costs. The objective of the firm is now simply stated and easily understood—to make money. But what the general public does not understand is that this seemingly crass dictum in practice would help solve numerous complex problems and provide the rider better service at a lower cost.

The management of privately owned firms is far more efficient than that of publicly owned or controlled firms, simply because of the difference in the pressures that managers face in the two situations. In publicly owned or controlled firms, not only are there fewer and smaller personal incentives to be efficient; political control adds a further and, in the end, disastrous thrust to fiscal myopia, to the acceptance of the expedient response, and an effort to solve today's difficulty at a greater cost tomorrow. This is in part because the period for the payoff from political decisions is short, often less than a year and seldom greater than two years. It is therefore no great surprise to view the political reluctance for the long-range solutions that inevitably incur short-run difficulties. It is expedient for the politician to curry favor now and leave the problems to the next election, the next administration, or the next generation of users. It is easier to take a popular stance on low fares today than to recommend the investment needed for a viable system tomorrow. Unfortunately, the outcome of this political exchange is worse for both riders and taxpayers.

While it is well recognized that private firms face greater pressures to respond to consumer wishes and to moderate costs, it is not so well recognized that private firms can withstand union pressures more easily. This is not to say that a powerful union cannot force inefficiencies and raise wage rates above competitive levels but to say that with any degree of union power the deleterious effects will be reduced. When a public authority like the NYCTA runs the subways, the unions recognize that they have access to the public treasury and general tax revenues; any deficits created by their own demands can always be filled through public monies.

Critics will say that while the above comments are well and good, experience has shown that no private company can run a transit system unsubsidized and that no private firm can raise the funds needed to rebuild the system. The answer is that experience has shown that when transit fares are held below economic levels by government fiat, incumbent firms go broke, and no one else will be interested in the economic equivalent of self-flagellation.

What is clear to even the most skeptical of critics is that there is an enormous reservoir of demand for relatively efficient transportation. The use of a car for a typical commuter is about one hour's drive plus about $30.00 a day. A commuter bus costs $6 to $10 a day, and it is inconvenient because of the necessity of sticking to a fixed and limited schedule. This is the currently allowed competition for the subway. If there were no price constraints, the city would be flooded with proposals for providing public transportation in innovative ways. If the lack of price constraints results in a profitable situation, one need not worry about the ability to raise the necessary capital funds.

The issue of financial viability has now been reduced to one with purely emotional content. Only the "rich" will be able to afford to ride the subway; so long as the subway is a monopoly the public will be gouged unmercifully. Much colorful language can be employed in the argument, but the true situation is far more prosaic. As usual in such debates, there is a subtle propensity for those enamored of municipal control and tax-based subsidies to argue both ways simultaneously — privately run systems are not financially viable because no one will use them at the profitable price (there is strong competition) and the subway is a monopoly and people must pay any price charged (there is no competition at all).

The truth of the matter is that subways face considerable competition, although for some trips subways would clearly be the preferred mode. Insofar as the subways are sold line by line and bus lines are sold separately, subways and buses provide competition for some trips as well as opportunities for cooperative service for others; for example, crosstown bus service linked to uptown-downtown subway service. Even from the outlying boroughs, express buses, car pooling, jitney cabs (if allowed), shared limousines, nonmedallion cabs, private cars, and motorcycles provide alternative modes of transportation.

Some idea of a market-clearing price can be inferred from several items of information. The Regional Plan Association estimated in 1980 that it would take a 45-cent fare increase (plus increases on the Long Island Rail Road) to raise $1 billion a year for rebuilding the system. After eliminating all subsidies and before realizing the existing and known potential for efficiency gains, an "average fare" of about $1.20 emerged, certainly less than $1.50. But even in 1986, fares within Manhattan could be 75 to 90 cents and only fares to the ends of the outer boroughs might reach $3.00.

If express buses can operate profitably in 1986 at $3.00 to $5.00 a ride as simple commuter operations, the subway could provide far better service for much less. Consequently, from this perspective, a maximum profitable price in 1986 from the outer boroughs is less than, say, $3.00 on average; short trips should be less than the current $1.

So far this discussion has ignored technological innovations, lowering the total cost of labor by substituting relatively cheaper capital equipment, and simple efficiency gains from work-rate changes. It has been estimated that relatively minor changes of this type can lower costs by 20 percent or more. Another example would be the elimination of token clerks, about 4,000 high-paid jobs, and another 3,000 "conductors." New rail lines seem to manage with only one driver.

A counterargument that can be raised at this point is that the price increases recommended will so lower demand that costs must rise even more. This argument is invalid on two counts. First, even accurate measures of the relative price responsiveness of demand would not be of much relevance in this situation, because what is at issue is the demand for a vastly improved system, not a higher price for the existing network. What is needed to calculate the effect on ridership is to evaluate the responsiveness of demand to increases in quality; it is the net effect of quality and price that will determine the gain in the ridership.

Second, the notion that cents per rider must rise if ridership falls can only be true for a system locked into overmanning. For most firms, if demand falls permanently, the firm shrinks to accommodate. It is usually only when demand falls to very low levels that one begins to experience serious increases in average cost to a fall in demand. The subways are by no means close to such a point.

Another argument made by those in favor of tax-supported systems is that if the subways were to charge the full economic cost, firms would relocate and New York City would lose jobs. The argument is false. First, it is true that transportation is a key issue in the decisions of firms whether to remain in the city or relocate, but it is *not* whether the fare is 60 cents or 75 cents or even $2.00 but the fact that employees are continually late, rushing off early to get a train, unwilling to work late, tired, irritable, and exhausted from inhuman conditions on the subway—in short, the abysmal level of services, or lack of them, is the problem.

Second, whatever the true costs of transportation in the city, the firm and its employees still pay the full costs no matter how low the nominal fare, because the shortfall must be made up in taxes. A viable New York City requires a viable transit system, and that requires a city government committed to open entry into the transit business, receptivity to innovative ideas, and above all the courage *not* to set price ceilings. Ironically, while this is the only strategy that can achieve a useful transportation network, it is the only one not yet tried by the city.

The most emotional issue of all concerns the poor. The nonworking poor seldom need transportation; attention here will therefore be focused on the working poor. Grant for a moment that these people would rather not work at all or would rather work locally than pay a higher subway fare. Employers would soon see their labor forces shrinking and would have to raise wages to get their workers back. In this case, then, the system is self-correcting. Further, fares based on distance traveled could lower fares for the working poor, since many work within their own neighborhoods and do not commute to Manhattan from the outer boroughs.

What can be done for the nonworking poor? The answer is not to keep fares artificially low for 95 percent of the population who can pay but to give an extra income subsidy to the nonworking poor and let them spend it how they will. Such a subsidy can be financed directly from the profits of the system paid to the city. But what if there are no profits paid in? This phenomenon can only be temporary, and there are two answers. First, since the firm is not making profits, everyone using the system is already being subsidized at the expense of the equity owners. Second, the city can finance the poor immediately in anticipation of future profit revenues.

For political reasons the city may wish to provide subway service to areas where alternative transportation is so cheap and efficient that the privately run subway system cannot compete. Under the existing scheme the city could use its profit share or any other revenue to purchase the extra service from the privately run system.

The final issue, and the most crucial one, is whether the proposed scheme is politically feasible. The opposition is powerful, but the answer can be yes. The TWU definitely does not want to see its members' pay reduced to that earned by their colleagues in private industry. All those who still believe others can be taxed to pay for their subway will be against the idea of paying their own way, no matter how inefficient and wasteful such a procedure is. There is a sizable body of people who firmly believe that only municipally provided services are desirable and that all such services should be paid for by taxing the "rich." Such people will only grudgingly compromise to accept some nonzero fare.

On the other side is the grim reality that the above proponents have reduced a once-great system to a shambles. Further, a number of people recognize that the only viable and affordable solution is to institute a private system of intracity transit like the intercity system. In any event, both New York City and the state can no longer afford to subsidize transportation at ever-increasing amounts because of the pressure of alternative and desperately needed capital expenditures on items less amenable to privatization, such as road repair, sewage plants, and street cleaning. Leadership, full discussion of the issues, and a clear recognition of the self-interest involved in many of the arguments may be the only way to escape from the transit morass.

Privatizing Waterworks

STEVE H. HANKE
STEPHEN J.K. WALTERS

"From 1838 to 1841, whilst examining the sanitary conditions of town populations, I found urban districts in England where there are two or three
sets of water-pipes carried through streets which might be as well or better
supplied under one establishment, [resulting in] bad and deficient supplies
at high charges to the public. . . . These competitions are what I then designated as 'competitions within the field of service.' As opposed to that form
of competition, I proposed, as an administrative principle, competition 'for
the field.' "

> Edwin Chadwick, Esq., *before the Statistical
Society of London, 1859*[1]

Edwin Chadwick's observations on the inefficiency of English water-
supply systems in the nineteenth century were remarkably prescient. He correctly
identified such systems as natural monopolies. Moreover, he proposed a novel
yet practical private solution to the problems inherent in natural monopolies. But
Chadwick's suggestions were not heeded. Consequently, England and Wales are
now served by ten regional, publicly owned waterworks systems that face no competition.

The conservative government of Prime Minister Margaret Thatcher has proposed to alter the current system of regionalized waterworks monopolies. The
Thatcher government has also announced that it intends to privatize the nation's
waterworks. The receipts from a public offering of the waterworks might exceed
the $9 billion generated by the sale of British Gas, the country's natural-gas utility,
in December 1986. The waterworks privatization would be the largest stock offering
in history.

The authors wish to thank M. J. Tixeront and M.F. Valiron for the valuable information about the
provision of water in France that they supplied during numerous conversations and in their lectures
on water management at the Ecole Nationale des Ponts-et-Chausees in Paris.

The objectives of privatizing waterworks are numerous. The most frequently cited goals include improving the economic performance and service functions of the assets; depoliticizing economic decisions; generating public-budget revenues through public-offering receipts; reducing public outlays, taxes, and borrowing requirements; reducing the power of public-sector unions; and promoting popular capitalism through wider share ownership.

These are, of course, ambitious goals. Critics question whether they are attainable and, if so, whether they are desirable. The discussion here is limited to the first objective of privatization — improving economic performance. The theory and evidence of the performance of private versus public enterprises are presented, focusing specifically on the applicability of Chadwick's concept of private competition "for the field" as a means for generating superior performance in the provision of water supply.

Private versus Public Enterprises

Private enterprises should be expected to be more efficient than public enterprises precisely because a private owner stands to gain enhanced wealth from improvements in efficiency, reductions in cost, and the like. To put it another way, a private owner stands to forgo wealth if improvements in efficiency, reductions in cost, and the like are not pursued. In essence, private owners face significant incentives to monitor the behavior of managers and employees so that they will supply what consumers demand and do so in a cost-effective way. Private owners are "residual claimants" who have a strong interest in seeing that there is indeed a residual, or profit, to claim.

Monitoring by owners can be quite costly. The necessity for owners to monitor managers, however, can be mitigated by providing the managers with compensation packages that include profit sharing or stock options. These packages are designed to make the managers' interests coincide with those of the owners.

The combination of monitoring and incentive compensation packages tends to make managers operate private firms in an efficient manner. If managers do not maximize owners' residual claims, however, the market for shares acts as a court of last resort. If the actions of incumbent managers are inappropriate, profits and share prices will be lower than they should be. This attracts corporate takeover specialists, because share prices that are relatively low enhance the returns from a takeover aimed at replacing current management. The threat of corporate takeovers thus helps discipline incumbent managements and generates an efficient provision of goods and services.

Pulic enterprises, by contrast, lack a "residual claimant" in any meaningful sense. Ownership shares in public enterprises generally cannot be bought or sold, so that takeovers are impossible. And it is rare to see the compensation of managers of public enterprises tied to their firms' performance. "Profits" generated via enhanced efficiency in a public enterprise could be refunded to taxpayers through tax reductions, but such refunds would be spread over many taxpayers, and any individual's benefits would be small. More important, taxpayers would be only one of the constituencies competing for these benefits. Before the "profits" were refunded, a variety of interest groups would try to see them spent in other ways. The taxpayers' costs of obtaining these benefits — such as acquiring information, lobbying, and monitoring elected officials — would be very high. Consequently, the incentive of any individual "taxpayer-owner" to monitor the behavior of public managers and employees is weak, and the likelihood of their shirking or acquiring various perquisites that increase production costs is greater than in private firms.

Though the preponderance of theoretical work suggests that private firms are more efficient and productive than public ones, it is only through examining the available evidence that the validity of any theory can be judged.

Numerous studies compare the performance of public and private firms. One of the most widely cited is David G. Davies's comparison of Australia's two inter-state airlines — one public, the other private.[2] Davies found that even though the private airline labored under heavy regulatory constraints it was more efficient: it carried 103 percent more freight and mail and 17 percent more passengers per employee than the public airline but earned 12 percent more revenue per employee.

Many studies show sizable cost savings in other private enterprises. Robert W. Poole, Jr., has documented significant savings in privately run air-traffic control systems, ambulance services, fire-protection services, park systems, and prisons.[3] E. S. Savas has documented enhanced efficiency in private postal services, security services, and refuse collection.[4] James T. Bennett and others have reported cost savings in privately run custodial-service firms, day-care centers, debt-collection services, schools, electric utilities, and ship-maintenance operations.[5] Kenneth W. Clarkson and William Rushing have found that private hospital administrators are more efficient than their public counterparts.[6] Hanke has found that public timber and grazing-land firms are less efficient than private firms.[7]

Most relevant to the central concern of this essay, W. Mark Crain and Asghar Zardkoohi have compared the performance of public and private water utilities in the United States.[8] They found that operating costs are significantly higher in the publicly owned utilities. Using 1970 data from a sample of twenty-four private and eighty-eight public water-supply companies, Crain and Zardkoohi established that public firms' low labor productivity and underutilization of capital equipment led to operating costs about 25 percent higher than in the private companies. Using a different data set, W. Douglas Morgan reached similar conclusions; Hanke found that customer cross-subsidization (that is, overcharging some consumers so that other consumers can be sold water at prices below cost) is more common in public water companies than in private ones.[9]

Though the great weight of empirical evidence seems to support the economic theory that private enterprises should be more efficient than public enterprises, it is possible to find examples of seemingly well-run public firms. John R. Baldwin, for example, reported that the Canadian airline industry, with a nationalized firm playing a key role, operated with higher load factors and lower markups than the privately owned (but at that time heavily regulated) United States industry.[10]

Richard Hellman has argued that some publicly owned electric utilities may also operate at lower average unit costs than regulated private utilities, though comparisons are clouded by water-rights differences and other disparities. All of these isolated examples, however, involve either comparisons with private firms that are heavily regulated as to rate of return — and regulation in itself implies a whole host of inefficiencies — or comparisons with private firms that have been vested with some sort of monopoly "rights."

But this is the crux of the problem regarding waterworks. Since water utilities generally qualify as natural monopolies, it may be that some form of government regulation of even privately owned utilities is inevitable. If so, perhaps some of the advantages of private ownership will be reduced or eliminated. In the presence of a true "natural monopoly problem," which necessitates some sort of government involvement, is privatization feasible?

The "Natural Monopoly Problem" and Franchise Bidding

An industry is usually said to be a natural monopoly if production can be conducted most efficiently by a single entity. This will generally be the case if unit costs are declining over the entire relevant range of market demand for a product — that is, there are massive economies of scale in the production of a good. Under this condition, having two firms in operation side by side would be undesirable and unlikely in the long run, since either of the rivals could expand output, experience lower unit costs, and drive the other from the market; a monopoly situation would "naturally" result. Only if a single firm captured the entire market and exploited all of the potential for lower unit costs through increases in scale would production be organized as cheaply as possible.

The water-supply industry is a straightforward illustration. A water pipe's capacity is roughly proportional to its cross-section area, while cost is roughly proportional to the pipe's circumference. If the cross-section area of a pipe is doubled, the circumference is *less than* doubled; therefore, doubling the volume of water to be transmitted between any two points less than doubles the cost, and the average transmission cost is everywhere declining. Not surprisingly, field data analyzed by Hanke and Roland W. Wentworth strongly support this theory.[12] Within any single area, therefore, more than one water utility will involve wasteful duplication of facilities.

On the other hand, any firm that is the sole producer of a commodity enjoys some measure of market power, and the fear has long been that *unregulated* natural monopolies would reduce output, charge prices substantially above costs, and thereby misallocate resources. To deal with the problem, government has generally recognized and licensed a single producer in markets identified as natural monopolies and then regulated the prices (or rates of return) received by these firms to forestall monopolistic conduct.

But rate regulation itself involves numerous problems. Since most rate regulation involves enforcing some sort of "cost-plus" pricing rule, regulated firms tend to allow their costs to drift upward—since, in most cases, they can be reasonably confident that rates will be set high enough to cover these costs and provide a "normal" return on capital. Harvey A. Averch and Leland L. Johnson have documented this tendency.[13] Obviously, it will be difficult for even a well-intentioned regulatory authority to determine which costs are letigimate; there is also a strong possibility that the authority will be "captured," come to serve the interests of the utility instead of the broader interests of consumers. Thus, one important study suggests, rate regulation can be completely ineffectual; in a comparison of regulated and unregulated electric power companies, George J. Stigler and Claire Friedland found no evidence that regulation resulted in lower prices or increased quantities supplied for the period 1912–37.[14]

Such observations have led economists and policymakers to search for alternatives to direct regulation that might better address the natural monopoly problem. One approach has been a revival of interest—begun by Harold Demsetz[15]—in Chadwick's concept of competition *for* the field. Chadwick recognized that those markets most cheaply served by a monopoly need not be afflicted with monopolistic conduct so long as there is meaningful competition for the rights to the monopoly franchise. In theory, if there is vigorous bidding for the franchise monopoly, the best of both worlds—avoidance of wasteful duplication of facilities and competitive prices—will be possible.

The crucial point is that the bidding for the monopoly franchise should not be in terms of a sum to be paid for the franchise but in terms of *the prices that the franchisee would charge and the services the franchisee would provide the public on award of the right to be the exclusive seller.* If the franchise were merely awarded to the bidder willing to pay the highest price for this exclusive right, competition would drive bids up to an amount equal to the present value of expected future monopoly profits in the market. This would filter these profits through the franchisee to whatever authority granted the franchise in the first place, but the net result would still be underproduction and overpricing of the product. By contrast, Chadwick proposed that an auction be held in which the franchise is awarded to whichever bidder promises the best combination of price and quality to consumers. Competition would then drive bid prices down to competitive levels for each possible level of service quality. So long as this bidding process is open and competitive, and so long as inputs to the production process are available in open and competitive markets as well, there is no need to fear monopolistic results even though a single firm has been granted rights as an exclusive seller.

Chadwickian theory is not necessarily reality, however, and scholars like Richard Schmalensee have expressed strong reservations about such franchise bidding.[16] One set of problems relates to the bidding process itself. Selecting a winner, that is, determining an optimal price structure and a mix of products, may be exceedingly complex, requiring the kind of expertise in the franchise-granting authority that one normally associates with a regulatory commission. In addition, there is no guarantee that bidding will be truly competitive; significant numbers of new firms may be reluctant to bid on a franchise that has expired when the previous franchisee is also in the bidding, since the previous supplier is almost certain to be better informed about actual cost and demand conditions than are the rivals.

Another set of problems relates to the likely behavior of the winning bidder during the term of the franchise contract. First, if the contract is for a reasonably long term, there must be some formula to allow for rate changes as costs, demands, and technologies change over time—or renegotiation must be allowed. If a formula approach is impractical and the latter approach is taken, the need for some sort of agency similar to a regulatory commission again becomes apparent. Such an agency will also be needed to police the franchise contract, since the agreement will not be self-enforcing. Another problem is that as the contract deadline approaches the franchisee may stint on maintenance and underinvest in new assets, leaving any resulting problems for the next franchisee. Indeed, since part of the return on any specialized assets (including knowledge about the firm or industry) might accrue to a subsequent franchisee, a finite contract term could imply a suboptimal incentive to invest in or maintain these assets.

These problems are serious but not intractable. Three aspects (selecting a winning bidder, specifying or renegotiating contracts, and policing the contract) require the existence of some sort of "buyers' agency" to represent consumers. Critics of franchise bidding have asserted that such an agency would, after all, be reduced to performing the same tasks that traditional regulatory commissions now perform—and with the same difficulties and potential for inefficiency or abuse.

But that need not be the case. The degree of technological complexity and swiftness of technological change in the relevant industry are crucial variables. Selecting a winning bidder may be difficult if technology has created a myriad of potential service options. But if it is possible to specify a limited number of service standards—as, for example, with water supply—awarding the franchise may not be troublesome at all. And where the pace of technological change is not too rapid—as, again, with water supply—it may quite easy to agree on a formula for rate increases, and the possibility of midcontract renegotiation may never arise. Enforcing the contract will also be facilitated in industries with a relatively limited number of service standards to be specified. The enforcement role of the buyers' agency is fundamentally different from that of the traditional regulatory commission. The buyers' agency in franchise bidding is merely enforcing a contract; there is no need for this agency to try to authenticate (as public utility commissions must) the franchisee's costs—a much more complex and difficult task.

The critics' doubts about the competitiveness of the bidding process are based largely on a misperception of existing suppliers' presumed advantageous position vis-à-vis new bidders. It is true that a current franchisee will know more about the market than a prospective one, but this in no way implies that bidding for franchise renewal must be less than fully competitive. Knowledge is an asset like any other; it must be created at a cost. That the current franchisee has already acquired the asset and paid the associated cost is irrelevant. Bids of current franchisees will incorporate a return to the knowledge asset that has been created, while bids of prospective franchisees will incorporate the capital cost of acquiring the asset. This will be equal to the interest rate times each bidder's cost of creating the asset; any bidder (including prospective franchisees) with a comparative advantage in creating this asset cheaply will be well situated to submit a winning bid.

The issue of a franchise holder's incentive to engage in suboptimal levels of maintenance and investment expenditure may also relate to the technological complexity of the industry. If the fixed assets of the operation may be feasibly inspected and evaluated by the authority, then the problem may be addressed by having the franchisee post a bond (to be forfeited and used to replenish any assets found deficient) as part of the contract. This would be similar to the process every tenant must follow in renting an apartment: a security deposit is posted as part of the lease agreement and forfeited if the apartment is depreciated more than normal. Obviously, the more complex the production process, the more difficult such an approach would be.

The nature of the water-supply industry, however, appears well suited to the franchise-bidding approach. The technology of water supply is well known and relatively static, and specifications about service standards ought to be readily formulable. Critics' qualms about the practicality of franchise bidding recede in such a context. The best evidence of this is that privately owned water-supply franchises have been commonplace in several areas; the track record of these systems will now be outlined.

Private Water Utilities in Practice

Practice likely preceded theory in this area. In his original article, Chadwick noted that the principle of awarding franchises to the bidder promising to charge the lowest price to consumers had already been undertaken in France in a variety of activities, including water supply.

The first franchise contract for water distribution in France was in 1782, when the Perier brothers were given exclusive distribution rights in Paris for a period of fifteen years. The charge was about one cent per liter. The Perier firm was later nationalized, however, and by 1854 the price of water in Paris had quintupled. While some other population centers (such as Avignon, Calais, Le Havre, and Cannes) were serviced by private water franchises as early as the 1850s, many municipalities opted to build and manage their own systems. Since 1950, however, many of these municipalities, including Paris, have turned to private companies to manage their systems. Today, about 55 percent of the drinking water in France is supplied by private companies.

Privatization of the water supply in France has generally taken one of two franchise forms, though at least two variants of these bear mentioning as well. The first form is the *concession*. In this system, a private company is entrusted with the construction (or, possibly, overhaul or modernization) of the facility as well as its operation. Such a system is especially advantageous when the municipality lacks funds for a major capital expenditure. The concessionaire advances all capital for construction and operation, assumes full responsibility (and risk) for monitoring, management, and maintenance of facilities, and collects payment directly from users. The contract is usually signed for a long-term period — generally thirty years — to enable amortization of the original capital outlay. The contract sets the price of the water with a formula including a fixed and variable component. For example, a user may pay a set monthly fee for access to a supply pipe of a certain diameter along with a variable charge based on the number of cubic meters consumed.

In the second system, *affermage*, the expenses for the installation of major civil works are borne by the local community; the private firm then manages the completed facilities and provides working capital. Such systems are popular when municipal financing can be provided at preferential interest rates. The contract contains detailed specifications for maintaining or upgrading facilities. All electromechanical, hydraulic, and metering equipment is the operator's responsibility, while civil works, water collection, and facility expansion are the responsibility of the municipality; pipe renewal may be the responsibility of either party. As in the *concession* system, a formula fixes the price of water; often, this formula contains a surcharge that the operator remits to the municipality for debt service.

Gerance, a variant of the *affermage*, involves roughly the same relationship between municipality and operator but more limited responsibilities for the private firm. The firm's pay is based on a tariff list agreed upon by the local authority. Yet another variant, *regie interressee*, involves management of a public authority by a private firm that shares in the revenues or profits. In theory, the municipality retains overall management; the firm is an agent of the municipality and is paid a percentage of revenues (to which may be added productivity bonuses or a share of net profits). This system leaves greater authority with the municipality but retains access to the technical services of a company with specialized knowledge and abilities. Franchise contracts usually include clauses specifying the quality of services, the minimum quantity to be supplied to each individual consumer, the mains pressure, and procedures for renewal of the contract, in addition to the clauses relating to maintenance responsibilities and a pricing formula.

The French experience demonstrates clearly that, at least in regard to waterworks, the franchise-bidding approach is a practical system. The technology of water supply and transmission is such that bidders may be selected, contracts drawn up and enforced, and maintenance and expansion conducted efficiently and at acceptable cost. While no comparative studies are available for the costs of private and public water-supply systems in France, the trend toward greater privatization (in a country not generally well disposed to the private sector) suggests that enhanced cost-effectiveness is a signal virtue of the private systems. Additional evidence of the superiority of the private French system of franchising is provided by the observation that "water professionals" are increasingly traveling to Paris to learn the most recent developments in waterworks management and technology.

The French experience, moreover, is not unique. In Spain, private water companies account for nearly as large a share of drinking-water requirements as in

France. Since 1914, French concessions have branched out and have set up systems in Italy, Brazil, Peru, Morocco, Indonesia, Kuwait, and several African nations (although some of these were expropriated during the 1960s). In Santiago, Chile, two private concessions operate in separate areas of the city, and in Guatemala City, Guatemala, a private concession shares the market with a partially public enterprise.

Conclusion

Both theory and evidence strongly support the notion that private supply is more efficient than governmental supply. Waterworks, however, are true natural monopolies; consequently, many argue against privatizating them. As they see it, privatization would simply transform a public monopoly into a private monopoly.

But that need not be the case. The benefits of large-scale, single-firm operations can be secured at competitive prices. This can be accomplished by employing Chadwick's system of franchise bidding in which the rights to a franchise are awarded to the firm that offers the best terms to the public.

Implementing such a system presents difficulties, of course. That such a system of private, competitive franchises is widely employed for waterworks in France, however, demonstrates that these difficulties can be overcome. Therefore, the question of natural monopoly should not enter into the debate over privatizing waterworks. The privatization of waterworks and the proper use of competitive franchising can and should generate substantial benefits for water consumers and reduced resource waste by society as a whole.

NOTES

1. Edwin Chadwick, "Results of Different Principles of Legislation and Administration in Europe; of Competition for the Field as Compared with Competition within the Field, of Service," *Journal of the Statistical Society of London,* 22 (1859): 384–85.

2. David G. Davies, "The Efficiency of Public versus Private Firms: The Case of Australia's Two Airlines," *Journal of Law & Economics* 14 (April 1971): 149–66. See also David G. Davies, "Property Rights and Economic Efficiency: The Australian Airlines Revisited," *Journal of Law & Economics* 20 (April 1977): 223–26.

3. See Robert W. Poole, Jr., *Cutting Back City Hall* (New York: Universe Books, 1980); idem, "Air Traffic Control: The Private Sector Option," Heritage Foundation Backgrounder No. 216, 5 Oct. 1982.

4. See E.S. Savas, *Privatizing the Public Sector: How to Shrink Government* (Chatham, N.J.: Chatham House Publishers, 1982).

5. See James T. Bennett and Manuel H. Johnson, *Better Government at Half the Price: Private Production of Public Services* (Ottawa, Ill.: Caroline House Publishers, 1981); James T. Bennett and Thomas J. DiLorenzo, "Public Employee Unions and the Privatization of 'Public' Services," *Journal of Labor Research* 4 (Winter 1983): 33–45.

6. See Kenneth W. Clarkson, "Some Implications of Property Rights in Hospital Management," *Journal of Law & Economics* 15 (October 1972): 363–84; William Rushing, "Differences in Profit and Nonprofit Organizations: A Study of Effectiveness and Efficiency in General Short-Stay Hospitals," *Administrative Sciences Quarterly* 19 (December 1974): 474–84.

7. See Steve H. Hanke, "The Privatization Debate: An Insider's View," *Cato Journal* 2 (Winter 1982): 653–62.

8. W. Mark Crain and Asghar Zardkoohi, "A Test of the Property-Rights Theory of the Firm: Water Utilities in the United States," *Journal of Law & Economics* 21 (October 1978): 395–408.

9. See W. Douglas Morgan, "Investor Owned vs. Publicly Owned Water Agencies: An Evaluation of the Property Rights Theory of the Firm," *Water Resources Bulletin* 13 (August 1977): 775–81; Steve H. Hanke, "On Water Tariff Equalization Policies," *Water Engineering and Management* 128 (August 1981): 33–34.

10. John R. Baldwin, *The Regulatory Agency and the Public Corporation: The Canadian Air Transport Industry* (Cambridge, Mass.: Ballinger, 1975), 200–205.

11. Richard Hellman, *Government Competition in the Electric Utility Industry* (New York: Praeger, 1972), argued that the TVA had favorable competitive effects on adjoining utilities. By contrast, Sam Peltzman, "Pricing in Public and Private Enterprises: Electric Utilities in the United States," *Journal of Law & Economics* 14 (April 1971): 109–47, argued that an average government utility-rate advantage merely reflects lower tax burdens.

12. Steve H. Hanke and Roland W. Wentworth, "Etudes statistiques de prix de revient pour les canalisations d'eau usee," *Techniques et Sciences Municipales – L'Eau* 75 (Octobre 1980): 517–18.

13. Harvey A. Averch and Leland L. Johnson, "Behavior of the Firm Under Regulatory Constraint," *American Economic Review* 52 (December 1962): 1052–69. For a survey of other studies of this tendency, see Elizabeth Bailey, *Economic Theory of Regulatory Constraint* (Lexington, Mass.: Lexington Books, 1973).

14. George J. Stigler and Claire Friedland, "What Can Regulators Regulate? The Case of Electricity," *Journal of Law & Economics* 5 (October 1962): 1–16.

15. Harold Demsetz, "Why Regulate Utilities?" *Journal of Law & Economics* 11 (April 1968): 55–65.

16. Richard Schmalensee, *The Control of Natural Monopolies* (Lexington, Mass.: Lexington Books, 1979), 68–73.

Privatizing the Public Domain

STEVE H. HANKE
BARNEY DOWDLE

The land area of the United States is about 2.3 billion acres. Ownership by governmental entities is significant. For example, the Federal government's holdings amount to about 33 percent of the total; state governments, 6 percent; and county and municipal governments, about 1 percent. Indian lands are 52 million acres, or 2.3 percent of the total. These Indian lands amount to a land area equal to the six New England states, New Jersey, and Maryland.

Recent Public Land Policy Pronouncements

Privatization, the transfer of land ownership from governmental to private entities, has become a major policy issue in the 1980s. The debate over public versus private land ownership began in earnest when President Ronald Reagan delivered his budget message for fiscal year 1983. In that message, the president endorsed the goal of privatizing Federal public lands: "We will move systematically to reduce the vast holdings of surplus land and real property, [since] some of this property is not in use and would be of greater value to society if transferred to the private sector. In the next 3 years we would save $9 billion by shedding these unnecessary properties while fully protecting and preserving our national parks, forests, wilderness and scenic areas."[1]

The Reagan administration made its views about public versus private land ownership felt again in 1984, when it endorsed the recommendations of the Presidential Commission on Indian Reservation Economies. Although the recommendations are directed specifically to Indian land, they apply to varying degrees to other parts of the public domain. The commission found that "extensive tribal government management and involvement in business development activity contributed to the failure of tribal enterprises. Merely separating the corporate functions of tribal enterprises from interference by tribal government and employing competent management will not achieve a privatization of tribal enterprises capable of offering profit motivation, private property ownership, nor individual freedom.

"Private ownership of tribal enterprises contemplates ownership of the means of production, private management, for-profit motivation and freedom for individual Indians or groups of Indians who have or share an interest in participating in business activity on an Indian reservation. Tribes could just as easily lease tribally held assets to their members as they presently do to nonmember businesses which use their resources. Existing businesses could be sold to tribal members, or ownership transferred by way of stock transfers, rather than per capita distributions of corporate retained earnings. Employee stock participation plans could also be offered. There is no one correct approach to privatizing tribal enterprises. There are, however, many possibilities for offering individual Indians incentives. There is no difference between a per capita payment from a tribal enterprise, a judgment fund, a mineral royalty or bonus, and a welfare distribution, where no opportunity exists for individual Indians to self-actualize or to succeed through individual effort."[2] The presidential commission, therefore, advocated privatizing communally owned reservation resources.

The Rationale for Federal Land Privatization

Privatization objectives vary. The most frequently cited objectives for Federal land privatization include the following:

1. The productivity of Federal lands would increase. With private ownership, it would be possible to obtain more commercial, recreational, and environmental outputs than with Federal ownership.
2. With increased productivity, not only would the value of lands be increased, but employment and economic activity would also be enhanced with private, rather than Federal, ownership.
3. Consumers would be served more effectively, and lands would be allocated to their most highly valued uses. After all, the only way that private-land owners can profit from their property is to employ it for the satisfaction of other people's wants. Serving consumers, of course, is the social function of private property.
4. Land sales would generate current Federal revenues.
5. The annual Federal costs (which incorrectly omit capital carrying charges) exceed the annual revenues generated from Federal lands. Privatization would therefore eliminate negative cash flows for the Federal government. This would benefit all United States taxpayers, who must now pay taxes to support the Federal government's retention of Federal lands.
6. A state and local tax base would be created. Western dependence on in-lieu payments from Washington would be reduced and federalism would be enhanced.
7. Land-use decisions would become less politicized. Both commercial and noncommercial land users would have to spend less of their time and money attempting to obtain land-use rights through political and bureaucratic processes.

The Rationale for Indian Land Privatization

The objectives most frequently mentioned for Indian land privatization are increased land productivity, increased employment opportunities, depoliticization of land-use decisions, and the establishment of a tax base. Present arrangements lead to two quite different defects. The first involves grazing lands, the second timber property.

Public grazing lands are typically subject to what is called the "tragedy of the commons," a condition that has occurred many times in human history. This tragedy, which is characterized by overuse and a loss in land productivity, would be eliminated through privatization. This beneficial aspect of privatization has captured the attention of some Indian leaders and merits attention.

To understand the tragedy, suppose a group of youngsters is given a free soda and straws. Next the straws enter the soda, which is common property; each youngster attempts to capture the maximum amount of soda as fast as possible before others can lay claim to it; and the soda is depleted at a rapid rate. Since, under these rules, each youngster knows that his friends will drink part of the new soda without contributing to its purchase, i.e., none has an incentive to invest in another soda. The only way the soda supply can be maintained is for the youngsters to convince an outsider to replenish it.

The soda analogy reflects the fate of lands held in common ownership. For example, Gary D. Libecap and Ronald D. Johnson found the tragedy of the commons being played out on the Navajo reservation, which is the largest reservation in the United States.[3] They found that common property (vague tenure) arrangements on the reservation have resulted in rapid increases in the number of sheep and goat herders. Consequently, overgrazing has occurred and the land quality has declined through a loss of palatable plant species and severe wind and water erosion. The result has been high livestock mortality, low lambing rates, poor wool production, and a fall in livestock-based income. To maintain their livestock, the Navajo have had to rely on feed-grain subsidies from the Federal government.

The second preventable defect applies to public timberlands. Indian lands as well as others are subject to a timber-harvesting principle (or in some cases, a modification thereof) called "nondeclining even flow." This harvesting principle is imposed on Indian tribes by the Bureau of Indian Affairs (BIA), a bureau of the U.S. Department of Interior. "Even flow" harvesting—which, in contrast to the tragedy of the commons on grazing lands, is characterized by an underuse of resources—would be eliminated through privatization. This beneficial aspect of privatization has captured the attention of some Indian leaders. Even flow, which is practiced on public lands, merits special attention because the privatization proposal that will be analyzed involves the privatization of public timberlands.

Nondeclining even flow requires annual timber harvests not to fall below an initially established level. With even flow, the timber-harvest rate is determined by inventory volumes and timber-growth rates. Hence, it is a physical, rather than an economic, concept. Economic costs and demands are not part of the determination of harvest rates. Consequently, even flow results in the noneconomic, underuse of timberlands. The principle is as follows. Timber is a capital asset. Hence, its proper management should be viewed as an investment or capital management problem. Capital costs (interest costs) are a part of the true cost of growing timber. These costs, of course, are not counted when the nondeclining even-flow concept is employed. Timber-harvest rates are determined by even-flow measures, not by costs; the guides to harvesting, therefore, result in rotation ages for timber that are much too long. Timber is allowed, in an economic sense, to become "overripe" before it is harvested, and too much timber is held in inventory. A corollary problem results: current output is too low relative to a correct measure of cost and market value.

The problems caused by even flow and its lack of consideration for capital carrying charges on timber inventories are most pronounced when this harvesting principle is applied to "overmature" forests. In these cases, the forests are not growing. What is more, they are subject to "blow-down" and disease, which are problems associated with old age. It would be economic to liquidate old growth, overmature timber rapidly, and then to replant forests. Even flow, however, does not allow for this type of inventory adjustment. In economic terms, even flow imposes excessive capital carrying costs on timberlands. By idling capital resources, the even-flow principle turns forestlands into resources that are roughly analogous to the Hindus' sacred cows. Moreover, even flow, which is required on most public lands, creates economic instability in the regions where public ownership of timberlands is dominant. With even flow, the amount of timber marketed annually is about constant. Consequently, during periods of weak demand, stumpage prices plummet; and during periods of strong demand, prices soar.

Barney Dowdle and Steve H. Hanke have shown that the Pacific Northwest, a region in which public entities own about 75 percent of the timber inventories, is paying dearly for even flow.[4] That harvest policy has not allowed for an economic liquidation of overmature timber. This, in turn, has resulted in an artificial "shortage" of timber going to market during periods of strong demand. Moreover, even flow has caused excessive price volatility in the region. To avoid artificial "shortages" and price volatility, the wood-processing industry of the Pacific Northwest has been migrating to the South, where most timberlands are privately owned.

Given this dismal record — overgrazing in some cases and inefficient timber cutting in others — why have Indians refused to advocate privatizing communally owned Indian lands? The major obstacle has been many Indians' perception that past efforts to privatize Indian lands — most notably the Dawes Severalty Act of 1887 — were failures. Consequently, most Indians view private property as an institution that favors the white man and as not well suited to Indian culture. But the real and imagined failure of privatizations under the Dawes Act had little, if anything, to do with the institution of private property per se.

The Dawes Severalty Act of 1887

Throughout the nineteenth century, Indian policy making was characterized by simplistic diagnoses of Indian problems, simplistic solutions, and stereotypes of Indians as uncivilized savages. During the early decades of the century, Indian policy was influenced primarily by missionaries who believed that the teachings of the Bible and acceptance of the Sabbath were the best means for civilizing Indians and integrating them into society.

The lack of success of this missionary approach led to the domination of policy making by nineteenth-century liberals. They believed that exposing Indians to private property rights and a laissez-faire economic system would enable them better to adjust to a civil society. The latter approach, as well as Indian stereotypes characteristic of the era, are well captured in the views of Merrill E. Gates, president of Amherst College and of the Lake Mohonk Conference of the Friends of the Indians. In his presidential address at the 1896 annual meeting of the conference, he observed that there was a "need of awakening in the savage Indian broader desires and ampler wants. . . . Discontent with the tepee and the starving rations of the Indian camp in winter is needed to get the Indian out of the blanket and into trousers." Moreover, he argued, these trousers needed to have "a pocket in them . . . a pocket that aches to be filled with dollars."[5]

The Dawes Severalty Act of 1887 was a product of such thinking. Most influential people thought that hard work, thrift, and a system of private property rights would encourage and enable Indians to acquire wealth and become integrated into society. The Dawes Act authorized the president to allot Indian reservation land to individual Indians. Heads of families were to receive 160 acres, while others were to receive smaller allotments. Indians were to receive full citizenship with the land transfers. Titles were to be held in trust by the United States government for twenty-five years, and then the land could be freely transferred. "Surplus" land — land left over after the allotments had been made — was to be sold on the market.

Since there were considerably more "Indian lands" than acreages that qualified for Indian allotments, almost half of the land controlled by Indians was declared "surplus" and removed from their control. Also, many of the Indians who qualified and received allotments sold their newly acquired lands. This further reduced lands under Indian ownership and control. In addition, and perhaps most important, Indians (as well as many white homesteaders) were not afforded common law protections that accompany property and contracts. Property rights and contracts were often neither enforced nor protected. William T. Hagan has reported that many Indians lost their lands "through tactics that ranged from deceit and duplicity to murder."[6]

With the passage of the Dawes Act in 1887, the land area controlled by Indians was reduced by 50 percent. Then, between 1887 and the so-called Indian New Deal of 1934, which reversed the policies set in motion by the Dawes Act, about 38 percent of the acreage that had been allocated to Indians under provisions of the act was transferred through sales and other means to non-Indians. Moreover, much of the land that the Indians retained was semiarid or desert land in the Southwest. This, along with the fact that the average parcel awarded to an Indian was 160 acres and farm prices were declining, resulted in a great deal of Indian ownership that was not economically viable.

Not surprisingly, the Dawes Act experience has led Indians to distrust private ownership. However, the institution of private property had little to do with the failure of the Dawes Act. Rather, its failure was the result of a poorly conceived Federal privatization policy and a frontier justice system that did not properly recognize and use the common law of property and contracts. In a misguided effort to ensure that they would not be exploited by private property institutions, Indians have favored communal ownership. In turn, this communal arrangement has ensured that the Indians would misuse their lands and exploit one another.

Privatization and the Siletz Indians

Indian views are neither monolithic nor static. The Siletz Indians, for example, have endorsed privatization. In the mid-1800s, the Siletz were moved from their native lands and relocated on a 1.2-million-acre reservation located on the central Oregon coast. Subsequently, most of this land was transferred from reservation status to other types of non-Indian ownership and use. By 1900, little of the original reservation was left.

In 1954, Congress formally terminated all relationships between the Federal government and the Siletz. Remaining reservation lands were transferred to the Federal government, and the Siletz no longer qualified for programs administered by the Bureau of Indian Affairs. With the adoption of the Siletz Restoration Act of 1977, however, the relationship between the Federal government and the Siletz was restored. Moreover, this act instructed the secretary of the interior to develop a plan for reestablishing a new reservation.

After the secretary's plan was presented, Congress reestablished the Siletz Tribal Reservation in 1980. The new reservation consists of 3,628 acres of land in Lincoln County, Oregon. These lands were previously part of the public domain. Most of the area consists of scattered parcels of timberlands located two to twenty-five miles from Siletz, Oregon. Government Hill, which is part of the reservation and the location of Siletz Tribal Headquarters, is a thirty-six-acre parcel located within the city limits of Siletz.

Since the restoration of the Siletz, which now have an estimated population of 1,806, and the reestablishment of the reservation, they have adopted economic self-sufficiency as their primary goal. This goal underlies the tribe's efforts to expand either its reservation or its members' land ownership, since the acreage, type, and distribution of land in the existing reservation are considered inadequate for achieving self-sufficiency. For example, tree farming on a land area as small as the existing reservation precludes the tribe from reaching its goal of self-sufficiency.

There are 12,000 acres of public-domain lands in Lincoln County, Oregon. They are similar to those lands in the existing Siletz Tribal Reservation and are scattered throughout Lincoln County in ninety separate parcels that range from 20 to 520 acres. These lands are owned by the Federal government and managed by the U.S. Bureau of Land Management (BLM). The Siletz think that the transfer of the 12,000 acres of public-domain lands would provide a means for them to achieve their goal of self-sufficiency.

A Cost-Benefit Analysis of Land Transfer

One must ask what are the benefits, if any, from transferring public-domain lands and what type of land ownership would provide the Siletz Indians with the most economic benefits. A cost-benefit analysis on two types of land transfers will answer these questions. The first is a transfer that would require the Siletz to add the lands to their existing reservation and manage them on a typical Indian communal basis. The second would require the Siletz to place the lands in private ownership and manage them on a for-profit basis. Three ownership arrangements will be analyzed—the "BLM Status Quo," the "Siletz Tribal," and the "Siletz Private."

BLM Status Quo. The 12,000 acres of public-domain land would be retained in Federal ownership. The BLM would continue to manage these lands. This plan provides a baseline against which the other two can be compared. Timber harvest schedules would be based on the "nondeclining even-flow" principle; that is, timber harvests would not be permitted to fall below an initially established level. Since Federal law prohibits the export of logs cut on Federal lands, the logs produced from timber-harvesting operations could not be sold in the foreign market.

Siletz Tribal. The 12,000 acres of public-domain land would be transferred to the Siletz. The lands would be collectively owned and managed by the Siletz under existing Indian trust law. Policies and management procedures would be subject to regulations of the BIA, and, in keeping with the agency's historical role in managing Indian timberlands, the BIA would remain involved in the planning and management. Timber-harvest schedules would be based on a modified version of the traditional "even-flow" principle. The modified version, which is commonly employed on Indian lands, allows for somewhat higher harvesting rates than the strict nondeclining even-flow principle. Logs could be sold in the foreign market because Indian lands are exempt from the log-export ban.

Siletz Private. The 12,000 acres of public-domain lands would be transferred to the Siletz and then to a private corporation. The initial distribution of stock in this corporation would be made to members of the Siletz and could subsequently be freely exchanged. Timber-harvest schedules would be based on cutting rates that would maximize the present value of the timberlands. Logs could be sold in the foreign market because private lands are exempt from the log-export ban.

The analysis of the three alternatives will be presented in a sequence of steps. The first step requires an estimate of the average annual land-management costs for the 12,000 acres. Based on an evaluation of management-cost data from Federal lands in the region (which include the 12,000 acres of public-domain land), the average annual land-management costs are about $25 an acre. This figure is used for the BLM Status Quo alternative.

The $25 an acre estimate is also used to evaluate the Siletz Tribal plan. The assumption that the costs are the same is justified because forest-management practices now used by the Siletz Tribe are not significantly different from those used on federally owned lands in western Oregon. Finally, for the Siletz Private arrangement, an average annual management cost of $10 an acre is assumed. This assumption is based on regional (western Oregon and western Washington) average management costs for privately owned timberlands.

Average management costs for privately owned timberlands are significantly less than for publicly owned lands because managers of private land face stronger incentives to manage timberlands in a cost-effective manner than do managers of public lands.

The second step requires estimates of the existing timber volumes by age classes and species on the lands proposed for transfer. These estimates provide a basis for determining timber harvest rates for each of the possibilities. By virtue of its age and size, most of the timber on the 12,000 acres is ready for harvest. The estimate of merchantable timber is 380-million-board feet (MMBF).

The third step determines how fast the mature timber inventory would be harvested under each arrangement. Scheduling timber harvests under the BLM Status Quo plan requires the use of the "nondeclining even-flow" principle. This approach precludes any reduction in an initially determined annual level of timber harvest. As a result of this constraint, scheduled rates of timber harvest tend to be uneconomically low. In other words, economically justifiable corrections of excess timber inventories cannot be made. Consequently, public timber-management agencies commonly carry a surplus of mature timber.

Based on BLM rates of timber harvest compared with timber inventory volumes elsewhere in western Oregon, the BLM Status Quo plan will result in an estimated harvest of five MMBF a year. Twenty-five years after the plan has been initiated, only 125 MMBF of the original 380 MMBF will have been harvested. Much of the original timber inventory will still exceed economically optimal harvest age.

The Siletz Tribal plan would not be constrained by the nondeclining even-flow rule. Rather, a modified even-flow approach would be used. Under the modification, a reasonable estimate of the annual timber harvest would be fifteen MMBF. This rate is consistent with the current planned harvest rate on existing reservation timberlands. Assuming that annual timber harvest was fifteen MMBF, the existing inventory of mature timber on the 12,000 acres could sustain such a harvest rate for at least twenty-five years. Timber growth rates, which are relatively high in Lincoln County, could enable this same rate to be continued for a longer period.

The Siletz Private plan would not be constrained by Federal or Indian reservation timber-harvesting policies or traditions. Since the objective for an owner of private timber lands is to maximize the value, this objective would be pursued under the Siletz Private arrangement. Thus the rate of timber harvest under the Siletz Private plan would be twenty-five MMBF a year, and existing mature timber inventories would be harvested within approximately fifteen years.

It should be emphasized that under the Siletz Private plan the new timber corporation would be subject to the same laws and regulations that govern other private owners of timberlands in Oregon. Consequently, regeneration of cutover lands would be required, streams would be protected from excessive logging damage, and logging slash (debris) would be managed to reduce fire hazards.

The fourth step is an estimation of timber prices to project timber sales receipts. Prices are assumed to be $100 an MBF for the BLM Status Quo plan and $125 an MBF for the Siletz Tribal and Siletz Private arrangements. Timber prices under both Siletz plans are assumed to be $25 an MBF higher than the BLM Status Quo arrangement, because the logs produced under these plans could be exported from the United States. Exported logs have commanded premium prices during the past few years. If the growth in trade with Pacific Basin countries continues, these premiums should average at least $25 an MBF.

With the estimates developed in steps one through four, the present value of the 12,000 acres can be estimated under the three ownership plans. Table 1 contains a summary of the assumptions and present-value estimates, which are about $2.0 million, $16.0 million, and $25.7 million for the BLM Status Quo, Siletz Tribal, and Siletz Private arrangements, respectively.

TABLE 1

Economic Value of Ownership Alternatives
(in 1985 real dollars)

Ownership Option	Timber Harvest Objectives and Marketing Constraints	Annual Timber Harvest[1]	Timber Price[2] (per MBF)	Average Annual Cost (per acre)	Annual Net Income and Residual Value[3]	Present Value at 10%
BLM Status Quo	Nondeclining even-flow	5MM for 25 years	$100	$25	$200,000 for 25 yrs.	$ 1,815,408
	Log exports banned				$167/ac. avg. value after 25 years	184,592
						$ 2,000,000
Siletz Tribal	Modified even flow	15 MM for 25 years	$125	$25	$1,575,000 for 25 yrs.	$14,296,338
	Log exports allowed				$1,500/ac. avg. value after 25 yrs.	1,661,328
						$15,957,666
Siletz Private	Maximize present value	25 MM for 15 years	$125	$10	$3,005,000 for 15 years	$22,856,269
	Log exports allowed				$1,000/ac. avg. value after 15 yrs.	2,872,705
						$25,728,974

Source: Steve H. Hanke and Barney Dowdle, "A Preliminary Economic Evaluation of the Transfer of Ownership of the Public Domain Lands in Lincoln County, Oregon, from the Federal Government to the Confederated Tribes of Siletz Indians of Oregon," April 1986, 1–31 (typescript).

[1] Based on 380 MMBF timber inventory and relevant timber-harvest objectives.

[2] Higher price for Siletz Tribal and Siletz Private options reflects removal of constraint on log exports.

[3] Residual values are based on value of the land and timber inventory being carried at the end of the respective planning periods.

If transferred from the Federal government to the Siletz under either the Siletz Tribal or the Siletz Private forms of ownership, the 12,000 acres of public-domain land would be significantly enhanced in value. The ratio of benefits to costs for transferring the public-domain lands to Siletz Tribal ownership is 8 to 1 and for transferring the lands to Siletz Private ownership, 12.9 to 1.

The Siletz have thus chosen to pursue privatization. They are now deliberating with Congress and the Reagan administration to transfer the 12,000 acres of public-domain land from the Federal government to the Siletz on terms that are similar to the Siletz Private ownership plan.

Conclusion

Indian policies in the United States have been subject to sweeping changes. These policies are now in a state of ferment. It appears that, with the privatization proposal of the Siletz, we are witnessing the beginnings of a new policy and the acceptance of an observation made by no less than Lord Keynes in 1936: "There are valuable human activities which require the motive of money-making and the environment of private wealth-ownership for their full fruition. Moreover, dangerous human proclivities can be canalized into comparatively harmless channels by the existence of opportunities for money-making and private wealth, which, if they cannot be satisfied in this way, may find their outlet in cruelty, the reckless pursuit of power and authority, and other forms of self-aggrandizement. It is better that a man should tyrannize over his bank balance than over his fellow-citizens; and whilst the former is sometimes denounced as being but a means to the latter, sometimes at least it is an alternative."[7]

Notes

1. Budget of the United States Government, Fiscal Year 1983 (Washington, D.C.: U.S. Government Printing Office, 1982), M18–M19.

2. Presidential Commission on Indian Reservation Economies, *Report and Recommendations to the President of the United States* (Washington, D.C., Nov. 1984), 41.

3. Gary D. Libecap and Ronald N. Johnson, "Legislating Commons: The Navajo Tribal Council and the Navajo Range," *Economic Inquiry*, 18 (Jan. 1980), 9–86.

4. Barney Dowdle and Steve H. Hanke, "Public Timber Policy and the Wood-Products Industry," in *Forestlands: Public and Private*, ed. Robert T. Deacon and M. Bruce Johnson (Cambridge, Mass.: Ballinger Publishing Company, 1985), 77–102.

5. See Robert F. Berkhofer, Jr., *The White Man's Indian*, Vintage Books (New York: Random House, 1978), 173.

6. William T. Hagan, "Private Property: The Indian's Door to Civilization," *Ethnohistory* 3, no. 2 (1956): 126–37.

7. John Maynard Keynes, *The General Theory of Employment Interest and Money* (New York: Harcourt, Brace, and Co., 1936), 374.

The Limits of Privatization

PAUL STARR

The traditional socialist program of nationalizing industry aimed to subject the economy to public control. But nationalization sorely disappointed expectations; public ownership did not make nearly as much difference as socialists had anticipated. In an ironic twist, conservative advocates of privatization are among the few in the West who are still convinced of the decisive importance of changing the locus of ownership. But it is not only nationalized industry that they want transferred to the private sector. In the United States, that would scarcely amount to a significant program. The original contribution of American proponents of privatization is that they would like to privatize the full gamut of public assets and services, including many forms of public provision, such as public schools, national parks, public-transport infrastructure, and prisons, whose origins and rationale fall comfortably within the ambit of the classical liberal state. In privatization they believe they have found a sovereign remedy against all ailments to the body politic, good for stimulating economic growth, improving the efficiency of services, slimming down the state, and expanding individual freedom, including the opportunities of disadvantaged minorities, too.

In a dismal world where trade-offs and compromises prevail, we rarely meet up with so happy a possibility of simultaneously making the economy larger, the government smaller, and virtually all of us better off. Then why has privatization made so little headway in the United States? Opposition, the conservatives say, comes from the same groups whom they identify as responsible for public programs: self-interested politicians, public employees, and beneficiaries with large stakes in public expenditure. The picture of our political life that the conservatives propose is a bloated, parasitic public sector blocking the bustle and growth of a more freely flowing private economy.

The task of this brief essay is to challenge both the specific claims made for privatization and the general picture of our political and economic world offered by its advocates. However, my aim here is not to present a mirror image of right-wing simplifications by suggesting that public provision is always better than private or that every activity in the public sector ought to remain there forever. A pragmatic public policy must recognize where private alternatives might work better and, by the same token, where new forms of public provision may ameliorate endemic shortcomings of the market. Most of all, it must recognize that markets are not natural creations; they are always legally and politically structured. Hence the choice is not public *or* private but which of many possible mixed public-private structures works best. And "best" cannot mean only most efficient, for a reasonable appraisal of alternatives needs to weigh concerns of justice, security, and citizenship.

For the sake of clarity, it may be helpful to define some terms. In this essay, *privatization* refers to a shift from publicly to privately produced goods and services.[1] Policies that encourage such a shift include (1) the cessation of public programs and disengagement of government from specific kinds of responsibilities; (2) sales of public assets, including public lands, public infrastructure, and public enterprises; (3) financing private provision of services — for example, through contracting out or vouchers — instead of directly producing them; and (4) deregulating entry into activities, such as first-class mail, that were previously treated as a public monopoly.

These forms of privatization vary greatly in their consequences. They differ, first of all, in the extent to which they reduce public spending and accountability. Contracting out, vouchers, and other systems for paying private providers generally do not obviate the need to collect taxes. And they do not eliminate, though they may reduce, the accountability of public officials for the results of the expenditures. By shifting only the locus of service production, they privatize the means of policy implementation but not the functional sphere of government action. These partial forms of privatization need to be sharply distinguished from the sale of assets and cessation of programs (sometimes called "load-shedding," a term which itself is politically loaded, since it defines public programs as a burden). Yet even the more thorough forms of privatization may involve indirect forms of public subsidy and control. For example, many proposals for asset sales and program termination contemplate the use of tax incentives to stimulate private substitutes for public services. Such incentives influence market outcomes and represent a source of lost revenue (that is, a tax expenditure). Hence there is no certainty that these policies lead toward budgetary balance.

The various forms of privatization also differ in their effects on competition. Two related processes, privatization and liberalization, need to be more carefully distinguished than they are in much discussion. In this context, liberalization refers to the opening up of any industry to competitive pressures. The opening up of public monopolies to private firms is a form of privatization that is also liberalizing. However, it is entirely possible to privatize without liberalizing, as Margaret Thatcher's government has demonstrated by selling shares of two monopolies (British Telecom and British Gas) without significantly subjecting either industry to competitive forces. Britain has substituted private monopolies for public ones and introduced new regulatory agencies to perform some of the functions previously undertaken through public ownership.[2] Conversely, it is also possible to liberalize without privatizing—that is, to introduce competition into the public sector without transferring ownership. For example, governments may require public enterprises or operating agencies to compete for capital or contracts from higher-level authorities. Indeed, it is even possible to nationalize and liberalize at the same time. In the early 1980s the French socialists both nationalized banks and liberalized financial markets. In other words, things are not as simple as they may first seem.

These distinctions suggest that privatization is not a single set of measures that logically or practically entail one another. Only ideologically and symbolically are they linked. There is an obvious, radical difference between partial and total privatization and a subtle but equally important difference between privatization and liberalization. By treating these heterogeneous measures as members of the same family, the advocates of privatization use the more moderate ideas, such as vouchers and contracting out, to gain plausibility for the more radical goal of government disengagement. Milton and Rose Friedman have said explicitly that they would prefer ending all public financing of primary and secondary education, except in hardship cases, but propose vouchers as a more acceptable first step.[3] In the most ingenious and refreshingly frank case for privatization, Stuart Butler has argued that the real objective should be to break up "public spending coalitions" to bring about a permanent reduction in the base of political support for government growth.[4] So, while privatization can be presented as a measure to improve the performance of particular services, the larger intention of some exponents is to reduce support for public provision altogether. Whether partial privatization would actually lead to disengagement (or even to lower budgetary costs) will be scrutinized below, but it is worth noting here that the more moderate forms of privatization are for its advocates stepping stones toward more radical objectives shared by only a small minority of Americans.

Privatization, Public Spending, and Economic Growth

The conservative proponents of privatization see a zero-sum relationship between government and the economy. The bigger the public sector, the smaller the private economy. The more public spending, the less private savings and investment. Hence, in this simple view, privatization is certain to increase savings, investment, productivity, and growth.

If government spending truly retarded economic development, the Western economies with the highest ratios of public expenditures to gross national product would grow the slowest. However, comparative studies show that not to be the case.[5] The conservative view of government as an economic black hole misses what government adds to the productive resources of society and overstates what government takes away. First, much public spending represents investment in human and intangible capital as well as physical infrastructure. In the United States, the structure of the Federal budget (which fails to distinguish capital expenditures) and the national income accounts (which treat all government expenditures as consumption) obscure these contributions of public spending to the country's capital stock and long-run economic development.[6] And, second, much of the contemporary increase in public spending has come in the form of transfer payments, which redistribute income but do not exhaust resources that would otherwise be available for investment. To be sure, some governments have heavily subsidized inefficient industries, but others have used public programs to reduce opposition to industrial change by cushioning workers against unemployment and retraining them for jobs in expanding sectors. The effect of government on economic growth depends principally on the character of its intervention.

The case for privatization as a means of bringing about deep reductions in government activity also neglects the contribution of increased public expenditure to economic stabilization. We have far from abolished the business cycle, but the cycle has been much less severe in the last half century now that the scale of taxation and spending provides governments with the tools of fiscal management that they formerly lacked.

Nor is there the slightest chance that governments will unload responsibility for the stability of the economy and the financial system. The voters will not allow it. Nor will the banks. When Continental Illinois was on the verge of collapse in 1984, the Reagan administration did not hesitate to rescue it. Governmental assumption of risk, whether for the potential insolvency of pension funds, savings and loans associations, or the international financial system, shows every sign of continuing. In these persistent patterns, there is a lesson about the limits of privatization. Though there is disagreement about the instruments of policy, there is no doubt that governments will continue to be held accountable for economic growth and security. Disengagement from macroeconomic management is impossible.

In the current conservative view, the public arena is nothing but a political marketplace where politicians, public employees, and competing groups of beneficiaries seek their narrow interests at the expense of the general welfare. Government expands because bureaucrats maximize their budgets and because beneficiaries with "concentrated" interests in program expansion exercise more political muscle than do taxpayers with "diffuse" interests in restraint. As an explanation for the development of the modern state, the theory is unpersuasive; it cannot explain the variations over time or across societies. If the influences on the budget were always asymmetrical, spending would have grown as much in periods when its growth was slow.[7] The narrowly individualistic view of political choice also provides a misleading account of contemporary politics. Contrary to expectations, the general performance of the economy in the United States seems to weigh more heavily in voting decisions than does the voter's individual economic experience.[8] Nor is the support for public spending as narrow as the conservatives suggest. By overwhelming margins the American public has consistently supported increased spending for most of the programs and services that governments provide.[9] While conservatives puzzle over the political failure of privatization proposals, they miss the most obvious explanation because it undermines their own theory of government growth. Their proposals for privatizing the welfare state make little headway because if introduced they would be vastly unpopular.

In this respect, partial privatization differs from the more radical forms. Where only the means of implementation are privatized, the opposition of public employees may be critical. But if programs now operated directly by government were shifted to private contractors and the providers of service under voucher systems, these private providers could scarcely be expected to exert less pressure for higher spending than do public employees. In regard to contracting out, Butler has acknowledged that privatization may not break up the "public spending coalitions."[10] The effect would actually be to enlarge them. Contracting out expands the set of claimants on the public treasury. By having defense equipment privately produced, we do not reduce the pressure on the defense budget. The defense companies and their employees are capable of determining their stake in higher military expenditures. By having highways constructed by private contractors, we do not reduce the pressure for bigger construction appropriations. By having health services under Medicare provided by private doctors and hospitals, we do not obscure from them their interest in higher Medicare appropriations. Indeed, Medicare has done for medical and hospital associations what no liberal persuasion could do—turned them into advocates of higher public spending. The same would be true of educational vouchers, which would add private schools, the families sending children to them, and their teachers to the set of claimants on education budgets. Today public- and private-school constituencies have distinct interests, but under a voucher system they would share an interest in setting vouchers at the highest possible money value.

Conservatives who favor privatization read the record as proving the superiority of private providers, but this is an act of heroically selective attention. Given the American experience with defense production, construction projects, and health care—all mostly produced privately with public dollars—it is remarkable that anyone could see a path toward budgetary salvation simply by shifting the locus of service production from the public sector to the private sector. Advocates of privatization show an undue tenderness toward private contractors and an undue hostility toward public employees. They indulge private contractors their history of cost overruns; they rebuke public employees for their history of wage increases. But their preference for private provision actually reflects a deep underestimate of the skills that private firms can deploy. They underestimate the capacity of contractors to manipulate to their own advantage the incentives that are held out to them for better performance. And they underestimate the contractors' capacity to influence political decisions, either illegitimately through bribery or legally through campaign contributions and lobbying. Missing from the case for privatization is any clear sense of feedback effects—the reaction back upon the government of the enlarged class of private contractors and other providers dependent on public money.

So, if partial privatization is to reduce public spending, it cannot be expected to achieve its effect by reducing spending pressure. Private firms have to be far more efficient. Some evidence does suggest that private producers have lower costs, but the picture is complicated by the following: First, contrary evidence from other studies shows no difference in costs or even higher costs among commercial providers.[11] Second, there are pervasive differences in the services performed by public and private organizations, particularly because of differences in their clientele, such as exist between public and private schools, hospitals, and social services as a result of the "creaming" of client populations by private institutions. Third, studies usually lack any evidence about the quality of services, thereby making it difficult to judge whether lower costs result from greater efficiency or deteriorating quality. And, fourth, some private firms' lower costs stem from lower wage levels and greater use of part-time workers with fewer fringe benefits. If privatization enables governments to cut wages and break unions, it is a means of imposing losses on public employees. If it enables governments to reduce services and allows providers to skim off the best clients, it is a means of imposing losses on beneficiaries. Neither of these ways of reducing cost has anything to do with improvements in efficiency. Perhaps the public wants wages and benefits cut. If so, voters and legislators should do so with their eyes open.

By emphasizing these considerations, I do not mean to suggest that contracting out is never a good idea. It is an important and valuable instrument of public management, but it is treacherous to generalize about its virtues. After all, if contracting were always superior to direct employment, no large corporations would exist. Everyone would be a contractor; no one would be an employee. When private firms decide to employ personnel to carry out a task, they choose bureaucracy over the market. There would be manifest disadvantages to contracting for many routine activities — among them a reduced ability to monitor performance and to reorganize production. Furthermore, contractors build up "local knowledge" (or what Oliver Williamson calls "asset-specific" information) that reduces parity among bidders at times of contract renegotiation.[12] These problems of monitoring and control arise for the public as well as the private sector. To be sure, contracting out may give government the flexibility of switching among alternative suppliers, thereby enhancing its bargaining power. However, the advantages are worthwhile only if the government can assure itself of both the reliability of services and the ability to maintain competition at later points of contract renewal. In many markets, competition is weak at the outset and may diminish over time. Initial suppliers often gain cumulative insider advantages. Other agencies or firms respect the "turf" of the current contractors because of an anticompetitive ethos (as in the nonprofit sector) or tacit agreements not to underbid (as in the East Coast trash-collection industry infiltrated by organized crime). As a result of these barriers to competition, contracting out may turn out to be a form of privatization that is less liberalizing — and more costly — than it might initially seem.

Vouchers may also produce disappointing and perverse effects. Consider the potential of educational voucher plans to increase the public budget. They would add at least part of the cost of educating students now in private schools, but, perhaps more important, they might have a general inflationary impact. Educational voucher plans resemble third-party health insurance. It is not a happy precedent. Unless barred by new forms of price regulation, private schools would likely raise their fees once vouchers were available. In particular, the high-quality private schools that prize their exclusivity might use higher prices to keep out undesirable students who cannot supplement the vouchers. Besides, like doctors and hospital managers, teachers and administrators in all kinds of schools could think of good things that need to be done with extra funds; and vouchers, like third-party health insurance, would dull the price-consciousness of "consumers," who are in any case less concerned about price than about quality (which, as in health care, they cannot easily judge).

One suggested cure for these problems is regulation of private-school fees, admissions, and other procedures, but new regulation would have the perverse effect of making private schools more public. Indeed, this fear of new controls imposed by legislatures or courts makes many advocates of private schools wary of vouchers or other proposals for public funding. There is a larger lesson in this case. Although privatization aims to shift services from the public to the private sector, it could end up making private institutions more like public ones. If public money flows to private providers, the voters and their representatives are likely to demand greater accountability. The courts are likely to demand greater compliance with constitutional protections of clients' and employees' rights. The very distinctiveness of the sector would probably diminish. In the extreme case, the privatization of public provision could turn out to mean the socialization of private provision.

Thus there is much reason to question the seemingly straightforward view of privatization as a means of reducing government. Butler's argument that privatization would change the dynamics of government expansion is unpersuasive on its face. Private contractors make aggressive lobbyists, as would other recipients of public funds under any proposal to retain government financing but to move production into private hands. Asset sales do provide a temporary budgetary boost, but only in exchange for public capital; a proper accounting would show no improvement in the government's net financial condition. Asset sales improve the long-run budgetary picture only if governments avoid future subsidies. However, privatization is no guarantee that subsidies will stop. Private companies are not bashful about asking for help, usually in the form of tax benefits. And if privatization occurs without liberalization, privatized monopolies can obtain subsidies through regulatory protection. In any event, subsidies to government enterprises are not a major budget item in the United States, and some of the agencies that the Reagan administration has mentioned as candidates for privatization, such as the National Technical Information Service (NTIS) and the Federal Housing Administration (FHA), have been self-sustaining.[13] The sale of the public domain could produce significant revenue, but the support for selling major portions of it is negligible. Even a commission appointed by President Reagan called for new funds to add to the public lands.

The one privatization proposal that could undoubtedly have major budgetary consequences is the plan for privatizing Social Security through "super IRAs" (individual retirement accounts). But rather than save money, the proposal would be a genuine budget-buster. Its chief architect, Peter Ferrara, says that current beneficiaries would continue to receive their benefits while workers would be allowed to take tax credits for contributions to enlarged IRAs that would ultimately assume responsibility for retirement income, Medicare, disability insurance, and other benefits.[14] But this plan obviously raises an immense "double-payment problem," since the payroll taxes now being collected are spent on current beneficiaries. The money going into super IRAs would have to come from somewhere. If workers were allowed credits against their payroll taxes for contributions to super IRAs, Social Security would require a vast infusion of general revenues; and if workers could take credits against their income taxes, then general revenues would fall sharply. Either way, the Federal deficit would increase dramatically. Ferrara's answer is that the new savings in super IRAs would so greatly spur economic growth that all would end happily; and to prove his case, he gives estimates of real returns to investment that are wildly out of line with historic patterns or any reasonable economic expectations.[15] President Ronald Reagan and Congress believed in one supply-side miracle when they slashed income tax rates in 1981, expecting to ride the Laffer curve back to solvency. Another such supply-side miracle and the country will be dead broke.

Choice, Equality, and Citizenship

The case for privatization includes other claims besides improved efficiency, budget savings, and increased economic growth. The key word is *choice*. Advocates claim that privatization will enlarge the range of choice for individuals while serving the same essential functions as do traditional programs. Thus, if Social Security were privatized, the Federal government would still require people to put aside funds for retirement but would allow them to choose their own retirement investments. Educational vouchers would not abolish laws requiring children to go to school but would allow families to choose which one. Asset sales and shifts of services from public agencies to private contractors might permit greater choice among suppliers.

Proponents of privatization maintain that greater choice would serve the interests of equity. The rich have always been able to afford private schools; educational vouchers would give the middle classes and the poor that ability. Social Security, they say, favors whites, whose longer life expectancy enables them to receive greater retirement benefits than do blacks; privatization would allegedly correct that bias. According to the privatizers, greater freedom of choice will generally lead to a more just distribution of benefits.

Choice is unquestionably the single strongest point in the case for privatization. The uniformity of public programs and services is often a grave limitation. Even where it is not logically required, the demands of equal treatment are often interpreted to prohibit heterogeneity in public services. Rules requiring uniform pricing also impede the production of varied services, especially those of high quality. These barriers to heterogeneity have long been a weakness of public services, but the problem grows more serious as personal income increases with economic growth. Larger numbers of consumers demand the more varied, specially designed services available previously only to those with the highest incomes. This demand for quality – or rather for different qualities – constitutes a source of dissatisfaction with the public sector that may be expected to grow.

Yet while recognizing the handicaps of the public sector in providing for variety, we ought not to accept uncritically the conception of choice that the privatization proponents offer. Individual choice in the marketplace is not the only kind. Democratic societies offer another mode of choice through political participation. Conservatives usually emphasize the drawbacks of political choice: preferences of outvoted minorities are not satisfied, and representation is imperfect. But there are reasons to prefer democratic politics to markets in the making of some decisions. Most obviously, each citizen gets one vote, but in the marketplace people with more money have more "votes." The democratic polity also does not simply register preferences; it subjects them to public discussion. Deliberation creates opportunities for criticism and mutual persuasion, for interest to confront interest, sometimes to discover common ground. The whole point of a republican system of government is to set in motion these processes. After all, with interactive computers we might now have the technological capacity to turn political decisions back to individuals voting at their keyboards. But those who think such instant democracy would be an improvement overlook the critical and (dare I say it?) deeply conservative function of public deliberation.

Privatization does not transform constraint into choice; it transfers decisions from one realm of choice – and constraint – to another. These two realms differ in their basic rules for disclosure of information: the public realm requires greater access; private firms have fewer obligations to conduct open proceedings or to make known the reasons for their decisions. The two realms differ in their recognition of individual desires; the public realm mandates equal voting rights, while the market responds to purchasing power. They differ in the processes of preference formation: democratic politics is a process for articulating, criticizing, and adapting preferences in a context where individuals need to make a case for interests larger than their own. Privatization diminishes the sphere of public information, deliberation, and accountability – elements of democracy whose value is not reducible to efficiency. If we are to respect preferences, as conservatives urge that we do, we ought to respect preferences for democratic over market choice where they have been long and consistently demonstrated. As Amy Gutmann has pointed out, individuals exercise choice as much when they vote themselves public schools – or for that matter other public services – as when they buy services in the market.[16]

Moreover, the removal of decisions from the public arena diminishes the individual incentive for participation. Public schools, in particular, are a principal motivation for the participation of parents in local elections; the vitality of local government depends on their involvement. Privatization of the schools would weaken the foundations of local democracy.

Democratic politics is more than an alternative mode of choice; government also opens up choices that are not available in the market. When markets fail to provide goods and services, voting enables the public to purchase them. Advocates of privatization concede the appropriateness of government intervention for public goods, but they say that except for a few cases (such as national defense) the public sector can as readily buy the services as produce them (and that even within the category of national defense much more can be privatized). However, the difficulty of privatizing some public goods is that public administration is essential to their character. I have in mind, first of all, the administration of justice, the exercise of coercive power (as in prisons), the collection of taxes, and other functions where the very appearance of buying and selling undermines the claim of the state to be acting impartially on behalf of the entire community — and, indeed, where the practice of buying and selling may undermine the capacity for disinterested judgment. Conservatives not only view politics too narrowly as a political marketplace; through privatization they would help to turn it into one.

In a variety of market failures, government intervention often expands the range of choices available to individuals. In the broadcasting industry, commercial networks and stations sell audiences to advertisers; the programs are merely bait for the audience's attention. But the attention of children has relatively little economic value, since it cannot be sold except to brand-name food and toy producers, who sponsor only a limited amount of programming, little of it educational. Educational programming requires action outside of the market, which in the United States has taken the mixed form of combined government and philanthropic support. Public broadcasting has expanded the diversity not only of programs but also of decision-making processes about programs, and it has given priority to educational and cultural values that have little influence elsewhere. Public provision has thereby expanded the alternatives offered by the broadcasting system as a whole.[17]

Social Security is another, though quite different, example of the capacity of government to open up possibilities closed off in the market. Insurance markets suffer from severe problems of moral hazard and adverse selection. By creating a single risk pool, Social Security provides protection to those who could not afford it at market rates.[18] The argument that Social Security penalizes disadvantaged minorities overlooks some crucial facts. Although blacks collect retirement benefits for fewer years on average, the progressive benefit structure of Social Security enables them to collect more during those years than they would from private policies. (In any event, private insurance firms could not charge blacks less than whites for annuities because it would be unconstitutional for them to use racial classifications. The only way for blacks to derive savings because of a lower life expectancy would be to buy less coverage.) The privatization of Social Security would, therefore, reduce the income of the black elderly and make many more of them dependent on means-tested welfare benefits. In addition, blacks and other disadvantaged minorities depend especially on the other components of Social Security, such as disability, health insurance, and survivors benefits. Because of their higher costs in these areas, many of them could not purchase privately the full package of Social Security benefits. On the whole, Social Security is a bargain for low-income groups. It is simply disingenuous of privatization advocates to claim that the poor would benefit from a change that eliminates the progressive benefit structure and sends them into a private market that for good reason is shy of serving people certain to have higher health insurance, disability, and survivors' claims.[19]

Conservative critics complain that broad-based public programs like public education, public television, and Social Security are poorly targeted; middle-class recipients get subsidies they do not need. This is an odd complaint to hear from those who often recommend the use of tax expenditures, which may be the least well targeted of all forms of public subsidy (and are even less controllable than entitlement programs, since they are not subject to the annual appropriations process). The benefits of public education and Social Security are distributed far more equally than those of the private markets they supplement or supplant, and, besides, the programs ought not to be seen narrowly as income transfers. We pay taxes for schools to educate not just some parents' children but the next generation of citizens. Even childless adults have a stake in the survival of their society. We do not pay Social Security taxes solely to sustain the aged but also to keep up a compact that rolls over from one generation to the next. These are the frameworks of a commonwealth. Linking the fate of the poor to the majority strengthens their common sense of membership in the nation. The poor gain more from the vigilance of middle-class voters than they lose from any scattering of scarce benefits. Narrow targeting of public programs promotes the political isolation of their beneficiaries; it particularly feeds resentments of the excluded lower-middle classes. As "welfare" so well illustrates, programs that target benefits on the poor can also target cutbacks. A large-scale shift of public services to private providers would contribute to further isolating the least advantaged, since private firms have strong incentives to skim off the best clients and most profitable services. The result would often be a residual, poorer public sector providing services of last resort. Such institutions would be even less attractive as places to work than they are today. And their worsening difficulties would no doubt be cited as confirmation of the irremediable incompetence of public managers and inferiority of public services. Public institutions already suffer from this vicious circle; most forms of privatization would intensify it.

Privatization must be seen not only as a technical instrument of policy but also as a political measure of symbolic consequence. When applied to the administration of justice and exercise of coercive power, the symbolic element is of paramount importance. Meting out justice is a communicative act; its public character ought not to be confused. And where the state represents the nation and seeks to speak with one voice, it needs public servants loyal to its highest interests, not private contractors maximizing their own. Witness the outrage over the Reagan administration's "privatization of foreign policy." The president's open encouragement, if not direct authorization, of private agents to provide congressionally prohibited military aid to the contras in Nicaragua violated the presumption that only lawfully authorized agents of government can make and carry out United States foreign policy. In other areas of national policy as well, there ought to be no ambiguity about public control. The national parks and wilderness are a common legacy, and the message of their management should be that they belong to no private party but to the people as a whole.

Privatization signals diminished access. When distributive justice is at issue, privatization signals a diminished commitment to include the poor in the national household. That is clearly the message that would be read from the privatization of welfare, if that phrase means reliance on the "spur" of individual poverty (as George Gilder and Charles Murray advise us) or on acts of private charity, even if encouraged by tax deductions or credits.[20] Relying entirely upon charity, as John Goodman recommends, would give no assurance that the poor would receive equitable treatment—that poor blacks, for example, would not be treated less favorably than poor whites.[21] The privatization of Social Security would carry the same message of indifference to greater inequality. Upon retirement, some people would find they had done well with their personal IRAs, but others who gambled unsuccessfully in the stock market would face personal ruin. The privatization of the schools would symbolize a final retreat from the already faded ideal of bringing the disparate children of a community under a common roof.

However, the symbolic load of privatization ought not to be a categorical objection to all the various measures that are covered by that term. As I indicated at the beginning, the term covers a heterogeneous set of policies, some more worthy than others. We need not accept or reject all the elements as a single package. Like corporations, states ought to be able to divest themselves of some activities and take on others. They should be able to contemplate exchanging or liquidating assets, to compare buying with producing services, and to entertain new forms of competition within the public sector or between public and private organizations. The postal service, for example, no longer has the same practical and symbolic importance in knitting together the nation that it once did.[22] Its historic function has been partly superseded by other means of communication, and the prospect of still further technological change will ultimately require a fundamental reconceptualization of its role. Yet, like the railroads, which have discovered immense value in their real estate, the postal service possesses assets that might be more productively used. Restructuring the postal system might well include asset sales, contracting out of some functions, and eventually liberalization of entry into first-class mail delivery.[23]

Housing provides another example of the potential for restructuring public assets. Unlike education and justice, housing is not a service that Americans believe government should produce and manage; it is a private good that exemplifies the demands for variety that government is poorly equipped to meet. Housing policy in the United States has always been highly privatized—too often in the interests of developers, one might add.[24] Public housing accounts for only a small portion even of the housing that government has subsidized. To be sure, those who live in public housing (and the many more on waiting lists) value it highly. But public housing projects might be privatized if they can be sold to tenant cooperatives that show promise of effectively operating and maintaining them. However, such sales ought not to rule out building new public housing where the private market shows no signs of responding to the needs of the homeless. In some areas of policy like housing, government ought to move its investments in a kind of rolling privatization — disposing of some public assets while augmenting others.

In adjusting the public-private balance, we need to be attentive, sphere by sphere, to the special practical and moral considerations that arise in each. No single remedy is appropriate to the vastly different problems that distinguish collecting taxes from collecting trash, running schools from running railroads, managing prisons from managing shipyards. Nor ought we to reduce our choices to a simple public-private dichotomy. We have a more extensive repertoire of intermediate options in organizational forms and modes of ownership, control, and finance. The illusory appeal of privatization is to provide a single solution for many complex problems. But if the idea of privatization has any merit, it is to force us to rediscover the rationale of the public services we need and to remind us, if we had forgotten, that the public-private mix ought not to be considered settled for all time.

NOTES

1. For a discussion of this and other conceptions of privatization, see Paul Starr, "The Meaning of Privatization," in *Privatization and the Welfare State*, ed. Alfred Kahn and Sheila Kamerman (forthcoming).

2. See John Kay, Colin Mayer, and David Thompson, eds., *Privatisation and Regulation: The UK Experience* (London: Oxford University Press, 1987); Samuel Brittan, "The Politics and Economics of Privatisation," *Political Quarterly* 55 (Winter 1985): 109–27.

3. Milton and Rose Friedman, *Free to Choose* (New York: Harcourt Brace Jovanovich, 1980): 161–63.

4. Stuart M. Butler, *Privatizing Federal Spending: A Strategy to Eliminate the Deficit* (New York: Universe Books, 1985); idem, "Changing the Political Dynamics of Government," in this volume, 4–13.

5. Peter Saunders, "Public Expenditure and Economic Performance in OECD Countries," *Journal of Public Policy* 5 (1986): 1–21; David R. Cameron, "The Expansion of the Public Economy: A Comparative Analysis," *American Political Science Review* 72 (December 1978): 1243–61; and, more generally, Robert Kuttner, *The Economic Illusion: False Choices Between Prosperity and Social Justice* (Boston: Houghton Mifflin, 1984).

6. See Simon Kuznets, "National Income: A New Version," *Review of Economics and Statistics* 30 (August 1948): 151–79; Robert J. Gordon, "$45 Billion of U. S. Private Investment Has Been Mislaid," *American Economic Review* 59 (June 1969): 221–38; John W. Kendrick, *The Formation and Stocks of Total Capital* (New York: Columbia University Press, 1976); and Robert Eisner, *How Real is the Federal Deficit?* (New York: The Free Press, 1986).

7. For the "public choice" view of government growth, see Thomas Borcherding, ed. *Budgets and Bureaucrats: The Sources of Government Growth* (Durham, N.C.: Duke University Press, 1977), and for a critique, see Richard A. Musgrave, "Leviathan Cometh — or Does He?" in *Tax and Expenditure Limitations*, ed. Helen F. Ladd and T. Nicolaus Tideman (Washington, D.C.: Urban Institute Press, 1981), 77–120.

8. The evidence against the public-choice view of political behavior is summed up in Gary R.

Orren, "Beyond Self-Interest," in *The Power of Public Ideas*, ed. Robert Reich (Cambridge, Mass.: Ballinger Publishing, 1987), 13–29, and Steven Kelman, "Why Public Ideas Matter," ibid., 31–54. For a theoretical response to public-choice claims, see also Carlisle Ford Runge, "The Fallacy of 'Privatization,'" *Journal of Contemporary Studies* (Winter 1984), 3–17; and for an experimental study contradicting economists' assumptions about free riding, see Gerald Marwell and Ruth Ames, "Economists Free Ride, Does Anyone Else?" *Journal of Public Economics* 15 (June 1981): 295–310.

9. This was true even at the height of the tax revolt when Proposition 13 passed in California. See David O. Sears and Jack Citrin, *Tax Revolt: Something for Nothing in California* (Cambridge, Mass.: Harvard University Press, 1982), esp. chap. 3.

10. Butler, *Privatizing Federal Spending*, 56.

11. For more skeptical readings of the evidence on public versus private ownership, see Robert Millward, "The Comparative Performance of Public and Private Ownership," in *The Mixed Economy*, ed. Lord Roll of Ipsden (London: Macmillan Press, 1982), 58–93; George W. Downs and Patrick D. Larkey, *The Search for Government Efficiency* (Philadelphia: Temple University Press, 1986); and Charles T. Goodsell, *The Case for Bureaucracy: A Public Administration Polemic* (Chatham, N. J.: Chatham House Publishers, 1983).

12. Oliver E. Williamson, *The Economic Institutions of Capitalism* (New York: The Free Press, 1985).

13. The proposals to sell the FHA and NTIS met instant opposition not only from Congress but also from the private sector. See "Experts Assail Plan for F.H.A.," *New York Times*, 16 Dec. 1985, and "Congress Wary on Plan to Sell Assets," ibid., 6 Feb. 1986. On the NTIS and, more generally, the privatization of information resources, see Paul Starr and Ross Corson, "Who Will Have the Numbers? The Rise of the Statistical Services Industry and the Politics of Public Data," in *The Politics of Numbers*, ed. William Alonso and Paul Starr (New York: Russell Sage, 1987).

14. Peter J. Ferrara, "Social Security and the Super IRA: A Populist Proposal," in *Social Security: Prospects for Real Reform*, ed. Peter J. Ferrara (Washington, D.C.: Cato Institute, 1985), 193–220. For a more extensive treatment, see Peter J. Ferrara, *Social Security: The Inherent Contradiction* (San Francisco: Cato Institute, 1980).

15. For a more extended critical analysis, see Paul Starr, "Social Security and the American Public Household," in *The Politics of Social Security*, ed. Theodore Marmor and Jerry Mashaw (Princeton, N.J.: Princeton University Press, forthcoming).

16. Amy Gutmann, *Democratic Education* (Princeton, N.J.: Princeton University Press, 1987).

17. New developments in cable and other technologies are unlikely to supply the broader educational and cultural needs that public television has met. See Paul Starr "Television and the Public Household," in *Television in America's Future — A Search for the Right Public Policy*, ed. Michael Rice (forthcoming).

18. Even as severe a critic of Social Security as Michael J. Boskin has acknowledged the need for a public program to overcome the problems of the insurance market. See his *Too Many Promises: The Uncertain Future of Social Security* (Homewood, Ill.: Dow Jones-Irwin, 1986).

19. For further development, see Starr, "Social Security and the American Public Household."

20. George Gilder, *Wealth and Poverty* (New York: Basic Books, 1981); Charles Murray, *Losing Ground: American Social Policy, 1950–1980* (New York: Basic Books, 1984).

21. John C. Goodman, "Privatizing the Welfare State," in this volume, 36–48.

22. Wayne E. Fuller, *The American Mail: Enlarger of the Common Life* (University of Chicago Press, 1972).

23. For discussion of policy options, see Joel L. Fleischman, ed., *The Future of the Postal Service* (New York: Praeger, 1983).

24. Gosta Esping-Andersen and Paul Starr have used the term *passive intervention* to describe government policies in health care and housing that excessively accommodate private provider interests in "Passive Intervention," *Working Papers for a New Society* 7 (July-August 1979): 15–25.

Uses and Misuses of Privatization

ROBERT W. BAILEY

When a consensus was reached in the late 1970s that redistribution through taxation and budgeting was becoming a less attractive policy for state and local governments in the United States, a series of new, off-budget policy instruments were advanced to provide localities and the Federal government with other ways to act in the presence of fiscal restraint. In both public policy and the academic literature, *limits* became the watchword — limits not only in fiscal resources but also in the ability of government effectively to influence social or economic direction: the limits of *état* power. Strategic planning, land-use planning, exactive zoning, community-sponsored public benefit corporations, public development corporations, public-private partnerships, and many other initiatives can be gathered under this umbrella. Indeed, not since the first half of the nineteenth century has such intense activity been seen in these areas.

One of the concepts in vogue is privatization. Although the concept itself is unclear, it might be tentatively defined as a general effort to relieve the disincentives toward efficiency in public organizations by subjecting them to the incentives of the private market. There are in fact several different concepts of "privatization," but this theme unites them all. Depending on the emphasis of the advocates, the theoretical grounding of privatization comes from either public-choice theorists, students of monopolistic behavior in economics, or political scientists with a prescriptive view of interest-group analysis.

This essay presents some of the limits to privatization; not so much to reject the concept — the introduction of a policy instrument can only be beneficial for the professional public manager — but to reduce its ideological character to practical guidelines. For privatization is not new. It has been tried and, at least in four cases in New York City, has not always succeeded.

Clarifying the Concept of Privatization

When words become political weapons, they often lose their clarity. *Privatization* is no exception. At least four identifiable policy initiatives are associated with privatization in current public-management discussions. No one of them excludes the others.

The first might be called "load-shedding through privatization." This is the oldest notion of privatization and the one most often used. Simply stated, it is the transfer of a service or operation from a public agency to a private organization. The classic example has always been sanitation services. E. S. Savas has argued that the private pickup of solid waste would result in greater efficiency. The traditional argument is that a network of private organizations, in competition with one another, would create an incentive for cost containment or even reduction. At least in New York City, according to the argument, the growing influence of public-employee unions, through their ability to withhold services or through campaign activities, had undue influence over managerial prerogatives. In collective bargaining, the "scope of bargaining" had expanded, and labor had become involved in decisions that in the past would have been left to management. By privatizing the service, this influence would be put into a more proper perspective. Similarly, the argument over education is that privatization through a "voucher" system would lead to more effective schools, since parents, who would have control over the disposition of educational resources, could choose from a number of different educational offerings. Obviously, schools would then attempt to upgrade their educational effectiveness; if they did not, they would fail to establish credibility among parents and could not attract enough students to succeed. In education and sanitation, advocates of privatization see the monopolistic nature of local-service delivery as the greatest impediment to government effectiveness. Competition is the recommended remedy via privatization.

The second definition is associated with the current debate in Western Europe and is less germane to the American discourse. In Europe and in most of the rest of the First and Third Worlds, governments hold state owned enterprises (SOEs). These institutions can be either fully or partially owned. What separates them from their American counterparts is that many of these SOEs are equity corporations, that is, they issue stock or some other instrument that can be shared with nonstate organizations. Many of the airlines in the world are owned by state entities in partnership with private investors. In Israel, the government is often in partnership with the Histradut, the organization of labor unions. Their jointly owned corporations often form partnerships with other organizations — public or private or even international, such as the Jewish Agency. Privatization here relates to the relative position of the government in SOEs. In Britain, Prime Minister Margaret Thatcher's government has privatized many SOEs by selling up to 100 percent of the Crown's ownership. In France, Prime Minister Jacques Chirac has "privatized" some of the financial-services industry that President François Mitterand's government had "nationalized." In many cases, such as Italy, the government has an overall holding corporation that manages the state's role in SOEs. A direct application of this concept of privatization is not useful in the United States. Public benefit corporations (PBCs) are found in the United States, but not since the last century has there been a significant number of public-private equity corporations.

Although there are similar issues of political and managerial accountability of PBCs and SOEs, they remain fundamentally different. American public benefit corporations usually issue debt, serviced by revenue streams derived from their activities. In the American environment, debt—not equity—is the key to understanding SOEs.

The third definition—one recently added to the nuances of privatization—is the sale of assets. The Reagan administration has proposed liquidating some of the Federal government's holdings to either raise revenues or end subsidies. The sale of Conrail in the Northeast and oil lands in the West are the best examples. Suggestions for the sale of home mortgages held by Federal financing corporations and the privatization of Bonneville Power and Tennessee Valley Authority facilities have also been made. What is really being proposed in these "privatizations" is the liquidation of assets for their cash value. The problem, though, is determining the market value of the asset being liquidated. In California the Federal government wants to sell lands with oil reserves at only eight times their cash flow, normally considered quite a low price by market analysts. In the Northeast, the sale of Conrail has become a political problem because one of the groups offering to buy it is a consortium of unions involved in rail transport. The government has not been enthusiastic about the offer and has been leaning toward one made by Norfolk Southern. But even if the political problems can be solved, there are others. Conrail, for example, has extensive real property holdings throughout the northeast corridor. In some cases—such as northern Philadelphia and Hudson County, New Jersey—how that land is used will have a tremendous impact on development patterns. Liquidating Federal assets for their cash value may provide some temporary relief to budget problems, but it may also have important negative effects on the public interests of localities. Here, too, privatization is a complicated policy whose long-term effects may outweigh short-term gains.

The fourth definition is "privatization" by contract. Here the concept becomes even less clear. It is an operational notion of privatization—in which a traditional responsibility of government is maintained but conducted by a private firm—and yet the état power of government is responsible for both the policy and the financial success of the "private" actor. The traditional source of such privatization has been in the provision of social services. Because most social services were begun by religious and voluntary organizations, there was a base of service and experience when government began to take on these responsibilities. In many cases, services for children, families, drug and alcohol dependency, and other social needs can best be delivered by these groups. The government contracts with them for their services, and referrals are made through family courts, criminal courts, government social-service agencies, and other organizations. A more recent example is the contracting out of research and analytical services. The U. S. Department of Energy privatizes, or contracts out, over three-fourths of its total budget. The bureaucratic advantage is that people are off-budget. They do not show up in the headcount or the budget and are outside the civil service system. The flexibility offered is enormous, of course, but so is the opportunity for abuse. On the state and local levels, there has been considerable pressure to privatize the management of special facilities, particularly convention centers, park lands, and sports facilities. In Tennessee an effort has been made to privatize the management of the state's correctional facilities. Privatization has been hailed as a way to reduce the operating costs of large facilities, relieving managers from the need to deal with public-employee unions and offering the "economy" of private market values — as it has in all four definitions.

Each of these definitions could be further refined and additional nuances introduced. The focus here has been more operational than ideological. Public managers do not really need an explication of the theoretical underpinnings of privatization, since their experience will likely diverge from it. Indeed, that point needs to be pressed: the ideological advocates of privatization so overstate its applicability, or so cloud it as a concept, that practical public managers who might choose to use it as a feasible policy instrument find themselves on the defensive among others who have been aroused to oppose privatization on ideological grounds.

The Twin Themes of Efficiency in Public-Choice Theory

Despite the confusion of what exactly is meant by the term *privatization*, there is a clear unifying thread in all its uses: maximization of efficiency. The assumption among advocates is that, inherently, private managers can deliver at lower costs services similar or superior to those of public managers. One can understand this. The constraints on public managers are tremendous — certainly greater than on private managers. There are the constraints of labor, the press, and the citizenry, all of whom hold public managers to a higher standard of accountability than private managers. And yet it should be pointed out that public management is simply different from private management. No homogeneity exists in the criteria of policy choice as there is in the private sector. There is no objective way to establish the price of public services and thus no basis for comparative analysis among competing activities for the investment of slack public resources. The government is required to be more open than a private organization. In short, the two are not directly comparable. A different set of skills is needed, as private managers learn when they take on previously held public responsibilities.

This standard point of debate in the difference between private and public management noted, the intellectual grounding of advocates for privatization should be taken seriously. Particularly in the large American cities, monopolies are formed by local governments to deliver services. The tendency for these monopolies to perform like all others — whether public or private — is great. The organization tends to absorb resources on internal preference scales. Since there is no need to create new products, innovation is low and research and development is neglected. Clients have few ways to express their preferences and no alternative when minimum service desires are not met. Because there is no unifying criterion of policy making in the public sector as there is in the private sector — i.e., profitability — assessing or pricing the comparative worth of services is difficult. In fact, the public sector offers one of the few arenas where service providers regularly generate their own demand. Thus the Pentagon generates Soviet threats as the Soviet military establishment generates American threats; and special education evaluation committees recommend services for 95 percent of the students referred to them.

The monopolistic nature of much of local service delivery is matched by a monopsonist character. Often, the local government is the only purchaser of a service or commodity. This is less to the advantage of the local government than it should be — that is, in establishing a monopsonist price — but it also opens local government to additional noncompetitive restraints. The actual service providers are unified through unions or professional associations. As the sole or major purchaser of services, local and state government may become hostage to the inefficiencies of single sellers of services. The monopsony reinforces the tendency toward internal preference scales and creates an extraordinary imbalance of power between the bureaucracy and the individual.

The combination of monopolistic government and monopsonist providers led in some cases to an imbalance within the public sector itself. In what political scientists call policy arenas — service areas where third parties come together to effect their interests — the combination resisted community responsiveness or, in the case of schools, responsiveness to parents and even resisted the fiscal authority of central political authorities. This dynamic contributed to New York City's financial crisis.

While all these patterns could be affirmed by more research elsewhere, there is also an irony. The same intellectual traditions that provide the underlying arguments for privatization — public-choice theory, theories of the firm, and monopolistic behavior — also provide an argument against it, at least on the state and local levels. While the pressures working against the effectiveness of local administration revealed by these traditions are clear, the same traditions reveal latent and indirect pressures toward efficiency. Charles Tiebout, in his classic 1956 essay on local expenditures, celebrated the relative fragmentation of jurisdictions in American federalism.[1] He noted that there would be individual or household-preference tables for public goods and individual or household resources available for tax effort. Both of these would vary but would be the underlying influences in deciding between what Albert O. Hirschmann, fifteen years later, would call "exit and loyalty."[2] Young families, for example, might be willing to suffer high taxation if the quality of education in public schools was superior to that in surrounding school districts. Senior citizens, most of them on fixed incomes, would likely prefer lower taxes and might tend to rely on the church and family for social services. Single people would likely prefer few services and low taxes.

According to the public-choice tradition, an incentive toward efficiency comes from different jurisdictions providing an equivalent array of services at different tax efforts. If one jurisdiction can meet the preference schedule of an individual, household, or organization at "Y" tax effort and another at "1.12 × Y," other things being equal, that individual, household, or organization will tend to move into the first jurisdiction or, located in the second, tend to "exit." As the difference between jurisdictional efficiency variables increases, it will inevitably meet "inertia advantages" and make it irrational for the individual, household, or organization to remain settled. Obviously, these factors will become more potent as inertia advantages are mooted by depreciating capital, a larger family, a change in jobs, or other factors that put location on the decision agenda.

The point here is not so much that monopolistic behavior is unobserved in the public sector — surely it is — but that public entities are limited monopolies: limited by jurisdictional borders. Geographic fragmentation presents an incentive ultimately and, over time, toward efficiency. There is, then, a tension between two competing implications of public-choice theory: one indicating that the monopolistic nature of local-service delivery will naturally tend toward inefficiency, another indicating that the geographic limits of states and localities create an incentive toward efficiency. Which of the two themes is more potent at any one time is to be determined empirically by social scientists. What is interesting for us here, however, is that the tradition on which advocates of privatization rest their most persuasive arguments is in itself ambiguous on the long-term outcomes that limited local public-service monopolies might effect. One conclusion might be that intervening variables — such as the quality of public management — might have greater influence over public-sector efficiency than either of the discussed theoretical implications of public-choice theorists.

Lowering Expectations for Privatization: Four Cases from New York City

Although privatization is now discussed in a theoretical framework, much of what is being advanced has been in effect on the subnational level for many years. Four cases from the experience of New York City indicate that the promises held out for privatization may not be fully met. The intent here again is not to dismiss the concept of privatization but by reviewing it in real rather than ideological terms to see its actual utility. The four cases are commercial refuse, proprietary vocational schools, school transportation services, and management of sports facilities.

Commercial refuse. There are two major structures of solid-waste removal in New York City. The city's Department of Sanitation removes the solid waste of the residents and not-for-profit organizations of New York. Private carters service the sanitation needs of commercial enterprises, including office buildings, restaurants, and retail outlets. This current dual structure of sanitation service is the result of privatization. In 1957 the city turned over delivery of sanitation services for commercial enterprises to private firms. Individual firms bid for contracts among commercial establishments needing sanitation services, and dozens of carter firms sprang up in New York.

From a theoretical standpoint, the citywide monopoly held by the New York City Department of Sanitation was broken up and an opportunity to provide the services previously delivered by the department was opened. The result, however, has not been fully beneficial. By the mid-1980s the efficiency expected by the privatization of commercial refuse had not been achieved. The proliferation of private carter companies is really misleading, since many are owned jointly by holding companies. In addition, either through formal or informal arrangements, the city has been divided into service districts or routes. Carter firms have agreed not to compete for business on the routes of other carters—an anticompetitive action. "Stops"—commercial establishments needing private carter services—are regularly sold between private carters if they decide to change the routing of their trucks or leave the commercial-refuse business entirely. There have been continuing rumors and several indictments indicating that organized crime has influenced the anticompetitive action of some private carters.

Even if the suspicion that organized crime is involved in private carting services is untrue, the efficiencies claimed for the privatization of the trade-waste industry have certainly not been obtained. Clients have no alternatives. When a mailing went out by the city to owners of commercial establishments, it was found that many were being overcharged by their carters, including a major office tower in midtown Manhattan. The lack of competitiveness puts upward pressure on carting fees. The monopoly has simply been switched from a public one to a private one. In addition, what might be expected as a benefit of privatization—that private carters would not have to deal with public-employee unions—is also hampered. Although there may be many private carters in New York City, there is only one union—the Teamsters. Its contract is citywide and binds nearly all private carters.

In 1987 it is clear that the privatization of commercial refuse has not achieved what might have been hoped for in New York City. The current policy discussions on commercial refuse concern greater regulation, particularly in regard to hazardous waste. Many private carters do not handle dangerous materials, such as asbestos and hospital wastes, in a proper manner. Despite a predisposition against taking on additional government responsibilities, the Koch administration is seriously considering eliminating the private carters.

Proprietary vocational education. Although one can point to a specific policy choice in the privatization of commercial refuse collection in New York City, no such decision was made about private vocational schools. There has been a conscious decision to regulate these schools, however, and to provide financing for them. An accumulation of regulatory and legislative initiatives in New York State leaves the clear impression that government wishes to meet the short-term, adult vocational-education needs being generated by the economy through private services.

Since the early 1980s the number of private vocational and business schools in New York State has skyrocketed: from 28 in 1980 to over 100 in 1986. Proprietary business and vocational schools offer training programs lasting from a few weeks to two years. Their curricula range from driver training, air-conditioning repair, and computer assistance to business skills. Many of these schools have long traditions and have made important contributions to their students and communities. But many have not.

Fueled by third-party payments—mostly student loans, New York State tuition assistance, and Federal Pell grants – the educational offerings of these schools have often been investigated. In some cases, there have been charges of outright fraud. Their primary market is students over the age of eighteen who have either dropped out of the public-school system or are among the new wave of immigration from South Asia or Spanish-speaking areas of the Caribbean and South America. The enrollment is overwhelmingly black, Hispanic, and female.

The State Education Department is responsible for regulating proprietary vocational schools in New York, but its resources are strained, and many of these institutions are affiliated with national chains and operate outside the jurisdiction of the department's officials. Compounding the problem is the fact that most of the state's inspectors are in Albany, while most of the schools are in New York City.

In a series of investigations conducted by state and city consumer-affairs advocates, legal-aid attorneys, and legislative staff, patterns of poor services and fraud were revealed. Many schools assessed students in terms of their potential for aid – and thus tuition – and were only secondarily interested in establishing needs assessment for their education. Some schools coached students skills tests during admission. Often students would be directed toward programs longer than they initially requested, thus ensuring eligibility for state and Federal assistance. Students were never informed that equivalent or better services were offered at their local community colleges at substantially lower cost. They were encouraged to incur debt. Some students signed loan applications without ever knowing that they were applying for a loan, and recruiters were paid a per head fee for students applying to schools. One school continued to recruit students and accept their tuition even though its lawyers were planning to file for bankruptcy.

The experience with private vocational schools in New York State over the past ten years raises some serious questions about privatizing educational services. Given the third-party payments available to students using these schools – essentially a form of the voucher system advanced by advocates of privatization – there was little incentive on the part of either the schools or the students to ensure the quality of education. Most students drop out. Since the schools can fill empty seats with new students and obtain new fees, the proprietors do not attempt to bring dropouts back to class. There is no evidence that competition has enhanced the career options or the quality of education for these students. The competition seems to be among the schools for students with the most potential for state and Federal aid. Of all sectors of the education community in New York State, proprietary vocational schools appear to be the least honest and the least effective.

School transportation. School transportation services in New York City are private. Although the city's school district provides for free transport of most of its pupils, the Board of Education contracts out the service. Five major bus companies compete for such services and the one overwhelming actor is Varsity Bus Company. Despite efforts by the Board of Education to expand the number of potential vendors and thus increase competition, there has been no dramatic increase in the number of bidders for school contracts. The capital and start-up costs for a new firm are high. Necessary safety equipment increases the costs, leaving both the school system and the vendors with difficult trade-offs between children and profits. Despite efforts to get minority and small firms into the school transportation business, the situation remains the same: one firm dominates the market and four others provide whatever check there is on monopolistic abuse.

Even if the city's Board of Education could expand the number of potential bidders, there is a hidden monopoly in the school transportation market. Although five bus companies are operating in the market, the real driving force behind the bidding process is the contract provisions between the drivers' union and the five companies. The two principal costs in delivering transportation services are the cost of the buses — again a near monopoly situation — and the cost of labor. While the drivers' union may strike the bus companies, they are also striking against the school system, pressuring the Board of Education to accept higher vendor fees, different work rules, or other contract demands legally binding only on the bus company. In reality, however, at least in labor terms, there is a clear monopolist-monopsonist relationship: the union is the sole provider of services, and the school system is the sole purchaser. Competition among the bus companies, even if effective, would have influence only at the margins of this transportation market. Privatization here has had only minor effects.

Management of sports facilities. If one of the definitions of *privatization* is contracting out managerial and analytical services, then current activities in sports-facilities management are germane. For many communities, sports and convention facilities have become signs of pride and have involved heavy capital investment. They are seen as part of the infrastructure cluster needed if a city is to obtain or keep a reputation as a regional center. How sports and convention facilities are built and managed is now generally seen as an aspect of economic development. Indeed, the Lilly Endowment in Indianapolis, Indiana, advised and partly financed the city's efforts to become "the amateur sports capital of the United States." One need not be a sports enthusiast to recognize its economic and business aspects.

One trend in all of this is for government — either a general-service government or a public benefit corporation — to build these facilities and contract out their management. There are several advantages to this. At its best, contracting out management puts personnel practices outside the civil service system and public-employee collective bargaining. Greater flexibility in personnel assignment and compensation packages should become available for the private manager of a public facility. In addition, there will be an incentive to maximize utilization of the facility, since private managers will make more money. The public manager would not.

Although the proper application of this concept of privatization holds out some hope for a more efficient use of important public infrastructure investments, again the New York City experience with private management of public facilities has been negative. The general-service government of New York City built two major sports facilities in the 1960s and 1970s: Shea Stadium at 24 million 1961 dollars and the new Yankee Stadium at 127 million 1974 dollars. They are managed in the on season by the principal tenants of the stadiums — the New York Mets and the New York Yankees – and in the off season by the New York City Department of Parks. In both cases, the on season is now only half the year, since two National Football League franchises, which had used the facilities at other times of the year, have left the city and play in the Meadowlands complex in New Jersey.

The terms of private management of both stadiums are laid out in great detail in tenant contracts with the city and give both the Yankees and the Mets broad authority over the management of these facilities. Among these are decisions on prices, concessions, scheduling, hiring of non-Parks Department personnel, use of office space, sale of advertisement and television rights, and many other issues. Thus, for at least half a year, the management of these stadiums is privatized. The privileges were so extensive in the case of the Mets that the subtenant for over twenty years, the New York Jets, claimed that its principal reason for leaving the city was management quarrels and poor contract provisions exercised by the Mets franchise. The New York Yankees, whose contract precluded use of the city-owned Yankee Stadium by any other organizations unless approved by the Yankee management, recently threatened to leave New York City if the city does not build more parking space for spectators. In addition, since the city did not negotiate either a share in television rights for the use of its own facility or an agreement that television rights would not be sold to pay-television operations, the Yankee organization has sold the rights to more than 200 games to a local sports cable enterprise with no revenue derived for the city. Even worse from a political vantage point, most of New York City is not yet wired for cable television. Fifteen years after it was rebuilt, the new Yankee Stadium can be seen as a direct public subsidy to a private business organization.

This experience is not frivolous. Better management by the city of its own sports facilities would have increased utilization, enhanced revenues, provided greater managerial flexibility, and provided some political accountability to fans who can no longer watch a baseball game at home. Although the relationship between the Department of Parks and the Mets and Yankees has always been described in terms of tenant and landlord, it might be better termed as the privatization of facilities management. In this way it could be seen how New York City can get more out of its investments, and other jurisdictions can avoid its mistake. Proper privatization of management to an independent firm might have given the city a better bargaining position and a greater revenue stream. The lesson to be learned from New York City, however, is that if the privatization of sports and convention-facilities management is to succeed, it should not be privatized to the principal tenants.

What to Watch Out For

The point in these four cases is not to reject all aspects of privatization but simply to show its limits. It is true that in New York City other factors – such as union strength, the scale of the city, and its politics and government – may have mitigated the potential privatization offers to other jurisdictions. Expanding the tools available to state and local – and even Federal – public managers can only yield good results. The wise application of privatization, however, is a difficult enterprise and should be weighed against local needs, the matrix of obligations and resources the manager confronts and the effects that privatizing may have on different groups in the jurisdiction or on other jurisdictions. One can be certain that New York City's experience requires public managers to ask questions and not to treat privatization in an ideological fashion. At least ten issues should be considered before policymakers and public managers make a commitment to privatize.

1. *Hidden monopolies.* Hidden monopolies mitigate the efficiencies expected from the breakup of a public monopoly. These monopolies could be in labor or in available vendors who might contract to deliver a service, or they could be in material necessary for the provision of a service. Surely, when there is a sole bid from one contractor, the potential for savings from contracting out will not be achieved. The potential for voucher systems to give parents an increased voice in education policy will likely be undermined in those states with a strong teachers' union. Hidden monopolies will work against the goals of privatizers. They will either have to accept this reality or be willing to bear the additional fiscal and political costs of breaking up a set of private monopolies in addition to the public monopoly.

2. *The continuing need to regulate.* Government will still need to regulate a delivered service even though it has been privatized, since privatizing a service does not leave the government without responsibilities. Issues of public safety, public health, and quality of service will arise. Private hospitals and nursing homes are regulated by every state, and it could be argued that they should be regulated even more. In the Northeast, where there is a strong tradition of private higher education, the private nature of colleges and universities does not preclude state regulation and licensing of higher educational facilities. In fact, it requires it. Meeting the public need through private action will inevitably lead to greater regulation of private activities, regardless of who delivers the service. There will always be a need to regulate such activities to ensure that the public need outweighs private interests. And costs will thus be incurred.

3. *The availability of a vendor.* Many advocates of privatization assume that a vendor will always be available to purchase a government asset or to contract the services needed to be delivered. But no organization wants to take on the responsibility to deliver services that, for the most part, lose money. No organization could deliver solid-waste management services for the city of New York – or any other large city in the United States for that matter. Despite the proposal by John Silber of Boston University to contract with the Boston School Board for the management of the school system by the university, no private organization has sufficient capital or human resources to deliver educational services to the children of any large city, county, or small state. No organization is large enough or has sufficient private capital to operate a privatized national airport or a system of air-traffic control. And these are comparatively easy cases when compared with the Social Security system, the U.S. Postal Service, or the publicly owned utilities throughout the country.

4. Transition costs. The theoretical literature on which privatization is based assumes perfect knowledge and mobility and that individuals will seek Pareto-optimality. Transition costs are rarely mentioned. But the public manager must face a different set of issues and assumptions, including the costs of disruption associated with transition, potential labor problems, vendors' failure to deliver, vulnerability to litigation caused by tort actions in transition, or poor management. Consider the potential loss of life — and the costs of litigation — during a transitional period if air-traffic control was privatized. Anyone who has ever overseen the transition from manual systems to integrated data base-management systems understands the loss of productivity, unintended costs, labor problems, and innumerable other issues that sometimes lead to questioning whether computerization was a good idea in the first place. Transition is a real, sometimes inestimable cost that could far outweigh the potential benefits of privatization. The public manager understands this. The theoretician may not.

5. Loss of economies of scale. Economies of scale may be lost if the operations of a government monopoly were transferred to many smaller private operating companies. The argument for *small* is efficiency through competition; the argument for *large* is economies of scale. Again, New York City refuse collection is an example. As the largest purchaser of sanitation trucks in the country, New York City can negotiate bulk sales with lower per unit costs. Moreover, the purchase is so attractive to manufacturers that they will cooperate with city officials in designing equipment particularly beneficial to New York. This allowed productivity managers to move from three-person trucks to two-person trucks in the Department of Sanitation, thus saving millions of dollars in labor costs and enhancing services. The fragmentation of educational services would also likely increase per pupil fixed costs for facilities, support services, transportation, nonpedogogic personnel costs, and other expenses. Although large public bureaucracies impede efficiency certain economies can be gained from the scale of public organizations. One option is to break up the organization to control bureaucratic inefficiencies. The other is better management to attain the full potential of scale.

6. The problem of estimating market value. If a public organization is to privatize (liquidate) some of its assets, how does it establish the price? The Federal government, for example, wishes to sell off certain oil properties in California, but their claim to market value is low when compared with standard measures of corporate analysis. In many areas of the country, localities are selling underutilized schools to developers. What is their value? Obviously, it could be argued that the price should be set in a competitive process. But if the asset is so large that only one or two consortia can bid — as in the case of Conrail — is the price set fair? And if the price is not at maximum yield, what has been gained by privatizing it? Is the government obtaining public-sector efficiency or subsidizing a private consortium by selling public assets at lower than market value? A traditional problem in public management has been the inability to set a price for the value of public services. In some cases, at least, the same may be true of public assets.

7. Contract compliance. How does the public manager ensure that a privatized service is meeting the terms of the contract? Although contracting out a service or management of a capital facility may offer certain benefits, it does not eliminate public responsibility. Contracting out day-care services does not end public responsibility for fiscal efficacy or—in the worst case—child abuse. In the latter case, is the government open to criminal or civil action because of the acts or omissions of its vendors? Like the regulation of services privatized, contracting out requires public monitoring of quality and the achievement of the public interest. If a locality contracts any services, an obligation remains that the providers abide by state and local health and education regulations, offer services as described in the contract, and review financial records. There will be auditing requirements, program evaluation, and investigatory needs if corruption or criminal activity is possible. All of this will add to costs and detract from services. As a practical matter, contract compliance will require a managerial unit to oversee vendor actions—another hidden cost of privatization.

8. *Lost opportunities.* In privatizing a service or an asset, the government may lose opportunities to effect better service or to act more efficiently. One reason the private sector may be perceived to be more efficient in the use of its resources is that there is an internal incentive for managers to lower per unit fixed costs and raise utilization rates of capital, i.e., profitability. There is no such incentive in the public sector. In fact, there is a disincentive. Even the effective public manager tends to see capital as it contributes to the provision of service he or she oversees, not its overall potential. Thus school buildings, sports and convention facilities, park land, and other government-held assets are underutilized, because the public manager is not focusing on maximum utilization but on minimization of cost in service delivery. In addition, effectiveness is rarely tied to utilization rates of capital, partly because—in most jurisdictions—the capital budgeting process is separate from the operating budget process. Maximum utilization of a sports facility, a convention center, a school, or a university could just as easily be obtained by public managers if they were more entrepreneurial. By privatizing either the asset or its management, options may be closed off that were never explored in the past.

9. *The costs of failure.* It is possible that many private actors who wish to take over public services will fail either from lack of quality—in which case government regulators will have to decide whether to cancel a contract—or because of bankruptcy, leaving clients without services. In either event, the public sector will have to provide the service as before privatization or bear the transition costs as the service is transferred to another private actor. It is clear that the service was of sufficient import for government to provide in the first place—before it was privatized—and so one can be fairly certain that there will be political pressure to guarantee service delivery. Again, a series of new start-up costs, transitional costs, legal costs, and the loss of service—a nonfiscal cost borne by clients—will follow as the inability of the private actor to meet public needs reminds public managers of their responsibility.

10. *The limits of governance.* Privatization redefines the relationship between what is public and what is private, what is of the commons and what is not. It

also changes the relative sets of social incentives and their relationship to the governing process. In the end, an unexpressed but present sense of legitimacy is also being privatized. From Adam Smith to current public-choice theorists, an ongoing effort has been made to provide an intellectual framework for the mobilization of private interests to the public purpose. In Smith's time, the application of the seeming reason of the market over the whims of the monarchy held out the promise of higher productivity and even "peace," the arbitrariness of the crowns being tempered by the reason of the market. The source of inefficiency and arbitrariness in public management today may well be the alliance of service providers, public-employee unions, and entrenched bureaucrats that has become the windmill against which privatizers are fighting. And yet economics does not exhaust governance. Privatization certainly offers the possibility that it will enhance efficiency and buttress the command, control, and accountability processes of the public sector. But it comes at the risk of a transition of allegiance from the state — in the French sense of *état* — to private actors. If the private actors are community-based, intermediate organizations, the outcome may be socially beneficial. If not, a sense of public legitimacy will have been squandered for marginal productivity enhancement — a trade-off that not only is unquantifiable but is even more dangerous to effective governance.

Conclusion

Privatization adds another policy instrument to the tools of the public manager and policymaker. If fully aware of the hidden costs, the potential for failure, and the inadequate guarantees for obtaining the efficiencies that theory indicates will accrue, policymakers can decide to privatize. For the public manager, it should not be a matter of ideology, however, but of informed judgment based on experience in public management and on policy analyses more exacting than is currently presented by advocates of privatization.

Americans' ideology often outpaces their behavior. George Kennan and Walter Lippmann saw it in foreign policy; Mark Roeloffs, on a domestic level. Americans may celebrate the market place, its ability to satisfy a wide variety of needs and desires, its tendency toward efficient distribution and utilization of resources, and its openness to those of sufficient means to obtain access. But Americans do not subject the things they hold most valuable to the market. The nurturing of children, the care of the elderly, the obtaining of basic educational skills, the provision of a minimum standard of living, minimum health care, and nutrition standards, for example, are not left to the market. For these, they rely on family, church, or state. It would, of course, be an exaggeration to claim that Americans delegate exclusively to family, church, and state the things they hold most dear and to the market those things they can do without; nevertheless, the point is made. Americans let the market establish the price of pork bellies, not the future of children.

It is true that Americans have always mobilized private interests for the public purpose. But they set limits on the process. Entrepreneurial generals, with self-financing and standing armies, would never be tolerated by the American people. And yet that fits the privatization model. Although privatization may provide a good tool for the public manager and add an interesting dimension to the political discourse, the concept — even after eventual clarification — will not offer as much as its advocates claim. Privatization will be applied only to things that the American people are not willing to risk; that includes every policy and program that several generations have put into place to protect themselves from the whims, uncertainties, instabilities, and unintended consequences of the marketplace.

Notes

1. Charles M. Tiebout, "A Pure Theory of Local Expenditures," *Journal of Political Economy* (October 1956): 416–24.

2. Albert O. Hirschmann, *Exit, Voice and Loyalty* (Cambridge, Mass.: Harvard University Press, 1970).

Privatizing Public Management:
The Grace Commission and Its Critics

WALTER F. BABER

The President's Private Sector Survey on Cost Control, better known as the Grace Commission, has provoked a spate of critical essays and enlivened the debate on efficiency and productivity in government. Not surprisingly, the work of the commission has renewed the debate over the utility of business concepts and practices in the public sector.

It has been decades since the private sector has been so well represented in Washington, D.C. Consequently, the debate over contracting out, service shedding, and other forms of privatization has expanded. It is being argued (at least implicitly) that the processes of decision and implementation in government can be subjected to the standards of the market. In short, the possibility has been raised that public management can be privatized.

The Grace Commission has provided a valuable opportunity to assess the quality of the public-private debate. The commission itself, however, did not address the issue. It simply asserted, in great detail and with considerable zest, the applicability of private-sector principles and procedures to public administration. And the commission has been criticized precisely for not stating or defending its assumptions on this score.

It is reasonable to assume that some critics of the commission have based their arguments on the premise that public-sector administrative problems are unique. And in taking exception to the commission report, they may have identified the hypothesized differences between public- and private-sector management that matter most to those who work in and around government. They may have also created the opportunity to bring some basic social-scientific research to bear on the issue by predicating their arguments on hypotheses subject to empirical investigation. This essay, then, will not critique the Grace Commission but its critics.

To assess the quality of criticism directed at the Grace Commission, it is necessary to create a simple data base. Using the Public Affairs Information Service, Business Periodicals Index, Reader's Guide to Periodical Literature, and Sage Public

Administration Abstracts, one can build a collection of references to the commission. These references can then be aggregated into generalized criticisms that will reveal the implicit distinctions between the private and public sectors.

Many of the references collected from these sources are either supportive of the Grace Commission or merely descriptive accounts of its activities. Many more, particularly those appearing in Federal government documents, contain only citations of the commission's findings. The remaining references assert, or strongly suggest, some inadequacy in the Grace Commission or its work. These criticisms can be characterized as personal, procedural, programmatic, or political.

Personalities and Procedures

Personal criticisms are directed at the character or behavior of key personnel on the Grace Commission — usually at J. Peter Grace. These personal criticisms are of three sorts. The first questions the basic integrity of the man. Grace has brought this upon himself to some extent by, for instance, claiming that food stamps are a Puerto Rican program. At best such remarks can be interpreted as evidence of a failure to recognize the uniquely public role of those acting in the name of government and the attention that public service draws to their behavior. A less charitable assessment would be that Grace has displayed an insensitivity to the plight of others or, worse yet, an overt form of racism. A second form of personal criticism questions Grace's qualifications to head an operation like the commission. In this vein, the *New Republic* observed that the president's efficiency expert "got where he is today by efficiently inheriting a shipping company."[1] The problem with both of these sorts of personal criticisms is that they do not speak to the substance of the issues raised by the Grace Commission. Grace might appear to some as a misanthrope of Dickensian proportions. But that in itself would not invalidate the work of a commission headed by him. And it must be noted that these ad hominem attacks shed no light on the question of whether private-sector management principles are applicable to the public sector.

A third category of personal criticism is more directly related to the substance of the Grace Commission's activity. In a hearing before the House Subcommittee on Economic Stabilization, Charles A. Bowsher, United States comptroller general, admitted to certain reservations about the Grace Commission. Bowsher expressed the fear that misstatements by commission members that major policy changes suggested by the commission were mere management improvements would engender such resentment that the positive aspects of the commission's work would be overlooked. Another criticism of this kind has been made by Charles T. Goodsell. Goodsell suggested that the commission and Grace himself have made broad and unsupported statements that are counterproductive even from the point of view of the commission's own goals. Specifically, Goodsell argued that "the report's contention that countless billions are wasted, plus Peter Grace's own habit of insisting that government is run horribly, undermines the public's faith in legitimate institutions" and further erodes morale in the Federal civil service.[2] Certainly, neither of these outcomes could advance the goal of efficiency in government. But, like the ad hominem arguments described earlier, these criticisms do not bear on the findings of the commission. And, though they may raise questions about the prudence and integrity of Grace and some of his subordinates, they do not address the differences between management in the public and private sectors.

Procedural criticisms of the Grace Commission differ from personal ones in that they relate to the methods employed by the commission in pursuing its goals. Writing under the pseudonym of Jeremiah Baruch, one Federal employee chastised the commission for its heavy use of anecdotal material. Goodsell has also complained that the issue-recommendation summaries accompanying the commission's proposals are flawed in that they typically begin with a "transparently biased question that contains its own answer."[3] But the most widespread procedural complaint has to do with the commission's methods for estimating cost savings. In a study of the commission report by the Congressional Budget Office and the General Accounting Office (CBO/GAO), dozens of commission procedures and estimates are questioned. But, more dramatically, the commission's own staff director, James Nance, a retired admiral, is reported to have assailed the validity of the task force's estimates and criticized its "slapdash ways of measuring savings" before resigning his post in March 1983.[4]

Related as these procedural criticisms are to the methods of analysis and presentation used by the commission, they cast doubt on the validity of the findings. But, like the personal criticisms, they do not directly address the issue of the applicability of private-sector management principles to the public sector. Sloppiness and incompetence, if that is what the Grace Commission is guilty of, are not unique to the private sector. And even if not all of the commission's 2,478 proposals are based on logically and empirically reliable analysis, that does not mean that they are inapplicable to the public sector. It only means that if they are applied they will fail to produce the desired results because they are incorrect. If neither the personal nor procedural criticisms directed at the Grace Commission advance the understanding of the differences between administration in the private and public sectors, the commission's programmatic and political critics should address this issue.

Programs and Politics

Programmatic criticisms of the Grace Commission usually relate to either the special management issues confronted by an agency at which some commission proposal is directed or, more generally, to the mission of that agency. Management issues raised by critics have to do with the complexity and interrelatedness of the tasks of public agencies, the problems of implementation that are unique to the public sector because of its scale and the complexity of its tasks, and the special characteristics and environment of public employees.

Many of the criticisms of the Grace Commission suggest that something is unique about the tasks facing public managers. *Complexity, ambiguity,* and *interrelated-*

ness are words often used in this connection. For example, the recommendation to allow local unit commanders in the armed forces to set both military and civilian personnel levels to reduce operating costs has been criticized for its potential interference with the rotational system that supports overseas deployments and the possibility that it might adversely affect the government's ability to meet treaty commitments. Commission recommendations on military retirement, it has been argued, ignore possible effects on manpower management, force profiles, and other personnel costs. These and other personnel recommendations directed at the military are also routinely criticized for failing to consider possible effects on combat readiness. Such realignments, based solely on budgetary criteria, could reduce military effectiveness because base facilities are often scaled in anticipation of emergency or wartime surge requirements. Closing these apparently underutilized bases would therefore reduce preparedness. Likewise, suggestions that some base commissaries be closed would increase consumer costs to military families. That could adversely affect rates of personnel retention, leading to increased training costs and, again, reduced preparedness.

Closely connected to these issues of complexity are suggestions that the commission has overlooked serious problems of implementation. For example, the commission proposal to reduce the size of government vehicle fleets fails to consider that over two-thirds of the vehicles owned by the Departments of Agriculture, Energy, and the Interior, as well as those of the Army Corps of Engineers and the Tennessee Valley Authority (TVA), are trucks used in remote areas where few opportunities for improved utilization exist. The commission also overlooked the fact that although shipping ammunition in fiberboard rather than bandoliers would reduce costs, it would also increase shipping damage and reduce readiness by increasing handling upon arrival. A commission proposal to require user charges for firewood cut in national forests suggests no way that the thousands of users (on millions of acres of land) can be identified and monitored; also, no cost-benefit analysis of the revenues generated and the costs of enforcement are provided. The CBO/GAO study of the commission's final recommendations is filled with a large number of these technical but telling points.

Finally, the Grace Commission has been criticized for ignoring the effect that their recommendations might have on the performance and retention of government employees. Changes in military pay, retirement, and benefits would be viewed by many as a reduction in compensation and would likely reduce retention rates, particularly among highly skilled enlisted personnel. The resulting increase in recruitment and training costs were not discussed by the commission. Also, the commission's recommendations for changes in the civilian General Schedule could affect as many as 188,000 Federal employees. Those individuals could be downgraded, resulting in lower morale, higher turnover, and lower levels of skills, all of which would lead to lower agency performance.

Another, somewhat broader, class of programmatic criticisms of the commission suggests that many of its findings are undesirable from the point of view of an agency's mission. The commission, for example, proposed a reduction in food-stamp benefits without addressing the issue of nutritional adequacy. It also proposed ways to improve debt-collection management in several Federal loan programs. But, as the CBO/GAO analysis of this recommendation demonstrated, the goal of improved debt collection conflicts directly with the mission of these loan programs in many instances.

Federal loan programs received further attention from the Grace Commission. The commission recommended that market practices be applied to direct Federal lending even though these programs are designed to benefit individuals who have been judged uncreditworthy by the market. Thus, by their very nature, these loans carry a high default risk. Additional default penalties, a typical market solution, might simply increase the delinquent borrower's financial burden and diminish his or her ability to repay. A commission suggestion that these direct loans be replaced with loan guarantees could reduce the ability of these programs to serve businesses and households with limited financial resources by providing a point at which market concerns could veto loans. The commission also recommended the consolidation of loans administered by the Department of Education and the elimination of its auxiliary loan programs. But the CBO/GAO study suggests that such a step could reduce Federal aid to students from the lowest income groups and deprive financial aid officers of the programmatic flexibility they need adequately to support these students.

Charles T. Goodsell provided a list of other commission proposals that also appear to ignore the missions of agencies. He argued that the proposals on Federal property management ignore the complexity, diversity, and symbolism of managing public buildings. He defended the Department of Energy against the charge that it employs an inefficient span of control by pointing out the agency's extensive use of contracting out. And he suggested that the commission's criticism of universal physical requirements in the military ignores the necessity for flexibility of assignment, especially in a time of crisis. Thus the programmatic criticisms of the commission, related both to issues of public management and to the missions of public agencies, begin to address the distinctions between the private and public sectors.

Political criticisms of the Grace Commission generally involve one or more of three concerns—a concern for law, fairness, or feasibility. Questions of legality are raised when commission recommendations might abrogate previous commitments undertaken by the government, deprive individuals of their constitutionally protected rights, or violate statute law.

Examples of legal concerns about Grace Commission proposals are most plentiful in the CBO/GAO analysis of its work. That study points out, for example, that allowing local unit commanders to set military and civilian personnel levels could violate American treaty commitments. A similar complaint is that proposals to cut civil-service retirement benefits would cause hardship for many retirees whose budgets are based on commitments by the government to provide a certain level of retirement income. This proposal also raises an issue of individual rights, since it might be challenged in court for depriving the retiree of his property right in his annuity. An identical criticism could be made of the commission's proposal to restrict short- and long-term disability benefits for Federal employees, since they possess a property right in their accumulated sick leave. The recommendations for improving income certification in means-tested programs may also entail the loss of the right of privacy without adequate safeguards against the improper disclosure of tax returns used for the purpose. Finally, statute law is purportedly endangered by the commission's recommendation that administrative law judges be prohibited from accepting new evidence on appeals of denials of disability benefits. This step, the CBO/GAO study asserts, would violate the Administrative Procedure Act of 1946.

Many criticisms dealing with the issue of fairness can also be found in the CBO/GAO study. For example, the proposal to limit growth in Federal spending for health care to the annual change in the gross national product (GNP) would either lower the level of health care (since inflation in this sector of the economy has consistently outpaced growth), or it would require recipients of these services to pay more, which many simply cannot do. Similar trade-offs with similarly negative implications would be forced on programs and services of the Defense Department and the National Institutes of Health. The commission's proposal to impose user fees for certain U.S. Coast Guard services would burden the fishing industry more than recreational boaters, increasing costs in that ailing industry by as much as 10 percent. A proposal to encourage electronic transfer of Federal funds by delaying checks mailed to individuals might present hardships to many of the elderly poor. Those recipients without bank accounts, currently 12 percent of the total, might be forced to accept bank service charges to ensure timely receipt of the checks to which they are entitled. And, finally, a proposal to eliminate excess hospital capacity by limiting certain reimbursements to hospitals with low occupancy rates could reduce access to care in rural areas that already lack many health services available in urban centers. All of these criticisms appeal to the basic sense of fairness. They also suggest that government programs are designed with the public-interest hypothesis in mind. But several other critics of the commission press the public-interest argument even more forcefully on this issue.

Fortune magazine, in its 16 May 1983 issue, expressed skepticism over the prospect of business people snooping around the agencies that regulate them. Goodsell has made the even more pointed comment that the Grace Commission seems to want citizens to pay not just what the services cost to provide but what the market will bear for government services. He attributed this to simple self-interest, the fear among business people of competition from government. He also cited a distinct bias in commission recommendations in favor of privatization and described it as another manifestation of self-interest.

A final category of political criticisms of the commission concerns feasibility. Here feasibility refers to the likelihood that a given proposal could be carried out without unacceptably negative side effects. The proposal to use tax returns to certify applicants for means-tested programs has been criticized for its potential to undermine the voluntary nature of the tax system, thus depriving government of the information necessary to certify applicants (or, in fact, to raise revenues). The suggestion to reduce progress payments to military contractors elicited from the CBO/GAO analysts the "marketwise" comment that this loss would have to be offset by some gain for contractors to maintain competition. More bluntly, Goodsell has argued that commission recommendations to cap entitlement programs are politically naive and that, for example, the closing of small, rural post offices would not be accepted, since it would contribute to the isolation of rural America from its government. All of these feasibility criticisms indicate, then, that the Grace Commission's proposals will fail because of their politically unacceptable consequences.

The Assumed Distinctions

Having cataloged various criticisms of the Grace Commission, it is now possible to suggest the authors' assumed distinctions between the private and public sectors. For this purpose, personal and procedural complaints about the work of the commission will be ignored because, whatever their value, they do not relate directly to the issue being considered.

It will be recalled that the programmatic criticisms of the commission are generally related to management and mission issues. In the area of public-agency management, problems of complexity, ambiguity, implementation, and the uniqueness of public-employee motivation are recurrent themes. The issues of mission raised by critics suggest that the commission's proposals miss the point because they ignore the fact that government programs are designed to create opportunities or capacities, compensate for market failures of some sort, or pursue ends that are largely symbolic in nature. The critics suggest, in sum, that government was created to do something fundamentally different from the things done by private-sector organizations.

Political criticisms suggest, by their reference to law and prior commitments, that government is held to a stricter standard of obligation and accountability than private industry. The issues of fairness (also raised in this connection) imply that government must operate in the public interest, heed appeals based on concepts of equity, and avoid even the appearance of a conflict of interest. And, finally, the argument that some commission proposals are politically infeasible assumes that government is more dependent than industry on the approbation of those outside of the organization. These assumed distinctions between the private and public sectors may be summarized as follows. As compared with the private sector, government:

- Faces more complex and ambiguous tasks.
- Has more difficulty implementing decisions.
- Employs people with different motivations.
- Is more concerned with securing opportunities or capacities.
- Is more concerned with compensating for market failures.
- Engages in activity with greater symbolic significance.

- Is held to stricter standards of previous commitment and legality.
- Has a greater responsibility to respond to issues of fairness.
- Must operate, or appear to operate, in the public interest.
- Must maintain some minimal level of public support above that required in private industry.

This list of the hypothesized differences between the private and public sectors is certainly not comprehensive. It probably does not even cover the entire range of differences assumed by the critics of the Grace Commission. But it does suggest which differences are most significant to the writers whose primary interest is in public management. It may be assumed, therefore, that these distinctions are relevant to the question of how widely private-sector management techniques and principles are applicable to the public sector. It cannot be assumed, however, that these hypothesized differences are empirically verifiable. In many cases, no methodology of inquiry is widely accepted. But it is possible to suggest some approaches to the empirical investigation of these difference hypotheses and to examine the existing evidence.

Empirical Approaches

Many of the distinctions implied or asserted by critics of the Grace Commission can be approached only inferentially, or by the use of indicators rather than direct measures. This does not mean that the notions are ill-conceived, only that the current state of social-scientific inquiry is not rigorous enough. An excellent example is the hypothesis that the tasks of public management are more complex and ambiguous than those in the private sector. One recent comparative study of public and private managers suggests that this difference may be more illusion than reality. Both sets of managers were found performing similar activities in a high-pressure environment that allowed them inadequate time for reflection and planning. Both were found to favor brief person-to-person interactions and oral communications. Both faced personnel shortages and rigid rules. And those in both groups thought of themselves as overburdened.[5] This study lends no support to the notion that public management is more complex or ambiguous than private management.

But a comparative case study of organization development experiences in both public and private organizations suggests an entirely different view. This work identified four key differences between the sectors. It pointed out that public organizations are characterized by multiple access points to multiple decision makers. A greater variety of individuals and groups with different and often mutually exclusive sets of interests, reward structures, and values were also found in public organizations. The lines of command in public organizations were also described as containing competing identifications and affiliations. And, finally, public organizations were found to be plagued by a slippage between managerial levels owing to the weakness of linkages between political and career officials.[6] This comparative study suggests that public managers confront a more complex and ambiguous task environment.

The question of differences in public- and private-employee motivation has been the subject of considerably more empirical research. A survey of public and private managers in Atlanta, Georgia, reported no difference in employee motivations. But other studies suggest that public employees are more risk averse than those in the private sector, with risk aversion measured as an index of insurance owned, use of seat belts, and smoking and drinking habits. Another survey of employee attitudes found stability to be most highly prized among state employees and least prized among those in the business sector. Results like these constitute the conventional wisdom on the subject of employee values and motivations in the public sector. But do the behaviors generally used to measure risk aversion actually reflect people's values, or do they simply indicate higher levels of education in public-sector employment? And is a finding that state employees value stability evidence of their innate conservatism, or does it merely suggest that they enjoy less of a universally prized commodity and therefore value it more highly? Recent findings suggest that security is less important to public employees and that, in fact, self-actualization has taken precedence over all other values in their minds. Clearly, the fact that widely accepted methods exist for studying the attitudes and motivations of public employees has not produced a consensus on the issue.

The contention that government is more concerned with securing opportunities or capacities than with producing products or services seems to be almost impossible to measure. But some indicators can be suggested. A concept of "values held in reserve" might be developed that would include capital resources retained by organizations, both private and public, against future use. This concept would have to include any undistributed corporate reserves and intentionally unused productive capacity in private industry. In the public sector an obvious example would be the reserve military capacity of the armed forces. If these values held in reserve were a greater percentage of net worth in the public sector, the hypothesis of an opportunity orientation in government would find empirical support. But no such comparison has been undertaken.

That government is more concerned than private industry with compensating for failures of the market seems self-evident. But this social function was once pursued almost entirely by nonprofit organizations. And it must be remembered that government has not rejected the use of market mechanisms in its attempt to counteract market dysfunctions. Government interventions in economic processes, in this country at least, generally take the form of manipulations of the market rather than the substitution of authoritative decisions. The issue is therefore not one of whether government's involvement in the economy is different but whether that obvious difference means that different decision rules and management practices are required. A similar question could be asked about the notion that government engages in activities with greater symbolic significance. It is probably true, but is it significant from a management viewpoint?

The argument that government is held to a stricter standard of legality might be addressed by discovering whether government agencies are more likely than private corporations to be defendants in civil or criminal court proceedings. Aside from the obvious technical problems with such an approach, it may miss the point altogether. The question is not who gets into more trouble but for whom is it more important to stay out of trouble. Everyone is aware that some major American corporations have made decisions about product-safety problems by weighing the costs of removing hazards to consumers against the losses they might incur if consumers are injured. These events seem to suggest that some businesses are not merely less sensitive to their legal obligations but actually contemptuous of them. But this kind of evidence is anecdotal, often based on experience with the very largest firms that routinely submit many issues to cost-benefit analysis. A better approach might be to discover whether reasons exist for public organizations to pay greater attention to issues of legality. This leads to one last set of differences between the private and public sectors.

Critics of the Grace Commission have suggested that management in the public sector is different because government must respond to issues of fairness, operate in the public interest, and maintain a level of public support greater than that required of private corporations. Again, all of these assertions accord with the conventional wisdom. But can any of them be verified empirically and, if so, do they make a difference at the level of management? This question confronts one of the most vexing issues in the analysis of human institutions: From the point of view of the individual's behavior, does the purpose of the organization matter?

Some empirical studies suggest that the differences in organizational mission between the private and public sectors do make a difference at the level of the individual. One survey of attitudes among job seekers found that those desiring positions in nonprofit organizations were more people-oriented, more likely to value qualities like self-acceptance, responsibility, flexibility, and friendliness, were less concerned with economic issues, and were more inclined to see themselves as close and warm in their interpersonal relations. Clearly, a process of self-selection is at work that may produce a different sort of employee in the public sector. Another indication that political issues (such as fairness) affect the work world of the public manager can be found in comparative studies of wages. Public-sector pay was found to be more equalitarian than pay in the private sector. A survey of government and business managers found that those in the public sector perceived a weaker relationship between performance and rewards. It also found that public managers feel more constrained by formal personnel procedures. All of these findings reflect the impact of a civil-service system that attempts to pursue both managerial and political goals. Finally, a comparison of female supervisors in business and government found that government presents a task environment that is more bureaucratized, more formalistic, and more structure oriented than that found in the private sector. Such a result can be attributed to the greater concern for accountability and responsiveness to political concerns in public organizations. So, in spite of the fact that the differences between public and private organizations are difficult to quantify, it is not nearly so difficult to measure the effect of those differences on the circumstances of public managers. But, of course, one must take the trouble to do so. It is here that public-administration academicians have failed their practitioner colleagues. But, ironically, the Grace Commission itself may have provided the best evidence possible of the differences between the public and private sectors and the importance of those differences for management procedures.

Reflexive Significance of the Grace Commission

One remark frequently heard about the Grace Commission is that its work demonstrates a lack of sensitivity to those in the agencies being studied. What this remark often amounts to is an accusation that the members of the commission have failed to understand the organizational culture and environment of government. It also suggests that those who lack a commitment to the public agenda are ill-equipped to aid in its pursuit. These are, of course, political judgments that are not universally shared. The United States is far enough away from the Great Depression, it seems, for some people to believe once again that something about private business makes it virtually infallible. But the Grace Commission demonstrated that it is impossible to separate management and policy. The commission was specifically charged to do so, but its report implies that what any organization is supposed to do imposes constraints on how it chooses to do it.

Government is different at the level of management because it is different at the level of policy. Hal G. Rainey has captured this relationship empirically in his study of the major differences in the perception of incentives in government and business. He concluded that "the enduring nature of these differences is related to characteristics of public administration which complicate the generic administrative problem of trading off between accountability and individual discretion." Public administration emphasizes "explicit, consistent, reviewable procedures" as well as the necessity that "technical decisions be buffered against excessive intrusion of political criteria." It is as if government is, and must be, constantly at war with itself and yet constantly responsive to citizen demands. The inability of the Grace Commission to grasp this essential truth and the inefficiencies and contradictions it implies is perhaps the best possible illustration of the differences between public and private management as well as the dangers inherent in the privatization of public management.

NOTES

1. "Amazing Grace," *New Republic*, 10 February 1984, 6.
2. Charles T. Goodsell, "The Grace Commission: Seeking Efficiency for the Whole People?" *Public Administration Review* 44 (May-June 1984): 198.
3. Ibid., 199.
4. "Grace Under Pressure," *Fortune*, 16 May 1983, 24.
5. Alan Lau, Arthur Newman, and Laurie Brodling, "The Nature of Management Work in the Public Sector," *Public Administration Review* 40 (September-October 1980): 513-20.
6. Robert Golembiewski, "Organization Development in Public Agencies: Perspectives on Theory and Practice," *Public Administration Review* 29 (May-June 1969): 367-77.

Status of State and Local Privatization

PHILIP E. FIXLER, JR.
ROBERT W. POOLE, JR.

State and local governments in the United States, more than any-where else in the world, are serving as laboratories for privatization. Virtually every type of service provided by governments — ranging from ambulances to zoning — is being provided privately in one form or another somewhere in the United States. For many "public services," such as residential garbage collection, vehicle towing, and day-care centers, private provision is probably more common than government provision. And the extent of privatization appears to be growing rapidly.

State and local privatization began rather quietly with the contracting out of "housekeeping" and support services — janitorial services in government buildings, vehicle maintenance, computer-center operation, and so on. Since government itself was the customer, it was less controversial to engage in a "make-or-buy" decision for these routine sorts of services. But the cost savings and sometimes greater accountability of private service provision soon led to an expanded scope for privatization. Moreover, because state and local governments were hit by the tax revolt of the late 1970s and the leveling off in Federal aid of the early 1980s, they began to look more favorably on shedding certain services to private enterprise, like ambulance service, garbage collection and disposal, and hospitals, or at least contracting them out. The 1981 tax law changes (especially the new, shorter depreciation lifetimes) also contributed to an expansion of privatization, with "turnkey" projects to finance, design, build, and operate costly infrastructure projects.

What has been learned about privatization from the ongoing experiments in the fifty states over the past decade? How likely is the continuation of the privatization revolution?

Growth and Cost Savings

There is considerable evidence to support impressionistic signs that privatization has grown tremendously in the United States since the early 1970s. Probably the best evidence is provided by a National Center for Policy Analysis (NCPA) comparison of the 1973 survey by the Advisory Commission on Intergovernmental Relations (ACIR) and the 1982 survey by the International City Management Association (ICMA).[1] Although the surveys differed in several respects, including sample size, service definitions, and number of respondents, NCPA's analysis of seventeen services covered in both surveys indicates significant growth in at least one privatization method—contracting out with for-profit firms. The NCPA analysis indicated that from 1973 to 1982 "the percentage growth ranged from 43% for refuse collection to 3,644% for data processing (record keeping)."[2]

Other indicators for specific services also support the proposition that there has been significant growth in privatization. A survey conducted by the Michigan Road Builders Association, for example, found that the state and local contracting out of road-repair and other highway services grew by 10 percent in the last three years. A comparison of the value of bonds sold to finance wastewater-treatment privatization projects in 1984 and 1985 shows a 400 percent increase. And an analysis of landfill surveys reported in 1975 and 1984 indicates an approximate 129 percent increase in contracting out for solid-waste disposal in landfills.

The 1982 ICMA survey also indicates that certain privatization methods are used more frequently in particular functional areas. For example, the predominant privatization method in public works-transportation, public safety, and support services is contracting out to for-profit firms. The three most frequently used methods for the private provision of health and human services are contracting out with for-profit firms and nonprofit organizations and relying on volunteers. The four most frequently used methods for private delivery of services for recreation, parks, and cultural arts are contracting with for-profit, nonprofit, and neighborhood organizations and enlisting volunteers. With regard to public utilities, franchising and contracting out to for-profit firms are the predominant methods.

One of the major factors leading to the growth of privatization has undoubtedly been the increasing number of state and local governments that have discovered the significant cost-savings potential of privatization. Almost every single quantitative, empirical study has confirmed this phenomenon, including a 1975–76 study of solid-waste collection sponsored by the National Science Foundation, a 1977 study of fire-protection services conducted by the Institute for Local Self Government, a 1983 study of solid-waste collection in Canada by researchers at the University of Victoria, a 1984 study of school bus transportation in Indiana by researchers at Ball State University and elsewhere, and a 1984 study of Federal support services in the Department of Defense as reported by the Office of Federal Procurement.

A 1986 study of urban bus transportation by researchers at the University of California, Irvine, found that privately owned systems were more efficiently operated and required less in subsidies than publicly owned systems.[3] However, the study also found that there was no significant difference in costs when publicly owned systems contracted out the *management* function for urban bus transportation. However, the authors of the study suggested that this exception to the findings of other studies of contracting out could be due to the high number of fixed-cost or percentage-of-revenue contracts and the fact that the management function is a small, nonlabor-intensive portion of a larger service function. This latter point is supported by the fact that there is some evidence that contracting out the *entire* transit function leads to cost savings of about 50 percent.

The most comprehensive study of contracting out was conducted by Ecodata, Inc., for the U.S. Department of Housing and Urban Development.[4] The 1984 Ecodata study compared government versus contractor delivery of eight public services by cities in the Southern California area. The study compared twenty different cities for each service, ten providing the service in-house and ten using contractors. For seven of eight services, direct government provision was 37 to 96 percent more costly than when provided by contractors. The one exception was payroll processing. But, as with the transit study, the researchers suggested that there could be special causes. Payroll processing, in contrast to other services, is not so much a separate, distinct service, because the cities themselves provide and process the raw data and distribute the checks. Thus, as with transit, the anomaly could be explained by the fact that the contractors were handling only a portion of a larger function and had no real comparative advantage. In sum, there is moderately strong quantitative evidence that privatization has grown dramatically and that it has yielded significant cost savings for a variety of services.

Review by Functional Area

As indicated above, routine support services are among the first areas to which privatization and partial privatization have been applied. Nineteen percent of the cities and counties responding to the ICMA's 1982 survey indicated, for instance, that they contract out for building and grounds maintenance with for-profit firms. There are many examples of cost savings from contracting out building and grounds maintenance. At the local level, Little Rock, Arkansas, contracted out its city hall janitorial services in 1977, cutting its total costs for this work by almost 50 percent;[5] Cypress, California, saved 20 percent, and Phoenix, Arizona, 57 percent. At the state level, Oregon State University, contracting out building maintenance to a for-profit firm, saved about 21 percent. California and Pennsylvania contract out for the cleaning of some state buildings.

Data processing is another support service often contracted out at the local level. A comparison of responses to the 1973 ACIR and 1982 ICMA surveys indicates that the rate of increase in contracting out for this service has been nothing short of phenomenal—3,600 percent. One of the first areas in this trend was Orange County, California. After contracting out its data-processing function in 1973, the county saved about 33 percent, according to one estimate.

Fleet maintenance and management is yet another housekeeping service that has been contracted out. In the 1982 ICMA survey, 28 percent of the reporting cities and counties contracted out with for-profit firms for fleet management and vehicle repair. An even higher number contracted out for maintenance of specialized vehicles: 30 percent for emergency vehicles and 31 percent for heavy vehicles.

Gainesville, Florida, began contracting out its vehicle repair work several years ago, with an estimated savings of 20 percent.[6]

The provision of food service in public facilities is another partially privatized support service. Many city and county cafeterias are franchised or contracted out, but perhaps more significant is the contracting out of food service in public institutions, such as schools, correctional facilities, and hospitals. One special district, the Evergreen School District near Vancouver, Washington, began contracting out for food service as far back as 1976, after many years of in-house provision. In contrast to the years of deficits under in-house provision, contract provision allowed Evergreen to operate in the black after the first year. In Oregon, Multnomah County contracts out food service at its correctional facility.

In recent years, after the success that many jurisdictions have had contracting out routine housekeeping services, some jurisdictions are beginning to apply this privatization method to higher-level support services, including those traditionally provided by professional-level personnel, such as attorneys and accountants. Probably the most frequently contracted-out support function is that of legal services. A comparison of responses to the 1973 ACIR survey and the 1982 ICMA survey indicates a 421 percent increase in the contracting out of legal services. According to the 1982 ICMA survey, 48 percent of the reporting cities and counties contracted out for legal services. Many small towns and cities traditionally contract out with local law firms to obtain legal representation and even a city attorney. But now larger jurisdictions are finding it advantageous to contract out public legal services normally provided in-house. For instance, Los Angeles County contracts out for some of its public-defender services. Shasta County, California, turned over its entire public-defender function to a local law firm after a study indicated that the cost of providing the service in-house was about one-third more than contract service. And in Washington state, at least seven local governments contract out for some public defender services.

Tax collection is also a professional-level support function that is frequently contracted out. The 1982 ICMA survey reported that tax-bill processing was contracted out by 10 percent of cities and counties, assessing by 27 percent, and delinquent tax collection by 18 percent. For property-tax assessment, an explicit industry has developed in many states. And "although some states forbid cities or counties to contract out for this service, Ohio actually requires contracting."[7]

Recreation and parks is another major functional area of state and local activity to which privatization and partial privatization have been applied. According to the 1982 ICMA survey, 19 percent of the reporting cities and counties used volunteers to provide recreation services and 12 percent contracted out with nonprofit organizations. For the operation and maintenance of recreation facilities, however, the predominant privatization methods were different: 9 percent contracted with nonprofit firms, 8 percent with for-profit organizations, and only 4 percent relied on volunteers. A comparison of responses to the 1973 ACIR and the 1982 ICMA surveys indicates that contracting out for recreation facilities increased by a dramatic 1,757 percent.

A major impetus for the contracting out of recreation services and the operation and maintenance of recreational facilities in California was Proposition 13. Most of the contracting out of recreation services has traditionally been to nonprofit organizations. The Hesperia Recreation and Park District, for instance, cut its budget by 37 percent by contracting out with the local YMCA for the provision of recreation services. But several California jurisdictions contract out with *for-profit* organizations for recreation and parks services. La Mirada, California, for example, began contracting out its recreation and park services to a for-profit firm in 1980, after the revenues of the independent park district previously supplying the service were cut by 50 percent.

Public utilities constitute another major functional area to which some type of privatization has been applied. There has been some contracting out of utility support-services, such as utility billing and meter reading to for-profit firms. Again, comparing responses to the 1973 ACIR and 1982 ICMA surveys, the contracting out of utility billing to for-profit firms increased by some 65 percent over that period. The 1982 ICMA survey indicates that 12 percent of reporting jurisdictions contracted with for-profit firms for this service, 8 percent had franchises providing service, and 1 percent contracted with nonprofit organizations. Lake Oswego, Oregon, contracts out utility meter reading to a private for-profit firm that uses innovative methods, such as requiring its readers to use motorcycles and to make tape recordings for later transcription.

Another major application of privatization to utility service is that of contracting out the operation and maintenance of water-supply or treatment to for-profit companies. In Pennsylvania, for example, a number of municipalities that took over regulated water companies supplying their area continued to contract out for water-system operation and maintenance. As a matter of fact, the Pennsylvania-based American Water Works Company, manages government-owned water and sewer facilities for more than 95 communities and serves over 500,000 people in Pennsylvania.

Recently, according to representatives of the American Water Works Association, several jurisdictions in other states have begun to contract out for the operation and maintenance of water supply or waste-water-treatment facilities, including Chandler and Scottsdale, Arizona; Decatur, Illinois; and Pampa, Texas. Several states have passed enabling legislation for wastewater-treatment privatization projects, including Alabama, Arizona, Arkansas, California, Colorado, Georgia, Louisiana, New Jersey, New York, Tennessee, and Utah.[8]

Public works and transportation are probably the general functions to which privatization techniques have been applied the most. Unquestionably, solid-waste collection and disposal is one of the earliest and most basic public-works services contracted out to the private sector. The most comprehensive United States study on the subject, sponsored by the National Science Foundation, indicates that as of 1976–77, about 62 percent of United States cities relied on some form of private provision of residential solid-waste collection (e.g., contract, franchise, private-competitive), although municipal agencies served 61 percent of the United States population. Major urban areas relying, at least in part, on some form of private collection include Atlanta, Houston, Los Angeles County, San Francisco, and Wichita.

As indicated earlier, there has also been a significant increase in contracting out for the operation and maintenance of landfills. A survey conducted by the Association of State and Territorial Waste Management Officials (ASTWMO) and *Waste Age* magazine in 1985 indicates that 444, or 6.4 percent, of publicly owned landfills are contracted out.

Contracting out has also been extensively applied to a variety of other basic public-works services. According to the 1982 ICMA survey, reporting cities and counties contract out 30 percent of their tree trimming, 26 percent of their street repair, and 9 percent of their street cleaning to for-profit firms. At the state level, there is also evidence of increased contracting of highway sweeping and repair. The state of Washington, for example, contracts out for some highway sweeping. And North Carolina has recently initiated a pilot program for the routine mowing of highway strips, cleaning up rest areas, and operating some drawbridges.

In the last few years there has been a significant increase in the use of another form of privatization for certain public works — waste-water treatment, resource recovery, and water supply. Essentially, this form of privatization involves a significantly greater role for the private sector, beyond mere operation and maintenance of existing facilities. It means the provision of "full services" on a "turnkey" basis, that is, financing, design, construction, operation and maintenance, and sometimes even ownership. A number of factors brought this about, including increasingly stringent environmental regulation, tax incentives for private infrastructure development, and a decline in Federal funding for these types of projects.

For these reasons, local jurisdictions across the country have initiated infrastructure privatization projects. Chandler, Arizona, began the first major waste-water privatization project when it entered into a service contract with a large engineering firm to purchase treatment-reclamation services from a $23 million, 5-million-gallons-per-day treatment plant to be constructed. At least fifteen jurisdictions have begun steps toward similar privatization projects since that time, including Auburn, Alabama; Baltimore, Maryland; Baton Rouge, Louisiana; Dowington, Pennsylvania; East Aurora, New York; Gilbert, Arizona; Greenville, South Carolina; Hubbard, Ohio; Jefferson Parish, Louisiana; Oklahoma City, Oklahoma; San Luis Obispo, California; Smithville, Utah; Snyderville, Utah; and Springboro, Ohio.

Transit is another major service area to which privatization and contracting out have been extensively applied. Some of the principal reasons include the increasing perception of the failure of local bus and fixed-rail systems, deregulation of smaller forms of transit like minibuses and taxicabs, and the discovery of the cost effectiveness of contracting out for some transit services.

The factor that characterizes all types of government-operated or -regulated transit services is probably increasing costs. Largely because of increasing costs, many jurisdictions decided to contract out for special transit services to meet low-volume demand, such as service on Sunday or at night and service to the elderly and the handicapped. Phoenix, Arizona, for instance, replaced costly, subsidized Sunday bus service with dial-a-ride service provided by a private taxi company in 1981. The city subsidy for this service has been reduced by an estimated 500 percent because of this switchover.[9]

Many cities' transit districts have become dissatisfied with the cost of municipal bus service, and several have begun contracting out or sponsoring peak-hour commuter service, including Houston, Los Angeles, and San Francisco. The Dallas transit district, however, leads the country. It contracts with Trailways for extensive suburban bus service involving hundreds of buses. And private (subscription, subsidized, or unsubsidized) commuter-bus service exists or has recently begun in Boston, Chicago, Los Angeles, and New York.

Westchester County, New York, contracts with sixteen bus companies to provide countywide service. The cost of operating Westchester County's contract buses is about 50 percent less than that of comparable New York City transit district buses.

Another major method of fostering the private provision of urban transit is deregulation. Transit deregulation is a growing trend. The Federal Trade Commission (FTC), for example, reported on a study indicating that from 1977 through 1982, 16 of 103 cities surveyed reduced entry controls, while only 3 increased them; 17 deregulated fares and 13 eliminated controls over fares; and 4 changed from mandatory to maximum fares. Cities deregulating entry or price included Berkeley, Sacramento, and San Diego, California; Charlotte, North Carolina; Phoenix and Tucson, Arizona; and Seattle, Washington.

Privatization is also being increasingly applied to another major functional area — health and human services. Nonprofit organizations seem to be providing more and more of these services. Recently there has been increasing interest in expanding the role of for-profit organizations in providing them. One manifestation of this trend is the willingness of nonprofit organizations to set up for-profit subsidiaries.

One of the first services that many local governments contracted out or otherwise privatized was hospitals. A comparison of responses to the 1973 ACIR and 1982 ICMA surveys indicates that the contracting out of hospital management and operation to for-profit firms increased some 53 percent. According to the 1982 ICMA survey, 25 percent of the reporting cities and counties contracted with for-profit firms; 24 percent contracted with nonprofit organizations; and 4 percent subsidized private hospitals. Several California counties, for example, contract out the management and operation of their hospitals to private organizations. Somona County, for instance, reduced its subsidy by more than 50 percent in the first year after turning over the operation of its county hospital to a for-profit chain.

In some cases, local public hospitals have been converted into private, nonprofit entities. At least eight major government-owned hospitals have been converted into private, nonprofit hospitals since 1980. Others have awarded management contracts to for-profit firms. And in a few cases, local governments — for example,

York County, South Carolina, and Detroit, Michigan — have turned over their hospitals almost completely to for-profit companies.

A recent trend is for some local governments and state universities to lease or otherwise contract out their teaching hospitals to the private sector. The most notable example is the University of Louisville, which leases its hospital to the Humana Corporation, renowned for its implantation of artificial hearts.

Several states also contract out for the management and operation of specialized state hospitals or health facilities. Florida, for example, contracts out the management and operation of its South Florida State Hospital, and Kentucky contracts out to a for-profit firm the management and operation of one of its four facilities for the mentally retarded.[10]

Other specialized health services in which there is increasing private interest include community mental-health services and alcohol-drug rehabilitation. According to the 1982 ICMA survey, 38 percent of reporting cities and counties contracted out for the operation of mental health and retardation programs or facilities to nonprofit organizations; 15 percent subsidized private organizations; and 6 percent contracted with for-profit firms. For drug-alcohol treatment programs, 38 percent contracted with nonprofit organizations, 12 percent subsidized private organizations, and 6 percent contracted with for-profit firms.

Public safety is the last, and probably most controversial, major function to which privatization is being applied. Fire protection is one example. Of course, essentially private volunteer organizations protect thousands of small towns and rural settlements. But the private provision of fire protection by for-profit firms is increasingly controversial. Today, even though the cost-savings potential is high, out of a total of thirty-six public agencies that contract out for private fire protection, only a few jurisdictions actually contract out for *general* (residential and commercial) fire protection, including Scottsdale, Arizona; Elk Grove, Illinois; and Hall County, Georgia. This, of course, is due to the intense political opposition to private fire protection. As a result, the latest trend is to contract out for specialized services, such as fire protection at airports. Five jurisdictions currently rely on private firms to protect their airports, including Sioux City, Iowa; Kansas City, Kansas; Manchester, New Hampshire; Reno, Nevada; and Dane County, Wisconsin.

Corrections is another controversial service for the application of privatization. At least three local governments now contract out for the management and operation of local jails to for-profit firms, including Hamilton County, Tennessee; Butler County, Pennsylvania; and Bay County, Florida. Ramsey County, Minnesota, contracts out the operation of its local women's prison to a nonprofit organization.

Several states, including New Jersey and Rhode Island, already contract out for the management and operation of juvenile corrections centers. Other states are interested in privatizing their prisons. Three Western states — Montana, New Mexico, and Texas — have passed enabling legislation to allow their cities and counties to contract out the operation of local jails. The governor of North Carolina has proposed a minimum-security prison for adult males. And Kentucky has gone as far as issuing an official request-for-proposal for a private, maximum-security prison. California's Corrections Department, however, has taken the lead. It recently contracted out the management and operation of several minimum-security, return-to-custody facilities for parole violators to for-profit firms.

Finally, police services are undoubtedly the most controversial public-safety application of privatization. Yet about one-fourth of the country's large and medium-sized police departments already deputize or give special police powers to private-security personnel. In Oregon, North Carolina, and Maryland the governor can designate private-security personnel as "special policemen" under certain circumstances. In one recent survey, 44 percent of public law-enforcement executives reported that local or state governments in their jurisdictions contract out with private agencies for the protection of public property, including schools, libraries, hospitals, parks, and government buildings. Private for-profit firms provide security for public buildings and facilities in Denver, Houston, Los Angeles County, New York, San Francisco, and Seattle.

Jurisdictions that have contracted out for the patrol of their public parks or housing authorities include San Diego and Norwalk, California; Saint Petersburg, Florida; and Lexington, Kentucky. Other jurisdictions contract out for traffic control or parking-lot enforcement, including the Arizona Department of Transportation, the University of Hawaii at Hilo, and the Eastern Idaho Regional Medical Center. Finally, there is some degree of contracting out for prisoner transport. For example, Santa Barbara County, California, contracts with private firms to transport some prisoners from faraway jurisdictions.

While there are no United States jurisdictions now contracting out for general police service, some have successfully done so in the past.[11] Currently, the only truly private police in the United States are in San Francisco, where the police commission licenses private individuals trained at the police academy to provide police-patrol services along certain "beats." The private police licensees, who are uniformed and armed, are hired by merchants in their patrol areas.

Overcoming Privatization Problems

While the dramatic growth in privatization has been quantitatively demonstrated and innumerable success stories published, a review of some privatization failures is certainly appropriate in any broad survey of the subject. Criticisms of privatization by the American Federation of State, County and Municipal Employees (AFSCME), for example, have focused on a number of problem areas, including unrealized cost-savings, low quality, corruption, lack of control and accountability, and reduced services to the poor.[12]

Unquestionably, as AFSCME and other critics have observed, contractors may on occasion bid too low to obtain a government contract and subsequently try to raise the price to make up for initial losses. AFSCME refers to this as "low-balling." If unable to recover initial losses, contractors may default on the contract, thus requiring the governments that depended on them to expand additional reserves in restarting public departments or in obtaining new contractors.

The city of Garden Grove, California, encountered such a situation. The city began contracting out its street-sweeping service in about 1977. After the city awarded a five-year contract, the contractor requested renegotiation because of substantial increases in the cost of labor and fuel. It was also clear that the contractor might default on the contract. The city knew it could not quickly bring the service in-house or obtain a contractor who could provide all of the service needed by the city. City officials feared significant price increases in the future.

But Garden Grove resolved the problem by dividing the city into two districts and rebidding the service. By doing so, the city was able to generate greater competition, because smaller bidders were capable of handling the service when the contract area was reduced in size. Moreover, the city reduced its dependence on a single contractor. The city public-works director was satisfied that the city had met its objective of increasing competition and reducing its vulnerability to price increases and service defaults.

Another potential problem is that of reduced quality of service. One approach to dealing with this problem is, of course, to develop detailed specifications and performance standards. In some cases, however, the contractor may be unable to comply with these requirements. Cypress, California, faced such a problem in contracting out janitorial service. After terminating one contractor, the city determined that it should modify its bidding process so that the bid would be awarded to the lowest, qualified bidder and not necessarily just the lowest bidder. Although there were minor losses in flexibility because of contracting out, the city was generally satisfied with the quality of service, and it estimated a cost savings of 20 percent.

The lack of accountability and control are other potential problems with privatization. These problems, of course, can occur in public as well as private organizations. The civil-service system, for instance, may prevent policymakers and public executives from imposing accountability and exerting control over a work force delivering a service. If a contract is badly drawn, similar problems could occur with contractors providing a service. But various jurisdictions have developed techniques that could help ensure accountability and control. Cypress, California, for instance, has the right to ask its custodial-services contractor to remove unsatisfactory employees and to deduct the cost of doing incomplete work from the contractor's fee. Gainesville, Florida, built incentives and penalties into its vehicle-maintenance contract. Hall County, Georgia, requires its contract fire chief to report to the city manager to discuss and resolve management problems and issues. La Mirada, California, requires its recreation-services contractor to take part in city staff meetings. Loma Linda, California, can adjust the contract price downward if its landscape maintenance contractor fails to perform the specified work. And Pasadena, California, requires its landscape-maintenance contractors to submit daily work schedules to city monitors. These are just a few of the techniques developed by United States local governments to enhance accountability and control.

Corruption can also be a problem when contracting out a service. AFSCME, for example, cites dozens of cases where the contracting out process was corrupted by payoffs, bid-rigging, price-fixing, and kickbacks. Such incidents have occurred in some of the country's largest cities, including Chicago, New York, and Philadelphia. Yet one must remember that there are tens of thousands and perhaps hundreds of thousands of contracts awarded each year by state and local governments. An in-depth, systematic analysis would likely indicate that although corruption is a problem, it is not a major one.

One example of corruption cited by AFSCME was the award of Union City, New Jersey, contracts to businesses owned by the mayor. But this obvious conflict-of-interest could have been easily avoided by requiring bidders to have no connection with current city employees or officials.

Corruption and many other problems are often due to flaws in the bidding or contracting-out process itself and are easily correctable. "The basic answer to the potential-corruption problem is to make use of rigorous, open-bidding procedures. Such procedures include a clearly defined Request for Proposal, spelling out the specific service requirements, written evaluation criteria, public access to all meetings and hearings, and written records dealing with the selection process."[13] An excellent source of workable procedures is *Contracting Municipal Services*, edited by John Tepper Marlin.[14]

A final problem that might arise in connection with the use of privatization is that of ensuring service to the poor. This is not so much a problem when government contracts out a service, because the service remains a tax-financed activity. However, when a privatization method that entails financing by service users is implemented (e.g., user fees, franchises, service shedding), a problem could arise — the same problem that faces many local governments that transfer their public hospitals to the private sector. One frequent strategy to cope with this problem is to reserve a portion of the proceeds from the sale to finance services to the poor. The state of Michigan used another approach in regard to patients treated at the Detroit General Hospital after that city turned over the hospital to a private organization. Michigan "agreed to reimburse the hospital for the costs of treating indigent patients not covered by federal Medicaid."[15] The use of vouchers is another possible method of dealing with this problem.

Barriers to Privatization

There are several potential obstacles to the continued growth of privatization. Two of these are in the hands of Congress. Federal tax laws greatly accelerated the move toward private development of infrastructure projects during the past few years. But critics have attacked the use of tax-exempt bond financing, investment tax credits, and short depreciation schedules that have helped make these projects attractive to private firms. The 1986 tax-reform legislation limits the extent of tax-exempt revenue bonds, repeals the investment tax credit, and increases depreciation periods. Some projects that would have worked out under the old laws will no longer do so, and hence, will not be built by private enterprise. Instead, being built by municipalities, they will remain off the tax rolls, generating neither corporate income taxes nor local property taxes. In the name of reducing "tax expenditures," the Federal government will actually lose revenue to the extent that the changes succeed in discouraging privatization.

Another potential barrier is Congress's circumvention of the Gramm-Rudman-Hollings Act of 1985. In spite of this spending-reduction measure, state and local governments could continue to receive significant revenues from the Federal government. Cushioned by these funds, they will be under less pressure to seek out more cost-effective means of service delivery, like privatization. For example, the Reagan administration has sought to terminate subsidies to local transit systems via the Urban Mass Transportation Administration. The loss of such subsidies would lead to drastic changes in local transit systems, with significant replacement of costly centralized service by lower-cost, flexible private providers. Continuation of the subsidies, however, will probably prolong the existence of today's bureaucratic-centralized systems.

Actual barriers to privatization exist in many states, generally embedded in state statutes or local-government charters. These barriers include outright bans on shedding or contracting out certain services, limits on the application of user fees and vouchers, laws requiring private contractors to pay employees as much as public employees receive, and laws imposing other onerous requirements on private firms. During the past few years a number of states have enacted privatization enabling legislation, usually to authorize privatization in a specific field (e.g., corrections, wastewater treatment) but sometimes to authorize general contracting-out. The Privatization Council published a compendium of state laws on privatization in April 1986.[16]

One of the major barriers to privatization continues to be employee opposition, which is often translated into political decisions not to privatize. Public employees fear that privatization will mean either the loss of their jobs altogether or at least a reduction in pay and fringe benefits. While either of these consequences may occur, public-sector managers in many jurisdictions have developed a number of techniques for reducing negative impacts on employees and thereby reducing or defusing their opposition.

There are three basic approaches: assisting those who go to the private sector, helping those who stay in the public sector, and easing the personal-adjustment process. One of the most important examples of the first approach is for the governmental unit that is contracting out a service to require the contractor to give the current government employees the right of first refusal for most or all of the jobs under the contract (generally excluding management positions). There are a number of variations of this provision; some governments require only that jobs be offered to current employees; others require that they be hired, at least for an initial period.

A newer technique is to assist public employees in forming companies to take over work previously performed in-house. One example would be to make the initial contract award on a sole-source basis to the former work force organized as a private enterprise. In subsequent rebidding of the contract, the new firm would have to compete against commercial bidders. The city of South Lake Tahoe, California, contracted out the provision of bus service to a company formed by two former city employees who engineered a buyout and designed an employee stock ownership plan. National Freight Corp. and Hovercraft Services are examples of successful British privatization that involved employee and management buyouts, sometimes for nominal sums.[17]

Another important way of reducing employee fear and opposition is to adopt a no-layoff policy. In such cases, the city government may decide that any net reductions in staffing levels due to privatization will be dealt with via attrition and transfers to other departments, rather than via layoffs. Both Los Angeles County (a leading practitioner of contracting out) and the Federal government have formal no-layoff policies. Attrition is especially useful if only a portion of a department's services are contracted out at one time, so that fewer people are affected at once. If attrition and transfer opportunities are too limited, a jurisdiction can at least adopt a "rehire" policy giving preference to those laid off.

Other options include using some of the money saved during the first year of privatization, either for one-time redundancy payments to the displaced employees or to pay for their retraining for other jobs. Another possibility is to provide incentives for early retirement. In Canada, for example, the government offered early retirement to older custodial personnel as part of its program of contracting out public-works cleaning services. Displaced workers may also be allowed to retain certain fringe benefits, at least for a while. When the Federal government transferred its Alaska Railway to the state of Alaska, the former Federal employees were allowed to remain in the Federal pension system.

Techniques for overcoming or defusing employee opposition have been spelled out in several recent publications. A detailed catalog of such methods is provided in *Employee Incentives for Privatization*, developed by the Federal government's Privatization Concerns Task Group and published by the U.S. Office of Personnel Management (OPM), and the OPM's "FED CO-OP: An Alternative Contracting Out Approach."[18] The issue is also addressed in the Council on Municipal Performance's excellent handbook, *Contracting Municipal Services*.

Conclusion

As should be clear from this overview, privatization has grown rapidly at the state and local levels in the United States. From the contracting out of mundane housekeeping services to the provision of such sensitive functions as fire protection, jails, and even police patrols and the provision of large-scale infrastructure, privatization has become an important new way for public-sector managers to provide needed public services.

What accounts for the popularity of privatization in the face of strong status-quo opposition? One very important factor has been the growing cost-revenue squeeze on government. Beginning with the tax revolts in the 1970s and continuing through the Reagan efforts to slow the growth of Federal spending, the era of big-spending government appears to be over — or at least suspended. Fiscal pressures have thus forced most governments to seek more for their money, usually through privatization.

Another factor is that the intellectual climate supports a turn away from government programs and toward private enterprise. Several decades of scholarly work under the headings of "law and economics" and "public choice theory" have applied the insights of economics to the political and bureaucratic realms. As a result, scholars, writers, and commentators today take a much less naive view of government administrators and public employees. They can now be seen objectively as people seeking to advance their own interests, like everyone else in society, rather than as textbook figures pursuing an idealized public interest. Moreover, several decades of empirical studies of government versus private provision of services have demonstrated the general superiority of profit incentives over bureaucratic incentives.

This intellectual shift is reflected in popular attitudes, which have grown increasingly skeptical of big government over the past two decades. Moreover, entrepreneurs have become the United States's new culture heroes. Thus it is hardly surprising that substituting competitive, entrepreneurial private enterprise for big-government bureaucracies would prove to be a popular program, when presented in those terms.

Finally, one would do well to appreciate the decentralized American Federal system. It is precisely the fifty-state, thousand-city system that has allowed the freedom to experiment with various forms of private service delivery. It has, moreover, given the economists and political scientists the diversity of examples and multiplicity of data points needed to draw empirical conclusions. And those empirical conclusions again and again point to the superior flexibility, responsiveness, and cost-effectiveness of privatization.

NOTES

1. *Privatization in the U. S.: Cities and Counties,* National Center for Policy Analysis (NCPA) Policy Report no. 116 (Dallas: NCPA, June 1985), 7.

2. Robert W. Poole, Jr., and Philip E. Fixler, Jr., "The Privatization of Public Sector Services in Practice: Experience and Potential" (Paper presented to the Conference on Privatization of the Public Sector, Department of Public Policy and Management, Wharton School, University of Pennsylvania, Philadelphia, Pennsylvania, 18–19 Sept. 1986), 3. Conference papers are to be published in a forthcoming issue of the *Journal of Policy Analysis and Management.*

3. James L. Perry and Timlynn T. Babitsky, "Comparative Performance in Urban Bus Transit: Assessing Privatization Strategies," *Public Administration Review* 46 (Jan./Feb. 1986):61, 63–64.

4. Barbara J. Stevens, ed., *Delivering Municipal Services Efficiently: A Comparison of Municipal and Private Service Delivery* [Summary], a report prepared by Ecodata, Inc., for the U.S. Dept. of Housing and Urban Development, June 1984.

5. James C. Mercer, "Growing Opportunities in Public Service Contracting," *Harvard Business Review* 61 (March-April 1983):178.

6. Harry P. Hatry, *A Review of Private Approaches for Delivery of Public Services* (Washington, DC: Urban Institute, 1983), 20.

7. Robert W. Poole, Jr., *Cutting Back City Hall* (New York: Universe Books, 1980), 161.

8. *Compendium of Privatization Laws* (New York: Privatization Council, April 1986).

9. Sandra Rosenbloom, "The Taxi in the Urban Transport System," in *Urban Transit: The Private Challenge to Public Transit*, ed. Charles A. Lave (Cambridge, Mass.: Ballinger Publishing Co. for Pacific Institute, 1985), 194–95.

10. Harry P. Hatry and Eugene Durman, *Issues in Competitive Contracting for Social Services* (Fall Church, Ill.: National Institute of Governmental Purchasing, Inc., Aug. 1985), 10.

11. Theodore Gage, "How to Buy Cops," *Reason*, August 1982, 23–28.

12. John D. Hanrahan, *Government for Sale: Contracting Out—The New Patronage* (American Federation of State, County and Municipal Employees [AFSCME], 1977); and *Passing the Bucks: The Contracting out of Public Services* (AFSCME, 1983).

13. Poole and Fixler, 13–14.

14. John Tepper Marlin, ed., *Contracting Municipal Services: A Guide to Purchase from the Private Sector* (New York: John Wiley & Sons, 1984).

15. Hatry, 72.

16. *Compendium of Privatization Laws.*

17. Madsen Pirie, *Dismantling the State: The Theory and Practice of Privatization* (Dallas: National Center for Policy Analysis, 1985), 43–47, 49–50.

18. Privatization Concerns Task Group, *Employee Incentives for Privatization* (Washington, D.C.: U.S. Office of Personnel Management, 1986), 19; and "FED CO-OP," Washington, D.C.: July 1986.

Privatization at the Federal Level

FRED L. SMITH, JR.

The key on the Federal privatization cash register struck most often has been "No Sale." For reasons ranging from ineptness to political resistance, the Reagan administration has been unable or unwilling to advance the cause of privatization. This essay documents this lack of progress, considers its causes, and suggests changes that will be necessary if privatization is ever to be "sold."

First-Term Privatization Attempts

During Ronald Reagan's first term as president, privatization became a policy position of the administration. As the term gained political potency, however, it was quickly captured by the forces of the status quo in and out of government. Agencies dusted off their conventional programs and found that "properly considered" these were "privatization efforts." But adopting the new label was only a way — largely successful — of resisting change. The most ambitious attempt to privatize during the first term was the Asset Management Program, an effort to sell large portions of federally owned land in the West, but the move was stopped within a short period.

This program and other first-term attempts to privatize were hampered by the absence of any commitment on the part of the administration to push privatization. Selling any asset involves transaction costs; the asset often needs to be refurbished, a marketing plan must be prepared, and many one-on-one confidential negotiations must begin. The sale of an asset involves up-front costs that should be recognized and approved. The White House did not create a privatization thrust and did not accept the need to spend money to make sales or to set up an appropriately funded and staffed sales program. Privatization was an intriguing new product, but it was given no marketing budget. The subsequent failure indicates the wisdom of the adage: "Build a better mousetrap and you'll have a warehouse full of better mousetraps — unless you pursue an intelligent marketing strategy."

The author would like to acknowledge the advice of Peter Young in the preparation of this essay.

Moreover, the thrust of the privatization effort was misguided from the beginning. Privatization was seen as a money-making scheme and was approached in budgetary rather than political terms. Thus programs both failed to catch the public imagination and alienated those currently benefiting from the government assets; their interests were largely ignored.

Government assets are rarely idle — merely inefficiently deployed. Those now benefiting from such assets might well favor the improvements possible from privatization and the bestowal of clear property rights, but they will vigorously oppose any policy that assumes that they have no "squatter's rights." A group that has used an asset for some time is generally believed to have some "right" to that resource; moreover, such resources have often been paid for in some sense. For example, grazing rights are tied to private rangelands, and the value of these rights (discounted for the possibility that the government might reclaim them) has long been capitalized into the selling price of this private land. To assume that it would be fair and equitable — as was sometimes naively done — to pay off the national debt by selling government land terrorized western ranchers and other groups who properly viewed themselves as having already paid a good price for these resources. The privatization effort ignored these prior claims, although the political realities clearly indicated that many powerful lobbying groups did "own" or at least had strong quasi-property rights in the resources in question.

The administration also failed to take into account the fact that traditional environmental groups had a major voice in anything that happens to wilderness areas, national wildlife regions, and scenic areas. Not to recognize these prior rights is to ignore political realities. Yet environmentalists were also ignored in the privatization drive, with predictable results.

The "highest price" approach to privatization also raised populist fears that the program was designed to transfer resources from the average citizen to the rich. Moreover, since most of those holding rights were in the West, as were the resources, privatization seemed likely to lead to a major revenue shift from the West to the rest of the country. Since westerners did not believe that they were responsible for the national deficit, they regarded this policy as prejudicial to their interests.

In addition, underlying this initial effort was the view that politics was not to enter into the sale of surplus assets. Government would find the highest price, take the money, and use it for "good things." Those less naive, such as former Secretary of the Interior James Watt, easily derailed the privatization initiative and defused its political support.

One of the more intriguing developments in the privatization debate during the first term was the tendency of Congress to pass legislation silencing the advocates of privatization. To stop those within the administration from raising embarrassing points about the recipients of Federal largesse, Congress simply banned any further study of such initiatives; government funds could not be used to examine the sale or transfer of selected resources.

A good example of such silencing was the ban on any study of privatization of power marketing administrations. William Niskanen, then a member of the Council of Economic Advisers, was assigned to chair a task force examining the possible sale of these relics of the socialist era of electric power. Congress immediately moved to pass bills to stop the task force. Indeed, when the administration again proposed privatizing the power marketing administrations, Congressman Vic Fazio (D., Calif.) and Senator Daniel Evans (R., Wash.) introduced bills reintroducing this "gag order."

Similar rows erupted over the possibility of privatizing military commissaries. These government supermarkets were established when American servicemen were stationed in remote regions where local facilities were inadequate to meet large military demands. Today, however, these facilities are found in highly urbanized regions of the country. Their current status provides merely another subsidy to the military, yet they are fiercely defended. A recommendation for their privatization in the policy report of the Heritage Foundation, "Mandate II," aroused much opposition, attracting more adverse comment than any of the other suggestions contained in the 500-page volume.

That Congress would oppose efforts to begin a debate is understandable. At its best, change would involve painful choices for Congress.

Conrail is a good example of poor marketing by the Reagan administration. The North East Rail Services Act (NERSA) of 1981 provided for the sale of Conrail as an entity. The Department of Transportation (DOT) sought bids from private railroads and other companies — they initially ruled out a public stock sale — and selected the Norfolk Southern Corporation as the winning bidder. The DOT then tried unsuccessfully to push this proposal through Congress. Eventually, John Dingell (D., Mich.), chairman of the House Commerce Committee, tabled the Norfolk Southern proposal and put forward legislation to sell Conrail as an independent entity by a public stock offering. The legislation passed within a very short time.

The failure of the DOT proposal illustrates some important lessons. Privatization is not advanced by antagonizing politically powerful groups. Privatization may require the defeat of certain interests; however, there should be no effort to expand the size of the opposition. The administration's effort to sell Conrail failed for this reason. DOT's decision to sell this line to one of the major competitors created substantial opposition from other railroads, from shippers who believed that they might be adversely affected, from political jurisdictions experiencing concerns similar to those of the shippers, and from western railroads. (The country now has three major eastern and three major western lines. The DOT plan would have eliminated one of the eastern lines; this would have left one western line without an eastern merger partner.)

Moreover, the DOT plan raised anew fears about the possible dangers of railroad "monopolies." These fears caused considerable problems for the industry and the administration in other areas of rail policy. An almost moribund industry was portrayed as the monolith of the past. Once again, politicians began to preach about the evils of monopoly and to request that the industry be legislated into competitiveness. This risk of reregulation is particularly troublesome for the railroad industry; unlike the trucking and airline industries, it is only partially deregulated. Indeed, the current level of economic regulation is excessive. The industry requires greater flexibility if it is to survive the heightened pressures from its deregulated competitors. The railroad industry also faces the problems of reduced demand for its services. Increasing inventory costs have led firms to substitute "higher cost" but more dependable trucking service for "cheaper" rail service. The range of questions that the DOT sale plan raised has made Congress far more reluctant to grant additional flexibility. In fact, the Conrail controversy has encouraged Congress to consider reregulating the railroad industry by modifying the Staggers Rail Act of 1980.

Furthermore, the DOT plan naturally alienated Conrail management, which knew it would lose its independence and some jobs if it were merged with Norfolk Southern. The Conrail workers feared a loss of their special stockowner status, which accounted for 15 percent of the corporation, as well as a loss of jobs. An analysis of privatization overseas would have suggested devising a privatization plan that could gain the support of all groups involved — workers, management, shippers, competitors, and states. The plan passed in Congress in 1986 did achieve this support. Had it been proposed by DOT in the first place, Conrail might have been sold much sooner.

Second-Term Privatization Attempts

President Reagan's first budget director, David Stockman, was not interested in privatization. Instead, he focused on attempts to cut spending on various programs through his unrivaled command of budgetary facts and figures. He mistakenly believed that Congress is influenced by rational arguments. After Congress voted to maintain most of the targeted programs, Stockman concluded that the budget could not be cut and left government to join the private sector. Privatization still has not been seriously tried.

Stockman's successor, James Miller, has been more enthusiastic about privatization and seems determined to make it a key part of his budget strategy. Privatization came back onto the political agenda in the 1987 budget. Proposals for privatization in the budget included the sale of five power marketing administrations, which accounted for 6 percent of all the electric power produced in the United States. The budget also proposed the sale of two oil fields owned by the Department of Energy, property owned by the General Services Administration, the Federal Housing Administration (which insures real-estate loans), the Overseas Private Investment Corporation, Export-Import Bank loans, and Amtrak, the ailing passenger railroad. The budget also included proposals to increase the number of Federal government services contracted out to the private sector.

President Reagan again outlined his support for the concept. In his introduction to the 1986 *Economic Report of the President,* he stated:

> The Federal Government has increasingly sought to provide services that can be more efficiently provided by the private sector. To address this problem, I have established

a working group to investigate which government functions could be effectively returned to the private sector. I have also included several initiatives in this area in the recently released budget. This strategy does not necessarily require eliminating services now provided by the government. Rather, it would make private alternatives available. Such a strategy ensures production of services that are demanded by consumers, not those chosen by government bureaucrats. It also leads to more efficient and lower cost production of those services, and often removes government-imposed restraints on competition.

This stress on the positive benefits of privatization indicated a welcome shift away from the previous fixation on fiscal advantages, but the new privatization effort still had serious deficiencies. Because privatization was presented as part of a budgetary strategy to reduce the deficit, many observers assumed that producing revenue was its only goal. But more important, no specific privatization plans were presented, enabling opponents to predict horrendous consequences.

Beyond proposing to transfer the power marketing administrations to the private sector, for example, the administration had no particular idea how to proceed. Many questions of the effect of privatization on electric rates, the environment, and Federal employees remained unanswered. The solution to these issues depends on the method of privatization. It is not surprising that few in Congress have enthusiastically embraced the idea when the outcome is unknown.

Few of the privatization proposals in the budget have become law. Some loan assets have been sold, and the sale of the Naval Petroleum reserves seems likely, but the prospects are poor for the other proposals. Such a record emphasizes the importance of crafting viable privatization policies rather than sending the idea haphazardly into the political process.

The administration must now construct this vital policy design. Foreign experiments provide examples of successful privatization in various economic and political circumstances. The success of British privatization indicates that privatization is as much a political process as an economic one. The support of important constituency groups affected by the privatization process is required. Naturally, this requirement has major implications for the design of a privatization policy.

First, a basic evaluation of the entity to be privatized needs to be carried out. The attractiveness of the entity to the private sector should be evaluated, for example, as well as its possible sale price and the viability and implications of different methods of privatization. The likely effects of privatization on the sale price of any products involved should also be considered.

Once the various options have been identified, a policy should be designed that not only avoids the most obvious pitfalls but also garners enough support to make it through the political process. This will mean building a coalition in favor of privatization. The first major tasks in forming a coalition are to identify all those involved with a single issue, find out their positions on privatization, note those already in contact with other groups, and identify each group's motivations and concerns.

The next step should be to meet with all interested groups, including those already publicly opposed to privatization, to seek common ground. Many groups will be hostile simply because they fear any change. They may be persuaded that they could benefit more from a new private operation. The most important part of this process will be to discover if their concerns might be met by modifying the privatization plan.

Not all groups, of course, will have the same concerns. Many will be contradictory. For example, some environmental groups favor the privatization of power marketing administrations because electric rates would go up, thus decreasing the demand for electricity and the consequent damage to the environment caused by the expansion of generation facilities. At the same time, heavy users of electricity could be persuaded to support such privatization only if they thought that rates would not rise steeply. Thus a policy must be devised that only partially meets each group's objective but satisfies each group enough to reduce its opposition.

Once such a policy has been devised, it will have to be explained in depth to all interested parties; as many as possible should be mobilized in support. Next, the key congressmen who have influence over a particular issue should be educated on the benefits of the specific privatization policy affecting their area. Members of the coalition supporting the privatization proposal should bring pressure on them.

This strategy implies working with the members of Congress whose constituents are directly affected by the proposed privatization and attempting to gain these members' support. The alternative strategy of working with members of Congress having no special stake in that issue is unlikely to succeed. Members of Congress will fight much harder to retain special privileges for their own districts than to eliminate those priveleges for others.

Attempting to put together a coalition of senators and congressmen from the Northeast, for example, to push for the privatization of federally subsidized power marketing administrations in the West is a strategy unlikely to succeed. It would be far better to attempt to persuade the senators and representatives from the West that such privatization need not necessarily harm the interests of their constituents.

It is important to take a bipartisan approach to privatization and to develop bipartisan support in Congress for it. Thus a top priority of a Republican administration should be to identify Democratic senators and representatives who might be persuaded to support privatization and convince them to take a lead on the issue. Now that the Democrats have regained control of the Senate, such a bipartisan approach will be essential.

Perhaps one of the most important advantages of presenting a comprehensive policy plan is the ability to "frame the issue" for each privatization attempt. For example, privatizing air traffic control should be presented as an attempt to "improve air safety." Selling the Tennessee Valley Authority (TVA) should be presented as an issue of "increasing local accountability and improving the service."

Buying Out the Interest Groups

There are some indications that some in the Reagan administration have learned from past failures and are adopting more innovative approaches to privatization.

For example, the Office of Personnel Management, under the leadership of Constance Horner, has developed a plan (the Federal Co-op plan) to allow government employees to share the benefits of privatization. The rather complex process allows Federal employees to form a new employee-owned company to carry out their function. The company would be guaranteed business for a specific time — perhaps five years — and then the contract would be open for bid.

This proposal has been prompted by the failure of the administration's "A-76" policy, named after Office of Management and Budget (OMB) Circular A-76. Together with OMB Circular A-25, which mandates user charges, Circular A-76 says that whenever the private sector can perform a given service or task at a lower cost than the government, it should be given the task. Circular A-25 reinforces this policy by stating that when government finds it necessary to provide goods and services to private parties, it should charge fees to recover the costs of its involvement. Thus no automatic subsidy is provided by the mere establishment of a government program.

These two policies together would greatly reduce the scope of government. Either government would not become directly involved or it would provide no direct subsidy. If such policies were enforced, there would be less support for government activities and services. Since in most cases the costs of government-provided services exceed those of private providers, users of government services would find themselves facing greater costs than if the service were provided privately. Thus, users would become a prominent lobbying force for privatization — as in fact they did for transport deregulation.

Unfortunately, the A-76 and A-25 policies are rarely enforced. OMB circulars provide some limited influence but are circumscribed by custom, law, or political timidity. Bureaucrats have become adept at carrying out the cost comparisons required by OMB Circular A-76. Of the 300,000 Federal jobs defined as commercial, only 30,000 are contracted out to the private sector. Circular A-25 has met a similar fate. User groups have exercised their political clout to ensure that user fees remain low. Moreover, as noted above, a long-established subsidy program is likely to have been capitalized in the transfer price of some other asset associated with that subsidized activity. For example, the Bureau of Land Management (BLM) has long charged low fees for grazing on the land that it manages. These "grazing rights" are linked to specific units of private land. A rancher, for example, may own a few thousand acres directly and also have rights to graze on some designated BLM acreage. The rights have value and are thus captured when the land is transferred. Many ranchers have in effect paid prices for land that included the estimated worth of the subsidy.

Because the failure to enforce A-25 initially has made it difficult and inequitable to enforce the circular today, no effort is being made to do so. That timidity reflects less a recognition of the equity stake of existing user groups than an unwillingness to accept the political nature of policy change. User groups involved in privatization fights must either be persuaded to support privatization or be defeated. In most cases, the fact that they hold at least some "quasi-rights" in the property in question suggests that these rights be recognized. Their greater value after full privatization might provide the incentive to persuade these groups to support privatization. Thus western lands could be offered at low prices to ranchers with grazing rights. Again, however, this "solution" may not attract other groups. If western lands, for example, were owned directly by the current holders of rights, they might use the land differently. Government upgrading efforts, such as chaining off unwanted bush, are often highly cost-ineffective and would thus be discontinued. Moreover, uses other than cattle ranching might be superior, leading the new owners to reduce their ranching efforts. Those now benefiting from the current use of BLM land (for example, meat processors) might therefore oppose privatization. Again, initial political research and "mapping" are essential.

The "Federal Co-op" plan being advocated by the Office of Personnel Management is one of the few administration initiatives that recognize this vital aspect of privatization. The usual simplistic view that privatization is like a private sale with only one buyer and one seller has caused considerable confusion. Political assets are controlled by politicians—in most cases, the full Congress and the White House. That group will have many conflicting goals, and it will be difficult to devise a scheme that will convince a workable majority that the plan is worthy of approval. The objective of political privatization must be to create such a viable privatization coalition.

The Federal Co-op plan implicitly assumes that this coalition can be attained by "buying out" the work force. The work force is indeed the most powerful unit in a large number of cases. Government workers can bring concentrated lobbying power to bear on Congress; they know how government works and are adept at defending their turf. Defusing their opposition to privatization would provide the key to success in privatizing many programs—but not all. The U.S. Postal Service, for example, derives its main political support from its work force. But many other groups may benefit from an existing Federal presence, and labor is only one of them. Those using the services or those selling to or buying from a government program may be more decisive. The power marketing administrations, for example, employ relatively few people. It is the users, not the employees, who provide the main political support for that program. Thus, in some cases, the Federal Co-op plan would attempt to "buy out" the wrong group and fail to resolve the political impasse.

The deregulation experience also demonstrates that labor may not be the decisive political force in many circumstances. Both trucking and airline deregulation occurred over the strong objections of both the firms involved and their labor forces. In retrospect, this opposition seems to have been largely misguided on the part of the companies, whereas the opposition of the labor force seems to have been entirely rational. A large part of the monopoly rents allowed by regulation were garnered in the form of higher salaries, reduced hours, and attractive fringe benefits.

Deregulation has been extremely painful to these labor groups. In the trucking industry, for example, the competitive pressures of deregulation has forced the

Teamsters Union to moderate its wage and benefit demands. Generally, these adjustments have occurred by attrition, by two-tier wage arrangements or by "givebacks" of selective benefits; nonetheless, the adjustments have been large. Similarly, airline deregulation led to lower salaries and benefits, but the total work force has increased in the airline industry.

That these deregulation efforts were successful indicates that even when strong worker opposition exists to a specific policy, it can prevail. In these two cases, the strong resistance of the unions and the protected firms was overcome by a strong political coalition of user groups (business and consumer) buttressed by a growing body of research indicating the negative effects of regulation. The realization that the benefits and necessity of economic regulation had been largely overstated and that such regulation created major losses to consumers became widely understood, making it possible for many people to become involved in the policy debate. That framing of the issue was significant and greatly favored deregulation.

All of this suggests that privatization need not always require that the affected workers be persuaded of the value of the policy shift. Privatization requires that one seek to map out the constellation of forces that support the existing government system of service provision and construct a countervailing coalition that will permit change. The first step is to map out the "force field" supporting the current program. What groups favor government provision, and for what reasons? What would lead them to support privatization? How strong are the relative groups involved in the issue? This mapping out of forces is a critical precursor to the task of changing forces.

The art of political change is something like the game of Pick-Up-Sticks. In that children's game, a number of colored sticks are allowed to fall down in a tangled interlocked pile. The task is to remove the sticks one at a time without disturbing the rest. That task requires that one estimate which sticks are critical to the current structure and which are not. Since there is no easy way to determine that without touching the sticks, there is a constant danger of misjudgment. Efforts to move the wrong stick can lead to the whole pile tumbling down and losing the game. Madsen Pirie, president of the Adam Smith Institute and a pioneer in the development of political strategies of privatization, has similarly stated that "dismantling a part of the public sector is like defusing an unexploded bomb. You have to analyze it carefully first, then devise the policy to cut the right wires before slowly extracting the detonator."[1]

Those seeking to privatize anything should first consider why the situation is as it is and then seek to develop a strategy that would allow a move to privatization. The workers, the users, or some other group may be the key to solving the political puzzle, or a combination of incentives may be required. For example, in the privatization of large companies or utilities in Britain, the workers have been allocated stock, the managers have been allowed to retain control, the public has been given the opportunity to buy stock, and the consumers have been guaranteed better service.

The privatization of public housing has progressed in the United States because such a politically sensitive approach has been adopted and the mapping of the political forces has been carried out. No doubt a traditional Republican approach would have involved trying to auction this housing off to private developers, and the resultant outcry would have gone on for years. Those interested in this issue seemed to have learned from the British experience, where more than 1 million public-sector houses have been sold to their tenants at heavily discounted rates. The support of tenant groups was gained for a similar initiative in the United States, and a privatization bill cosponsored by Jack Kemp (R., New York) and Walter Fauntroy (D., District of Columbia) passed the House of Representatives in 1986 with heavy bipartisan support.

That the support of user groups is vital for a successful privatization drive has also been appreciated by Ralph Stanley, administrator of the Urban Mass Transit Administration. He has brought transit consumers to Washington to testify in favor of privatizing bus services. The effect on the relevant committees was powerful. Stanley has also understood the need to sell privatization. Among other educational activities, he has commissioned a film on the success of privatized transport, organized a series of conferences on transport privatization, and brought successful transport privatizers from other countries to the United States.

In most cases, however, the Reagan administration is still too timid and ill-informed as to the mechanics of privatization to advocate innovative privatization solutions. Another government "solution" is often advocated rather than full privatization. The lease of Dulles and National airports to a regional commission rather than their outright sale is a good example of this. A politically attractive privatization package could have been devised. Legislation to privatize airports has been passed in Britain, for example. Yet the DOT made no such attempt, and when some individuals and organizations proposed privatization as an alternative to the DOT, they were criticized for rocking the boat.

Lack of confidence has led administration members to compromise their own ideas to accord with some preconceived notion of "political reality." Before most ideas are presented to Congress, so many compromises have already been made that the new idea often differs little from existing policy. One form or degree of government control is recommended as a substitute for another. In fact, the more radical suggestion is often the more "politically realistic" one. Witness the success of the radical version of tax reform rather than the bundle of compromises originally considered by the Senate Finance Committee.

It seems that tinkering with the status quo will be the probable administration response to the crisis in the air-traffic control system, rather than genuinely attempting to free the system from the clear inadequacies of political control by adopting a proper privatization solution like that advocated by Robert Poole of the Reason Foundation.

A political coalition to support full privatization could be created. Unless some means are found to remove the constraints now creating delays throughout the air-travel system, there will be substantial pressures to reregulate the airlines. That prospect threatens the gains of deregulation and creates the forces that might bring about privatization.

Airlines are extremely dissatisfied with the present system and, through the Air Transport Association (ATA), have proposed an alternative — a government corporation funded by user fees. This scheme, however, is far too timid. By the time that Congress would enact such a proposal, so many provisos will have been added that it will differ little from the status quo, and most of the deficiencies of political control will remain. The ATA and the DOT have begun to realize this risk.

Business aircraft users could also be brought into a privatization coalition. The system is so unreliable that they cannot be sure of getting to meetings on time. They would probably be willing to pay more to a private user cooperative if it enabled the system to eliminate delays. Private airplane owners are also dissatisfied with the present system and could be persuaded to support a privatization solution. Because they do not often use the en route system, they would not be much affected by increases in the user cost there. Because they generally use small airports, however, they would benefit greatly from reductions in landing fees resulting from lower cost air-traffic control services at airports. Such costs could be cut significantly if these services were no longer the responsibility of the Federal Aviation Administration but contracted out to private firms. It remains to be seen whether the Reagan administration will advocate such a privatization package.

Conclusion

At times, advocates of privatization have acted as if there were some magic wand that would simply "make privatization happen." They have been slow to realize that the structure of forces responsible for each government program is likely to be unique and that a unique strategy will therefore by required in each case. Politically, they should look for targets of opportunity, be creative in the arrangements made to develop the transfer, and create opportunities wherever possible.

To make privatization a political reality, it will be necessary to conduct specific issue-management campaigns for each major initiative. This process requires that the "sales force" consider the analytic questions likely to be raised by the sale, ensure that these facts are understood and communicated by the media, develop a dominant coalition of groups favoring privatization, and recruit members of Congress to support and guide through the transfer. This process requires considerable skill in understanding both the nature of privatization and the realities of politics. Privatization failures to date suggest that these two skills are not widely shared by similar people — at least not in the Reagan administration.

Privatization around the World

PETER   YOUNG

Privatization, now a worldwide phenomenon, is growing in its extent and impact. It is taking place in more than seventy countries around the world, a number that expands every year. The movement started in Britain, and most proponents of privatization still draw their inspiration and the bulk of their examples of success from that country. The following partial listing of public-sector bodies that have been privatized in Britain illustrates the extensive progress that has been made:

Amersham International; British Rail Hotels; English Channel Ferry Service; British Petroleum; British Aerospace; Britoil; Cable & Wireless; Associated British Ports; Jaguar Cars; the National Freight Corporation; several shipyards; Hoverspeed; 1 million public-sector housing units; British Telecom; the Royal Ordnance Factories; the Gibraltar Dockyard; forests; land and buildings belonging to a variety of public-sector bodies; and the contracting out of various local-government and hospital ancillary services, such as the maintenance and cleaning of government buildings, the testing of trucks and public vehicles, laundry, cleaning and medical care in the armed services, and the rest rooms at Kings Cross railroad station.

Next on the list for privatization is British Gas, which will be followed by British Airways, which will in turn be followed by the British Airports Authority, Rolls Royce, and the Water Authorities. Much has already been written about British privatization,[1] however, and it is more useful to concentrate on the extent of privatization in other countries, about which less is known.

Privatization in Developed Countries

Since the appointment of Prime Minister Jacques Chirac in March 1986, privatization has been a top priority in France. The principal economic minister has been renamed the minister for finance, the economy, and privatization; and the French privatization program may exceed the British program in size. The first three companies to be privatized are Saint-Gobain, a glass and engineering group;

Banque Paribas, the investment bank; and Group des Assurances Générales de France, the second largest French insurance company. These will be followed by a multitude of other banks, finance houses, insurance companies, and large industry groups. The previous Socialist government, moving tentatively toward privatization, had already sold some subsidiaries of state companies.

Turkey has sold the Bosporus Bridge and the Keban hydroelectric dam and has called in foreign consultants to advise on the privatization of thirty more state concerns. The sale of the state airline, Turk Hava Yollari (THY), began with the sale of an initial percentage of THY equity to its employees; shares are also being sold to the general public, and a final sale of shares will go to Turkish and foreign companies. The largest state bank, Türkiye Cumhariyeti Ziraat Bankasi, has announced plans to sell its shares of nineteen companies.

The socialist-led government in Italy has also begun privatizing. The state holding company, Instituto per la Ricostruzione Industriale (IRI), has raised $1.59 billion by selling some of its shares in various enterprises, such as the Aeritalia aerospace company and the Selenia electronics company. Forty percent of Sirti, a subsidiary of the Societa Finanziaria Telefonica (STET) telecommunications company, was sold for L200 billion, and the state-owned Banca Nazionale del Lavoro, the largest bank in Italy, is offering 25 percent of its shares to private investors and more to its employees.

Spain has started a privatization program as well. Socialist Prime Minister Felipe González has called the bloated Spanish public sector a "white elephant graveyard." The national car manufacturer, Seat, has been sold to Volkswagen, and plans have been announced to sell a state-owned ball-bearings factory and to hive off sections of high-technology companies.

The state airline, Iberia, may also soon be privatized. The state holding company, Instituto Nacional de Industria (INI), has sold its textile firm, Textil Tarazona, and has also sold its stake in the Spanish subsidiary of AB Svenska Kullagerfabrik to the Swedish parent company. The Spanish truck- and bus-manufacturing company Empresa Nacional de Autocamiones, S. A. (ENASA) has been sold to General Motors.

The West German government has concentrated on three general areas of privatization — industry, transport, and banking. A portion of the Berliner bank has already been sold; two smaller banks, as well as service stations on the autobahn, trucking concerns, and tourist offices, are being readied for sale. In 1984, the West German government reduced its shareholding in the Veba energy group from 43.7 percent to 30 percent by selling 4.4 million shares. Partial privatization is proceeding for VIAG, an energy, chemicals, and aluminum company; Prakla-Seismos, a geophysical research and development company; and IVG, a diversified finance, property, and engineering company.

The Social Democratic prime minister of Portugal, Aníbal Cavaço Silva, has committed his government to a privatization program, blaming state domination of the economy for keeping Portuguese standards of living behind those of most other European countries. In a speech to Parliament announcing his intentions, he stated: "Nothing justifies our remaining on the bottom rung in Europe. We are determined to put an end to the resignation and impotence imposed by our giant state machine."[2]

In Israel, the stock of Elta Electronics, a state-owned company that makes sophisticated military systems, is soon to be floated on the Israeli stock exchange. The government hopes to raise around $13 million from the initial issue, some 60 percent of which is expected to be bought by the country's work force. In August 1986, a government committee approved the $14 million sale of the state's 29 percent interest in Haifa Chemicals, a fertilizer producer, to a group of New York investors. The government is also soliciting bids for the 71 percent state share of Paz Oil Co., Israel's largest marketer of petroleum products. A 20 to 25 percent stake in Dead Sea Bromine Co., a subsidiary of state-owned Israel Chemicals Ltd., is to be placed as a public offering in New York. Other subsidiaries may follow.

The Canadian government has sold two unprofitable airframe manufacturers, Canadair and De Haviland; Canadian Arsenal, an arms-manufacturing company; as well as mining businesses, such as Eldorado Nuclear, a uranium producer, and Kidd Creek Mines. De Haviland is being sold to the Boeing Corporation for $170 million. Also sold was most of the government's stake in the Canada Development Corporation and Northern Transportation, a marine transport service. Teleglobe Canada, which handles overseas telephone calls, is being sold.

In a statement announcing the privatization of these concerns, Robert R. de Cotret, president of the Canadian Treasury Board and chairman of the Ministerial Task Force on Privatization, said that "a key element of the government's commitment to good management is our policy for the privatization of commercial crown corporations which no longer fulfill a specific public policy purpose."[3]

Even strife-torn South Africa is turning to privatization as a means to invigorate its shaky economy. State intervention in and regulation of the economy has been extensive in South Africa. The public sector is a bastion of white privilege, employing 46 percent of the white labor force of 2.6 million. Now the South African government has established a special committee headed by three cabinet ministers to draw up proposals for the privatization of public-sector enterprises, and President P. W. Botha revealed that the government had been carefully studying the British privatization experience.

Three forms of privatization are under consideration: the transformation of state enterprises into public companies, with shares issued through the stock exchange; the purchase by private companies of state assets on a tender or private-allocation basis; and a management buy-out option under which the management and employees of smaller state undertakings would be encouraged to take over ownership.

SASOL, which produces oil from coal, has already been successfully privatized, and future privatization targets are expected to include the South African Transport Services Board, which runs the state airline, the rail network, harbors, and other transport services; ESCOM, the electricity-supply corporation; and the South African Iron and Steel Industrial Corporation (ISCOR).

Japan has also begun privatizing its relatively small public sector. Legislation was passed in 1984 to transfer the telecommunications system, Nippon Telegraph and Telephone (NTT), and the state tobacco and salt monopolies to the private sector. The profitable NTT became a private company on 1 April 1985, and its monopoly was ended. Although privatization was fought tenaciously by a combined bureaucratic and trade-union lobby, the government pressed ahead since it thought that the continuation of the state monopoly would endanger long-term technological modernization.

Privatization of the unprofitable Japan National Railways (JNR) is in progress. The plan is to split JNR into six private regional firms and two national private firms, one for the bullet passenger-train network and the other for the JNR freight interests. JNR's substantial land assets will be sold to pay off some of its debts. The government hopes to divest itself of other unprofitable concerns as part of a wider strategy to reduce state spending and the budget deficit.

Privatization has been highly regarded in Japan. The minister for aviation has proposed that it should be applied to Japan Air Lines (JAL) in order to restore public confidence after the Boeing 747 disaster in 1985. The Council for Transport Policy, a government advisory panel, proposed in December 1985 that the JAL monopoly on international routes be ended and that Japan's two other airlines be allowed to compete on all international routes. This policy is seen as complementary to the sale of JAL.

Privatization in Communist Countries

A specter is haunting the communist world — the specter of private enterprise. The most astonishing developments are occurring in China. In a case of partial privatization, workers in three state-owned factories in southern China have invested $2.9 million to buy 30 percent of the enterprises. After buying shares, the *China Economic Daily* reported, many of the workers became more concerned about issues of production and management.

Some state-owned homes in China are also being sold. Six thousand apartments, for example, were on sale in Shanghai in 1985. Buyers had to contribute a third of the 18,000 yuan ($6,000) price, the balance to be paid jointly by the state and the employer. The Shanghai municipal authorities are also launching a lottery for would-be home owners as part of a campaign to stimulate savings. Half of all the households in the city of 11 million people have opened savings accounts that entitle them to lottery tickets and the chance of winning a new home.

There has been an explosion of private enterprise. Since 1978, privately owned restaurants and shops have been opening at four times the rate of their state counterparts. A whole street in the Manchurian city of Harbin is given over to the sale of new privately made vinyl sofas, and similar free markets are found in cities such as Canton, Shanghai, and Chengdu.

Even the principle of state ownership of land is now under attack. A recent national symposium featured speakers arguing in favor of privatizing state land. They alleged that current "building costs and rent regulations are quite unrealistic.

The more buildings you erect the more money you lose."[4] In the northeast city of Shenyang, the first stock exchange since 1949 has been opened. It is an experiment to help companies and stockholders obtain cash and ensure a more effective use of capital, according to the republic's Central Television.

Cuba is also experimenting with privatization. A law passed by the Cuban national assembly privatized most public housing in 1986. Under this law, state tenants who paid about 10 percent of their income in rent will own their homes, subject to a twenty-year mortgage with the Banco Popular del Ahorro. Up to fifteen years of repayments will be deducted for the years of rent already paid, and mortgage payments will thus roughly match current rents.

In Hungary, private food production is nearly half of the total output, and a growing number of private businesses are opening. People invest to make a profit and even lease state factories for private gain. According to Zoltan Palmai, the owner of the new Victoria Hotel in Budapest (the only private hotel in the Soviet bloc), "only private enterprise can save our economy."[5]

Even the Soviet Union is experimenting with privatization. In Estonia, some radio- and television-repair services became worker-run enterprises for profit. Radios and televisions are now repaired in less than two days, instead of the usual two to three weeks. Similar experiments are being carried out with other service-sector jobs.

In November 1986 the Supreme Soviet passed a new law legalizing a range of private-sector activities. Soviet citizens will be permitted to go into business to provide a range of service functions and small-scale manufacture. The law allows twenty-nine types of private enterprise, including the repair of cars and household appliances, the use of private cars as taxis, and tutoring in music, shorthand, and languages. The manufacture of clothes, small agricultural implements, furniture, shoes, toys, cosmetics, sports equipment, and souvenirs will also be permitted. It will not be legal, however, to employ people to carry out these tasks.

Tass, the Soviet news agency, indicated in an analysis that "government-owned services were in a monopoly situation, dictating to consumers the kinds and range of services, their quality, cost, duration of fulfillment, and so forth." Tass added that private repairmen usually worked "better and faster than the government-owned services."

More substantial privatization seems likely to follow. Leonid Abalkin, economic adviser to Mikhail Gorbachev, has described plans to introduce private production co-operatives in 1987. Abalkin said that the proposal, already approved in principle by the Communist party leadership, would allow private citizens to join together to manufacture items or provide services. The cooperatives would pay some tax to the state but keep the rest as profit, divided among co-operative members. Albalkin predicted that the co-operatives would constitute 10 to 12 percent of national income within the next decade. In an interview with the Soviet periodical *Argumenty i Fakty* he said that the country needed a change as radical as V. I. Lenin's "New Economic Policy," the 1921 measure that temporarily returned most of the economy to private control.

Privatization in Asia

In many developing countries, privatization is no longer just an intriguing idea but a real part of government policy. Socialist rhetoric has been abandoned, and governments are dismantling their public sectors. In most cases the privatization candidates are those enterprises that obviously belong in the private sector, such as hotels and textile factories, but some countries are tackling more difficult concerns, such as telecommunications networks.

The most progress toward privatization is taking place in Asia. In Sri Lanka, Minister of Finance and Planning Ronald de Mel has stated that the government will refrain from any activity that the private sector can do better and will transfer to the private sector some activities now run by the state. The telecommunication system is for sale, and the bus system, formerly a monopoly of the Sri Lanka Central Transport Board, has been deregulated and privatized. Some unprofitable textile mills were also sold and are now making a profit in private hands.

In July 1986 the thirty-year-old National Milk Board was replaced by Milco, a public limited liability company that will sell 49 percent of its shares to Sri Lankan milk producers. In August 1986 the Sri Lanka parliament voted to liquidate and sell the remains of three public corporations, the State Fertilizer Corporation, the Tobacco Industries Corporation, and the National Packaging Materials Corporation. International tenders will be invited; inquiries about the State Fertilizer Corporation have already come from India, Pakistan, and Iraq.

Privatization has become an important part of Bangladesh's New Industrial Policy, which was introduced in 1982. Concern about mounting public-sector losses, together with pressure from international and bilateral lending agencies, forced the government to take action. About thirty-five jute and thirty-seven textile mills, with about 40 percent of the production capacity in these two industries, have already been sold, as well as four newspapers, three magazines, and around 1,000 smaller businesses. A 49 percent government stake in the International Finance and Investment Commercial Bank has been reduced to 40 percent and will eventually reach 5 percent. Holdings in the Bangladesh Shipping Corporation are also being sold, and government stakes of 35 to 40 percent in various foreign-owned companies, such as the General Electric Company, Philips, Pfizer, and Bangladesh Tobacco are being reduced to 10 to 20 percent.

The Bangladesh government is embarking on the privatization of some larger targets. President Hossain Mohammad Ershad has announced: "We will start first with banks, then fertilizer factories, then paper mills, taking out the big industries first. We will sell the shares. That will generate funds, and the stock market will be activated."[6] Three of the four state-owned commercial banks will be the first to go. The finance ministry intends to sell 10 percent of the Rupali Bank to the public through the stock exchange by the end of 1986. That will be followed by another 39 percent and stakes in the other two, Agrani and Janata.

M. Syeduzzaman, cabinet minister and financial adviser to the president, has said that the policy is partly aimed at spreading shareholdings among smaller investors. He estimated that the percentage of the country's industrial assets owned by the government has already been reduced from 85 percent in 1972 to around 45 percent in 1986. President Ershad hopes that the main left-wing opposition alliance, headed by the Awami League, will have "an understanding" with the government on the privatization policies. That seems likely, since the opposition is becoming more private-sector oriented. One of its most prominent leaders, Kamal Hossain, is involved in establishing a subsidiary of the Al-Baraqua Bank of Saudi Arabia in Bangladesh, 70 percent of which will be owned by Saudi interests.

The privatization already carried out has been successful. The process was smooth, with little disruption of production and no strong public protest. The press and the private sector welcomed the change in policy. Employees of the textile mills were given the option of leaving with the benefits earned while the state operated the mill or accepting an employment contract with the new owners for one year. After privatization, the new owners could reduce employment to acceptable levels by means of attrition and removing "phantom" workers. By mid-1984, privatization had been shown to be a clear success; the mills that had suffered losses under state ownership were making substantial profits.

Rajiv Gandhi, the prime minister of India, said that the public sector "has spread to too many places where I feel it should not be."[7] The government has set its face against any more takeovers of "sick" industrial units in order to save jobs and will sell or close down twenty-six "sick" state-owned textile mills. It has also decided to involve the private sector in areas that had been solely a state preserve. In June 1985, for example, the central government asked state governments to consider involving the private sector in laying express toll highways as an alternative to the existing toll-free highways.

Pakistan has privatized some 2,000 rural rice, flour, and cotton mills and contracted out the maintenance of small wells and irrigation projects to the private sector. Finance Minister Mahbubul Haq, a champion of privatization, is planning to sell shares in a variety of government-owned corporations. The government hopes that revenue from privatization will become a major source of revenue and help it reduce its reliance on deficit financing. The budget for the fiscal year 1986-87 relies in part on privatization revenues.

The Malaysian government has committed itself to extensive privatization. "As far as possible we prefer the privatized bodies be owned by Malaysians," said Daim Zainuddin, minister of finance. "However, if there is inadequate capital locally, then we will consider tapping foreign capital markets."[8] The Malaysian Telecommunications Department will be turned into a government-owned corporation, which will then hive off selected functions to the private sector. The Malaysian Airlines System (MAS) will become a private corporation over a period of three years; 30 percent of the shares were sold in October 1985, and a joint government-private company, Aerospace Industries Malaysia, will take over the air force's maintenance facilities.

A bypass road in the Kuala Lumpur area has been leased to a private company, Shapadu, which manages the road. In addition, a number of services are being contracted out. For example, waste-management services in Kuala Lumpur have been contracted out to a British firm, GIS Waste Services. A general hospital is now run by a consortium of doctors in the Kuala Lumpur area. The government also intends to sell hotels, car parks, a lottery, water supplies, and a container terminal near Kuala Lumpur.

In 1984 the government allowed the introduction of a private commercial television station, breaking the government's own radio and television monopoly. The station, TV3, has had an invigorating effect on broadcasting in both Malaysia and neighboring Singapore, where advertising rates have declined because of the competition. The private sector is enthusiastic about the privatization program. One local merchant banker said: "The interest is enormous; proposals abound to privatize everything from sports complexes to municipal car parks."[9]

In the Philippines the public sector constitutes a major drain on the country's resources. The Aquino government plans a major privatization program. A cabinet plan calls for the government to withdraw from economic activities "to allow the private sector to become the prime mover of growth."[10] More than $6 billion worth of assets in various companies, many abandoned to bankruptcy by former President Ferdinand E. Marcos or his cronies, are earmarked for sale, including the Commercial Bank of Manila, the International Corporate Bank, the Pilipinas Bank, the Resort Hotels Corporation, the Bataan Pulp and Paper Mills, Inc., and Delta Motor Corp. Also for sale are many million dollars worth of banana, coconut, and sugar plantations formerly controlled by Marcos and his associates.

In Thailand a privatization program was started despite strong opposition from vested interests, including retired military officers appointed to the boards of many state corporations. In January 1985 the government decided to privatize through the stock market parts of the Electricity Generating Authority of Thailand and Thai Airlines International. It is also trying to privatize the Bangkok bus operations and part of the telephone system.

Taiwan, which still has some trappings of corporatism despite a rigorous free-market policy in most areas, is considering offering stock to the public in state steel, shipbuilding, chemical, and construction operations. "The time has come for privatization,"[11] said Y.Y. Wang, vice chairman of Taiwan's Commission on National Corporations.

In the Near East some Arab countries, notably Jordan, are considering privatization. The Jordanian government has identified five possible privatization targets, of which the largest is the Royal Jordanian Airline, worth around $0.5 billion. In Syria, candidates include the Damascus bus service, the water authority, an operation for processing tomato paste, and the government pension fund.

Privatization in Latin America

Privatization is beginning to make inroads in Latin America. José Sarney, president of Brazil, has announced a major change in economic policy toward privatization and promotion of the private sector. "Rarely in our history have we had such an opportunity to change the nature of Brazil's economic process," he has declared. "Leadership of the economic development process should now pass to a private sector freed from the shackles of statism."[12]

President Sarney has accepted the sales list of eighty-nine public-sector companies identified by the previous government, headed by General João Baptista de Figueiredo. Of these, twenty had been sold, and twenty-seven had been merged or transferred to local authorities. Sarney's government will sell the remaining forty-two as well as an additional twelve that he himself has identified.

The Sarney government's first task has been to determine the extent of the public sector, which has spread so widely that no one knows its full size. More than 20,000 federally owned companies and official bodies have been found, but this is nowhere near the total.

The Brazilian privatization program is likely to take three forms. State-created companies that play no strategic role in the economy, usually service or supply subsidiaries of large corporations, will be privatized. Former private-sector companies that were taken over by the government because of financial difficulties will also be sold, transferred to state and municipal governments, or closed. Private capital will be introduced into the large state corporations, such as Petróleo Brasilerio, SA, oil monopoly, the Valo do Rio Doce mining company, the Centrais Elétricas Brasileiras, SA, electricity utility, and the Siderurgica Brasileira, SA, steel company.

Raul Alfonsin, president of Argentina, has adopted privatization as an important part of his economic revitalization program. During Peronist rule in the 1940s and 1950s, large sectors of the economy were nationalized, contributing significantly to Argentina's economic decline. Today state-owned firms require vast subsidies to remain afloat; they account for 35 percent of public expenditures. Not much has been actually sold to date, but plans are ambitious. The sale of a travel agency, an industrial pipe manufacturer, and a ceramics factory has raised $4.6 million. This amount may seem slight, "but at least we have privatized something," commented Norberto Bertaina, state secretary for development. "In the past everyone talked about privatization but no one did anything."[13] President Alfonsin announced the sale of another six state companies — the Sociedad Mixta Siderurgica Argentina steel company and five petrochemical firms — and his Radical party is preparing legislation that would allow him to privatize 748 wholly or partly state-owned firms, although some of the largest money losers, such as the state airline, would be excluded from this list.

Central America is also becoming active in privatization. The government of Honduras has passed a divestiture law that allows for the sale of publicly held commercial businesses. The state-owned National Housing Finance Agency has been abolished and the functions and staff of the Honduran Banana Corporation have been greatly reduced. The private sector has been allowed to enter the lumber export marketing field, which was a solely public-sector function under the aegis of the state Forestry Development Corporation. The government of Guatemala is analyzing its paraestatals with a view to privatization.

The government of Grenada has formally announced a privatization policy, sold several hotels, and returned the possession of agricultrual lands to small farmers under long-term leases. Similarly, in the Dominican Republic the government has leased large tracts of land to private investors for export-oriented food production. There are plans to privatize the Dominican state corporation (CORDE), which owns thirty-two industrial, agricultural, and commercial enterprises.

Jamaica has sold or leased most of its sugar-refining and hotel interests. A total of eleven state-owned enterprises has been sold, five more will soon be privatized, and an analysis of another thirty targets is being carried out. The lease of a major public hospital-outpatient clinic to a private health-care corporation is also being studied. Some 2,000 acres of state-owned farm land out of an intended 10,000 acres have so far been leased to private farmers. In November 1986, the National Commercial Bank was privatized by means of a public stock offering; 40,000 Jamaicans applied for these shares.

Costa Rica has taken an innovative approach to privatization. With local currency provided by the U.S. Agency for International Development (USAID), a privatization trust fund has been established. The fund will buy the shares of subsidiary companies now owned by the Costa Rica Development Corporation (CODESA). The fund, itself a private entity, will then sell the subsidiaries to private investors. The proceeds of the sales will be used to replenish the fund and buy more state enterprises. USAID is providing outside consultants to help the government to determine the value of the companies' assets in order to establish minimum selling prices. The trust recently bought the first of the concerns, a major aluminum company, which it will soon offer for sale. A cotton mill, a sugar-processing plant, and several smaller enterprises will follow.

Another enterprising policy has been adopted in Belize, where farms owned by the Banana Control Board have been sold to the farmers who previously worked on them. The American consultants Equity Expansion International assisted the farmers in raising loan packages totaling some $750,000 from financial institutions to purchase about 2,000 acres from the Banana Control Board and to undertake the expansion of an additional 2,000 acres in the future. The funds were raised on the basis of the commercial viability of the projects and will be repaid out of future profits. The role of the Banana Control Board has been changed to a regulatory one, and its staff has been reduced from eighty to fourteen employees.

In March 1984, Mexico privatized 73 of its 467 nationalized companies. These were mainly small companies. On 6 February 1985, the Mexican cabinet decided to liquidate, dissolve, merge, transfer, or sell 236 state companies and agencies during the year. So far, however, less than a third of the 236 companies, together with minority government interests in thirteen other companies, have been put up for sale; only twenty-six companies have actually been sold.

One of the more significant sales, though, was that of the Nacional Hotelera chain on 28 October 1985 to a private Mexican investment group backed by two state banks as minority partners. The purchase price was set at 27.2 billion pesos, which is $84 million at the official exchange rate. Other companies for sale include bicycle factories, textile mills, luxury hotel chains, supermarkets, automobile-parts manufacturers, and nightclubs.

Yet private-sector critics of the government argue that the privatization program should strike closer to the heart of the state's vast industrial empire. Such critics single out for privatization the huge conglomerates like the National Company for Popular Subsistence (CONASUPO), the food importer, wholesaler, and retailer, which had losses of $930 million in 1985; Fertilizantes Mexicanos (FERTIMEX), a fertilizer manufacturer that lost $295 million in 1985; the Sicartsa Steelworks, with a $245 million loss in 1985; and the Federal Electricity Commission, which received $735 million in subsidies in 1985. One problem with the sale of such large entities is the possibility that heavy job losses might have adverse political effects on the ruling Institutional Revolutionary Party (PRI). In May 1986, the government took the politically difficult decision to close Fundidora Monterrey, Latin America's oldest steel mill. Some 11,000 workers who lost their jobs burned their PRI party membership cards in protest. Mexican leaders are eager to protect their political power base in labor groups. Another reason cited by Mexican politicians to explain their slow progress in privatizing is the desire to keep "strategic" industries out of the hands of foreigners. Demands that private investors be allowed into areas legally reserved for the government, such as railroads, power generation, and the extraction and refining of oil, have been rejected. These politically sensitive industries were controlled by foreigners before nationalization.

Nevertheless, the Mexican privatization drive does represent a reversal of the policy of public-sector expansion that had been pursued for the previous twelve years. The PRI, in power since 1929, has acquired more than 900 companies over the decades as part of its policy of maintaining employment and extending its influence. In 1985 state industries accounted for 45 percent of the Federal budget and spent 17 percent more than they had been allocated. They also contribute heavily to the Mexican foreign-debt crisis. In March 1986 the Finance Ministry reported that state industries owed foreign banks $29.2 billion, a foreign debt larger than that of most governments and half as large again as the total debt of the Mexican private sector.

Extensive divestiture has occurred in Chile, where thirteen corporations and eighteen banks were sold between 1974 and 1983. Some failed and had to be rescued by the government, but overall the experience has greatly strengthened the private sector. In 1981 Chile privatized its pension system, creating ten Administrators de Fondos Previsionales (AFPs) to provide old age, maternity, general health, and other insurance. Shares of these AFPs are now being sold, as are shares in the power company, CHILECTRA, and two large banks that the government had taken over after their collapse in 1983. A genuine capital market is emerging and the issuing of shares is increasingly popular.

Privatization in Africa

Progress toward privatization has been slower in Africa than elsewhere, but efforts are now accelerating. Socialist models have been more thoroughly appl' ed in Africa than elsewhere, and the continent has severe economic problems. "The positive role of the private sector is to be encouraged," acknowledged the Organization of African Unity in a major reversal of philosophy in 1985.[14] But conditions for privatization are difficult in Africa, particularly because of a lack of capital markets. Privatization, however, is long overdue and much needed, since the huge quantity of resources in Africa are being absorbed by inefficient state enterprises. Babacar N'Diaye, the Senegalese president of the African Development Bank, has commented that such enterprises are "a drain on so many countries with limited capital resources. Privatization is vital for the resuscitation of the region's depressed industries."[15]

N'Diaye has noted that privatization efforts are under way in countries like Gambia, Ghana, Guinea-Bissau, Ivory Coast, Malawi, Mali, Somalia, Sudan, Tanzania, Togo, Tunisia, Nigeria, Uganda, and Zaire. The extent of the efforts varies. In Togo all of the country's public-sector enterprises are for sale. In Kenya a government task force on privatization has been considering the divestment of the more than 400 enterprises wholly or partly owned by the state. These nationalized concerns have been a financial disaster for Kenya. Direct equity and loan investments by the government rose from $24 million in fiscal year 1970-71 to almost $117 million by 1979, constituting 16.5 percent of total government expenditure. Privatization progress has been slow because of concerns about sales to foreigners or minority ethnic groups. Nevertheless, President Daniel arap Moi is firmly committed to privatization. In his inaugural address on 12 October 1983, he said: "There will be a switch of some investments from Goverment-owned institutions to the private sector. It is quite clear that the Government is unnecessarily involved in commercial ventures which could better be handled by the private sector."[16] Competition with some state-owned monopolies is being allowed. For example, Uplands Bacon, which had dominated the pork-processing industry in Kenya, went bankrupt after a new private company captured most of the market.

In Nigeria, President Ibrahim Babangida plans to sell the government's interest in more than 160 companies, including breweries, hotels, and appliance manufacturers. To the south, Guinea closed all six of its state-owned banks in late 1985 and replaced them with new banks in which private shareholders have a stake. In Malawi, the government is proceeding with the privatization of the components of the Agricultural Holding and Marketing Corporation (ADMARC). The government of Morocco professes to be in favor of privatization and is developing a comprehensive privatization strategy to be implemented over the next six to eight years. As of 1986, however, all that can be reported is the government's agreement to privatize ten fertilizer sales points. The Ivory Coast has liquidated its national trading company along with unprofitable hotel and rice operations.

The government of Rwanda plans to privatize the Office de Valorisation Industriel des Bananes de Rwanda (OVIBAR), its banana-production company, and is seeking offers from private investors to purchase either the entire plant or portions of it, such as the banana wine, juice, and paste-production units. The government of Mozambique favors privatization of those portions of the construction and building-materials industries that are viable and liquidation of the remainder.

In Gambia, plans are proceeding to privatize the Gambia Produce Marketing Board and a sawmill.

Even in Tanzania, once the foremost exponent of socialism in Africa, privatization is on the agenda. Before his retirement as president, Dr. Julius Nyerere conceded that his brand of African socialism had failed, largely because of Tanzanian resistance to collectivization. The policy had resulted in a foreign debt of $3.5 billion, an annual growth of only 0.9 percent, and a per capita income of $240. Now the government plans to boost food production by allowing private investment in commercial farms and removing controls on exporters. Nyerere's successor, Ali Hassan Mwinyi, has warned Tanzania's 430 state-owned companies that they will have to survive without subsidies.

Privatization in the Pacific

The small islands of the Pacific have been plagued by the same kind of public-sector problems as larger countries. Privatization is attracting a great deal of interest among the islands' leaders and has actually begun in some places.

The island that has the highest degree of privatization is American Samoa, a territory of the United States, where the Democratic governor, A.P. Lutali, has launched a full-scale privatization effort. He has already privatized a 3,000-ton dry-dock and ship repair facility, known as the Ronald Reagan Marine Railway. The third largest employer on American Samoa, the railway is now under a long lease to Southwest Marine, a San Diego-based firm. Industry observers expect the shipyard to make a profit the first year and anticipate a 25 percent return on investment within the next two years. In addition, Southwest Marine intends to expand the facility and bring more business to the Samoan economy. By contrast, the shipyard lost $1 million in the last year of government operation.

Full privatization of the American Samoa Power Authority, vehicle and motor-pool maintenance, garbage collection and disposal, and management of the hospital and the hotel are at various stages of contract negotiation. "Nearly everything except the schools and roads are on the drawing board," said Governor Lutali, ". . .but even those have not been ruled out."[17] Privatization seems to have been accepted by government employees, probably because of skillful lobbying by Governor Lutali and the care taken to cushion employees in the transfer process.

Another United States Pacific territory, Guam, has a $100 million deficit and a large government that employs over one-third of the island's work force. Former Governor Ricardo J. Bordallo, a Democrat, unveiled a "deficit elimination plan," the centerpiece of which is the privatization of government services. "There is a genuine commitment to privatization at the highest levels of government," Governor Bordallo announced.[18] His successor, Republican Joe Ada, will continue the initiative. There is no shortage of privatization targets. The Federal bureaucrats who created the Guamanian government in the years after World War II modeled it on the Federal government. The result was a vastly oversized government that stifled economic growth.

A few minor services have already been privatized with good results. One example is the vehicle-inspection service, which in the public sector was a major target of criticism from people who had to wait in line all day to get their cars inspected. The service was privatized, and there are now three private vehicle-inspection stations in Guam. Customer service has improved dramatically. "Corruption has also sharply declined," said David Santos, director of the Department of Revenue and Taxation.[19] The animal-quarantine station was also successfully privatized.

Future privatization targets are likely to be somewhat larger. The local newspaper, the *Pacific Daily News*, is campaigning hard for privatizing the Guam Telephone Authority, which is profitable but very inefficient. "People complain bitterly about lack of service, lack of dial tones, and inability to get telephones," according to one editorial in the newspaper.[20] Other services under consideration for privatization include garbage collection, school transport and dining services, the Port Authority, the Public Utility Agency (the water and sewage system), and the Guam Power Authority.

To the north, in Saipan, American billionaire William Millard, owner of Computerland, has organized some local investors into a company to buy the electricity and water utilities. He thinks the utilities should be sold to a large number of local people, an idea that will also broaden capital ownership on the island. The plan has received the enthusiastic backing of local political leaders, such as Saipan Lieutenant Governor Pedro Tenerio, who has called it "a great concept."[21]

These developments in the Pacific territories of the United States owe much to a drive for privatization initiated by Richard T. Montoya, assistant secretary for territorial and international affairs in the U. S. Department of the Interior, which in many ways functions in relation to the Pacific territories as the USAID does for other developing countries. Montoya has provided advice and technical assistance on privatization and has sponsored an extensive education effort.

The lead set by the United States territories seems likely to be followed by other Pacific islands. Amata Kabua, president of the Marshall Islands, has requested that the American investment bank E. F. Hutton advise on the privatization of public services, including power supply and distribution, communication services, and sea and air transport services. He said, "I believe that privatization of these functions will lead to more efficient and cost effective services and will contribute to the economic development of my country."[22]

The Lessons of Experience

Reviewing these experiences to determine what works and what does not in privatization, one is somewhat hampered by the fact that most privatization efforts in the Third World are very recent and cannot be easily judged. Some lessons, however, can be drawn from the limited experience to date.

One must first ask what are the objectives of privatization in a particular case and what are the worries of the politicians in charge. In developing countries, one of the main objectives of privatization is usually to stem the huge tide of losses from inefficient public-sector bodies. But this is rarely the only concern. Politicians are usually unwilling to allow the transfer of assets to foreigners or to unpopular minority groups. They also seek to avoid large job losses that might cause enough unrest to threaten their hold on power. Generally speaking, they are prepared to suffer the losses if the only alternative is a sale to foreign interests and massive job losses.

The privatization that has been most successful is that which has recognized these realities. Privatization, in developing countries as in the West, is essentially a political process, not an economic formula. Attempting to attain the maximum purchase price regardless of other factors is a strategy that has greatly hampered privatization in many developing countries. Some governments have set unrealistic prices for various concerns and then waited for the flood of local bidders. They have been surprised when none or only a multinational emerged.

To succeed, particularly in countries with poor or nonexistent capital markets and weak private sectors, privatization must be much more imaginative. The evidence suggests that only imaginative privatization has succeeded or may be succeeding. The sale of textile mills in Bangladesh to local entrepreneurs with special protection for the employees can already be declared a success. The sale of the Banana Control Board farms in Belize to those who worked on the farms also seems to have worked well. The use of a revolving trust fund in Costa Rica to purchase state companies, rationalize them, and then sell them to local private investors is an innovative solution to the problem of lack of local funds. The forthcoming sale of the National Milk Board in Sri Lanka to Sri Lankan milk producers has encountered less opposition than an outright sale to the highest bidder or closure.

Privatization works best when it is seen as a positive process, not just as a means of repairing damage. When it is advocated for its potential to invigorate an economy, to spread wealth among ordinary citizens, to improve services, and to create functioning capital markets, it has a better chance of success.

A prejudice against foreign involvment in privatization may seem regrettable, but one must remember that it was wholesale foreign ownership of Third World economies that contributed in large part to the initial wave of nationalization. If one wishes to avoid creating the conditions for a second wave of nationalization, privatization to local investors is the most sensible course. The most useful role for foreign investors is to take a minority holding and provide the management expertise that may be lacking in the indigenous private sector.

It is regrettable that few basic utilities have been privatized in the developing world. Privatization of telecommunications is proceeding in Sri Lanka and Malaysia and is on the drawing board in a few other countries, but little else has been planned. This is unfortunate, because privatization of utilities provides the biggest benefits for consumers and citizens generally, both in improved service and in economic growth. The telephones do not work; they would after privatization. The ports are run inefficiently; they could be a focus for growth after privatization. These large concerns also offer the possibility of organizing stock flotations. That makes the task of satisfying interest groups, such as employees and managers, much easier and also offers an opportunity to widen local capital ownership. Efficient management of such facilities will act as an important spur to economic growth. After all, who would invest in a place where the telephones do not work, the electricity is unreliable, and the sewage mixes with the drinking water?

Insufficient attention has been given to the formation of employee companies as a means of privatization. It has sometimes been talked about as an option, but little thought has been given as to how it should be done. This form of privatization is more difficult technically, but it is much more rewarding politically. There also seems to have been little attention paid to the privatization of land and of public housing, both means of spreading capital ownership and of benefiting the poor.

If privatization in the developing world is to succeed, the real challenge must be recognized. It is obvious that Western companies can run efficient telephone or water companies at hugely reduced cost and vastly improved service. They take over all garbage collection and save the government money. But the real challenge is to use privatization to create local ability to run utilities on a commercial basis, to turn government employees into entrepreneurs, to spread capital ownership among the population at large, and to create a climate of profit making and risk taking that will permit sustained economic growth.

Conclusion

These examples from around the world, including the Communist bloc, demonstrate that there are no limits to privatization possibilities. Throughout the world, socialism has been revealed as a failed ideology. It neither delivers the goods nor provides the motivation. In some instances the rhetoric will probably linger on, but most countries will want to dismantle their socialist institutions and policies.

The available evidence suggests that a privatization revolution will sweep the world in the next decade. It is already well under way. Although it will clearly take longer than ten years to privatize the Soviet post office, advocates of privatization should see that as a long-term goal.

Notes

1. See Madsen Pirie, *Dismantling the State* (Dallas: National Center for Policy Analysis, 1985); and Peter Young, "Privatization in Great Britain," *Government Union Review* 7 (Spring 1986):1–23.

2. Peter Wise, "Premier Acts to Dismantle State Industries," *Washington Post*, 14 Dec. 1985.

3. Text of statement by the Honorable Robert R. De Cotret, chairman of the Ministerial Task Force on Privatization and President of the Treasury Board, 2 Dec. 1985.

4. Jasper Becker, "Shanghai Betting on Homeowning," *Guardian* (London), 13 Nov. 1985.

5. Andrew Borowiec, "Hungarian Business Strives to Post Profit Despite Bureaucracy," *Washington Times*, 26 Sept. 1985.

6. John Elliott, "Bangladesh Set to Privatize Banks," *Financial Times*, 21 May 1986.

7. Mohan Ram, "Retreat from Public Empire in Rajiv's India," *Far Eastern Economic Review,* 25 July 1985.

8. Quek Peck Lim, "Why Malaysia Means Business," *Euromoney,* Feb. 1985.

9. Ibid.

10. John Greenwald, "A New Age of Capitalism," *Time,* 28 July 1986.

11. Ibid.

12. "Privatization: Everybody's Doing it Differently," *The Economist,* 21 Dec. 1985.

13. Greenwald.

14. Ibid.

15. "Privatization Moves in Third World Grow," *Journal of Commerce,* 6 March 1986.

16. L. Gray Cowan, *Divestment and Privatization of the Public Sector: Case Studies of Five Countries,* USAID, Dec. 1983.

17. Donna Dudek, "Privatization is Samoa's Answer to US Budget Constraints," *Wall Street Journal,* 7 July 1986.

18. Personal interview with the author.

19. Ibid.

20. "GTA May be Ripe for Privatization," *Pacific Daily News,* 12 March 1986.

21. "Businessmen Privatizing Utility Services," *Pacific Daily News,* 4 June 1986.

22. Letter to Jay Moorhead, vice president, E.F. Hutton.

Index

100473

3657   67   C-S